Psychopathology and Therapeutic Approaches

An introduction

Stephen Joseph

palgrave

First published 2001 by
PALGRAVE
Houndmills, Basingstoke, Hampshire RG21 6XS and
175 Fifth Avenue, New York, N.Y. 10010
Companies and representatives throughout the world

PALGRAVE is the new global academic imprint of St. Martin's Press LLc
Scholarly and Reference Division and Palgrave Publishers Ltd (formerly
Macmillan Press Ltd).

ISBN 0-333-76110-3

This book is printed on paper suitable for recycling and made from
fully managed and sustained forest sources.

A catalogue record for this book is available from the British Library.

10   9   8   7   6   5   4   3   2   1
10   09 08 07 06 05 04 03 02 01

Printed in Malaysia

Contents

List of Figures and Tables

Figures

Tables

Preface

Why do people develop psychological problems? All of the various therapeutic approaches employed by counsellors and psychotherapists are based on particular models of psychopathology which attempt to explain why it is that some people and not others come to develop psychological problems. Explanations for psychopathology might focus on, for example, biochemical imbalances in the brain, unconscious conflicts and repressed desires, irrational thinking and maladaptive learning, conditional regard and thwarted personal growth, or damaging social and economic structures. These are the main explanations that are usually put forward by therapists to understand why psychological problems come about.

The first aim of writing this book was to provide an introduction for counselling and psychotherapy trainees to the different models of psychopathology and the various approaches to therapy. This is a book that looks at some of the main ideas behind the practice of therapy. What I aim to do is to introduce the trainee counsellor and psychotherapist to the essential ideas that inform the different schools of therapy. I also want to introduce the biomedical approach, the transpersonal approach, and the sociocultural approach, which are often overlooked or marginalised in books on therapeutic approaches. We are not only psychological beings, but we are also biological beings who live in a social world and who have spiritual needs. It is no longer appropriate to ask which of these is the correct way to understand human beings, each of these aspects of human experience are worthy of study. It is only through their combined understanding that we are able to appreciate the richness of what it means to be human. Each chapter contains a brief account of a particular model of psychopathology and its associated therapeutic approaches. Following an introduction to counselling and psychotherapy in the first chapter, the second chapter describes biomedical and medical approaches, the third chapter psychoanalytical and psychodynamic approaches, the fourth chapter behavioural and cognitive approaches, the fifth chapter humanistic and transpersonal approaches, the sixth chapter social and cultural approaches, and finally in chapter seven, eclectic and integrated approaches are discussed. The book is not intended to be comprehensive in scope but simply to provide an accessible introduction to the novice about psychopathology and therapeutic approaches. The main theorists to be discussed are: Freud representing the psychodynamic approach; Ellis and Beck representing the cognitive-behavioural approach; and Rogers representing the humanistic approach, as it their work that is most often the focus of introductory counselling and psychotherapy classes. Several case examples run throughout the book to help illustrate the different therapeutic approaches. Although these examples are based on real people, the cases reported here are amalgams of several different people and all details have been changed so that no one person is identifiable.

The second aim of writing this book was to introduce the counselling and psychotherapy trainee to the main ideas behind the scientific method and the role of evidence-based practice. Evidence-based practice is becoming an increasingly important topic in the field of counselling and psychotherapy. However, counsellors and psychotherapists tend not to get exposed to the scientific method in their training. In the first chapter I will discuss why we should be interested in scientific methods, how as human beings we have ways of deceiving ourselves and how the scientific method helps us to verify what we think we know to be true. In the second chapter on biomedical and medical approaches, I will discuss the scientific role of classification and the use of ex-perimental methods to test out the effectiveness of particular treatments. In the third chapter on psychoanalytical and psycho-dynamic approaches, I will discuss the logic of the scientific method and the concept of falsification. In the fourth chapter on behavioural and cognitive approaches I will discuss how the scien-tific method leads to an orientation which favours observable and measurable behaviour. In the fifth chapter on humanistic and transpersonal approaches, I will discuss how some of the ideas about human nature do not lend themselves easily to the applica-tion of the scientific method. In the sixth chapter on social and cultural approaches, I will discuss how, despite the ambition of the scientific method to be objective, what we know is often heavily imbued with the values of Western society. In the final chapter I will return to the concept of evidence-based practice and critically evaluate its place in the profession of counselling and psychotherapy. As counsellors and psychotherapists I think we owe it to ourselves to be scientifically literate, to be able to weigh up scientific evidence for and against an argument, and to know for ourselves the boundaries of scientific enquiry. If the reader comes away with an understanding of why therapists should be interested in the scientific method then I feel I will have been successful.

I hope that trainees in counselling and psychotherapy, as well as those thinking about embarking on professional training in counselling or psychotherapy, will find this book useful in understanding the various approaches to therapy. Although I have largely aimed the book at trainees in counselling and psychotherapy, students in the social and behavioural sciences who are taking final year options in relevant subjects such as clinical or health psychology will also find the book useful. The book may also be useful to those seeking counselling or psychotherapy in helping them to understand more about the different types of therapy and what therapists actually do. I have also included some information in the first chapter which I hope will help guide anyone seeking help through the range of different mental health professionals and professional bodies.

STEPHEN JOSEPH

Acknowledgements

Many people have contributed in different ways to this book. First of all, my thanks go to Vanessa Markey for her support and encouragement during the writing of this book. Grateful thanks also to Delia Cushway, Rob Hooper, and Richard Mauger for their very helpful comments on earlier versions of the manuscript. I would also like to thank the anonymous reviewers for their comments and feedback on an early draft of the book, and the friends and colleagues over the years for their discussions around many of the issues and topics in this book, as well as for their support. In particular, I would like to thank Chris Armitage, Chris Lewis, Cindy Salmon, Elaine Fox, Gill Wyatt, Jackie Masterson, Jerome Marshall, Julie Elliott, Kay Garvey, Kevin Dutton, Leanne Andrews, Maureen Haynes, Nick Troop, and Tim Dalgleish. Grateful thanks also go to Keith Povey for his editoral services and to Frances Arnold and Alison Dixon at Palgrave for their encouragement and editorial support.

S. J.

1

Counselling, Psychotherapy and Psychopathology

Introduction

Helen walks into the therapist's office. The therapist smiles and offers her a seat. Helen sits down and within seconds she bursts into floods of tears. The therapist hands Helen a tissue which Helen uses to wipe away her tears. Slowly, Helen begins to tell her story, and the therapist begins to build up a picture of how Helen feels so tired all of the time, finds it difficult to get out of bed in the morning, is unable to take an interest in things, has lost interest in her appearance, constantly feels like crying, wonders what the point of it all is and has thoughts of taking her own life. Socially, Helen has withdrawn from her family and friends, rarely accepting invitations to go out, behaviour which seems so out of character for Helen. Her friends have always thought of Helen as outgoing and gregarious and are now worried about her, wondering what has caused Helen to behave so differently to the way she usually is with them. Helen's employers have also warned her about persistent lateness and she is now at risk of losing her job. How should we, as therapists, go about helping Helen with her problems?

Someone else, Alex, tells the therapist of how he finds himself exploding in a rage at the slightest provocation. His behaviour, he says, has cost him his marriage and several friendships. In the latest episode he had been out drinking with his work colleagues to celebrate a birthday, but as the evening wore on he became increasingly irritable and towards the end of the night attacked one of his colleagues beating him to the ground and kicking him until he was pulled away by the others. Now even his job is at risk as a result of his temper. How can the therapist help Alex to understand his rage and help him find ways to deal with his feelings more effectively?

Different therapists will give different answers to the question of how we might help Helen and Alex. In this first chapter, the roles of the counsellor and psychotherapist will be discussed and the different models of psychopathology will be briefly introduced. The main focus of the chapter, however, is on how each of the different models reflects a particular way of looking at how psychopathology develops and how, in turn, our understanding of how psychopathology develops influences our choice of therapeutic approach. Broadly, the problems people bring to counselling and psychotherapy are either those that have their origin in the remote past of the person's life or those that arise from current stressful situations. The particular models of psychopathology and approaches to therapy will be discussed in greater detail in subsequent chapters.

A further focus of this chapter, and one that will run throughout the book, is the question of whether therapy is an art or a science. This is a pivotal question, the answer to which will shape the future development of counselling and psychotherapy as a profession. Some would argue that the methods of counselling and psychotherapy, like any medical intervention, must be shown to be effective using the methods of traditional scientific research. Using traditional scientific research, it is argued, we can build up an understanding of what causes psychopathology and which therapies are most effective in alleviating psychopathology. More will be said about the methods of traditional scientific research and how we might go about conducting such research. Others would, however, argue that counselling and psychotherapy are unlike medical interventions and that the tools of traditional scientific inquiry are limited in what they can tell us about what goes on between people in a therapeutic encounter. It might be said that here we are beyond the boundaries of traditional scientific enquiry and we would be better inclined to listen to what the philosophers, poets and mystics can tell us about how to live our lives. Can these two approaches to understanding counselling and psychotherapy be reconciled? Views from both perspectives on this issue will be presented. Let us, however, first turn to the question of what is meant by the term psychopathology.

Psychopathology

Distress, deviance, dysfunction, and dangerousness

What is meant by the term psychopathology? Psychopathology is a term that refers to the branch of psychology that is concerned with abnormal workings of the mind. It is a term also used to refer to abnormal psychological conditions. Someone may behave in a way which could be seen as abnormal in a statistical sense, that is to say they behave in a way in which most people do not, and it is in this sense that the term 'abnormality' is often used by psychologists and psychiatrists. However, it is a term which many counsellors and psychotherapists dislike and disown as it elicits negative images of the person and leads us to think of psychopathology in a particular way. So, although this is the definition of psychopathology given in many text books, I share this discomfort and I will generally avoid the term 'abnormality', defining psychopathology instead with reference to whether the thoughts, feelings, or behaviour of the person are distressing, dangerous, deviant, or dysfunctional, terms used by Comer (1998). At one time or another many of us will feel emotionally upset (*distress*), perhaps we will do something that is harmful to ourselves or to another person (*dangerous*), do something that seems really odd or strange to other people (*deviant*), or have difficulty functioning in our everyday lives (*dysfunction*). This is often a useful way to think about psychopathology and it is sometimes helpful to spend some time thinking about the concepts of distress, deviance, dangerousness, and dysfunction and how they apply to examples of behaviours that we might consider as psychological problems.

So, thinking back to Helen, we might say that her thoughts, feelings, and behaviours are a form of psychopathology insofar as she is clearly emotionally upset (distressed), having difficulties holding down her job (dysfunctional), at risk of harming herself (dangerous), and behaving out of character (deviant). Although this helps us to begin to understand how to think about psychopathology, it is not easy to define psychopathology exactly. The more distressing, dangerous, deviant, or dysfunctional the thoughts, feelings, and behaviours are, and the more obvious these thoughts, feelings, and behaviours are to others, the more likely we are to consider them as psychopathology. The more extreme the behaviours, the more easily we can see them as psychopathology. Helen and Alex provide two examples of the ways in which people can behave in ways that might be considered as forms of psychopathology. Both Helen and Alex recognise that they have problems in functioning effectively and have sought help.

In contrast, Matt is a young man who has worked since leaving school, has several close friends whom he sees regularly, and all of his friends would agree that Matt has always been someone who seems happy with life, content with himself, and who has a bright career ahead of him. However, in the last few months, Matt's friends have noticed that he is acting very strangely compared to the way he usually is with them. Matt has taken to spending more time by himself, refusing invitations, and saying that he has important work to do for the benefit of the world. His parents too have noticed that they often hear voices coming from Matt's room as if he is talking with someone but they know that he is alone in his room. They are becoming increasingly concerned about Matt. Matt's parents have suggested that he visits the doctor but Matt refuses to go along saying that nothing is the matter with him. In contrast to Helen and Alex, Matt may not consider himself to have a problem and he is less likely to seek out help voluntarily. However, he might be considered as dangerous and deviant by his parents and friends who are likely to bring Matt to the attention of psychiatric and psychology services. The different roles of these mental health professionals will be considered shortly, but for the moment what this illustrates is that counsellors and psychotherapists are likely to encounter different forms of psychopathology than psychologists and psychiatrists. Counsellors and psychotherapists are more likely to work with people like Helen who are emotionally distressed and who have sought help for themselves, whereas psychiatrists and psychologists will also work with people who are a danger to themselves and who other people consider as needing help.

Psychiatric classification

There is no doubt that psychological problems can become overwhelming in intensity and duration causing a person to behave in extremely dysfunctional and dangerous ways, and in ways which are unusual for this person, or unusual for the society he or she lives in. As we have seen we might define such experiences as psychopathology. Furthermore, psychopathology is a term that refers to a range of seemingly very different psychological problems. As we will see in Chapter 2, one of the tasks of modern psychiatry has been to try and define various forms of psychopathology, and psychiatrists have produced a classification system of so-called psychiatric disorders. Certainly, most people will not meet the strict criteria necessary to be diagnosed as suffering from a psychiatric disorder. The diagnosis of a psychiatric disorder implies that the person is suffering in a way that is inappropriate to the way they usually are or is disproportionate to their circumstances, and when we refer to psychiatric disorders we are usually dealing with very severe and chronic conditions. Many of the terms used to describe psychiatric disorders may already be familiar, and in the above examples it might be that Helen would be diagnosed as suffering from major depressive disorder, Alex from a disorder of impulse control, and Matt from the disorder of schizophrenia. Other so-called disorders include panic disorder, posttraumatic stress disorder, obsessive-compulsive disorder, anorexia nervosa, and bulimia nervosa to name but a few of the more commonly known disorders. We shall look at some of these in more detail in subsequent chapters.

However, although there are advantages to understanding psychopathology in this way, the classification of psychiatric disorders remains controversial and, as we shall see throughout this book, it is very difficult to draw a clear line between 'normality' and 'abnormality', to be able to say where psychopathology begins. This is particularly true in less extreme cases than those we have just considered. How emotionally distressed or dysfunctional does a person have to be for them to he considered as suffering from a psychopathology? How long does emotional distress or dysfunction have to last, and how severe does it have to be, for it to be considered as psychopathology? In certain situations it would seem to be perfectly normal to be emotionally distressed, for example, when we are anxious in response to some threat or when we are sad in response to some loss. It is not unusual to be anxious before taking an important exam or to feel sadness at the loss of a loved one. But what of someone who always feels nervous when going into new social situations or someone who remains grieving for years after their loss? Would we say that these are examples of psychopathology?

Answers to such questions will often depend on which perspective is taken on the nature of psychological suffering. Certainly, problems in living are widespread. Nelson-Jones (1984), for example, draws attention to the difficulties experienced by the majority of people, how most of us struggle to be autonomous in the way we live, and how Maslow (1970) used the term 'psychopathology of the average' to describe most people's level of functioning. We shall come back to the issue of difficulties in distinguishing 'abnormal' from 'normal' behaviour later, in Chapter 6, when we go on to discuss the work of Rosenhan (1973; 1975). Rosenhan conducted a now famous experiment in a real life situation showing that psychiatrists' diagnoses were influenced by the social context. The experiment raised important questions about who decides, and on what basis, what is 'normal' and what is 'abnormal'. Much work has accumulated telling us that considerations of what is 'normal' and what is 'abnormal' are not value free. Rather, considerations of 'normality' and 'abnormality' are bound up in cultural and historical contexts (see Littlewood and Lipsedge, 1993). Consequently, as already mentioned, the term 'abnormality' is one that a lot of counsellors and psychotherapists are uncomfortable with.

Nevertheless, the question of whether some experiences represent abnormal workings of the mind is one that we must take seriously. Many psychiatrists would argue, not surprisingly because of their medical background, that certain psychological problems such as schizophrenia are caused by abnormal biological states. Consequently, counselling and psychotherapy are seen as inappropriate for such problems and perhaps even harmful to the patient. The person suffering from such a condition requires instead some form of biochemical intervention. Of course there are those who strongly disagree with this position and we will consider the arguments for these respective positions in later chapters. But as it is so difficult to define exact boundaries between 'normal' and 'abnormal' behaviour, it might be helpful in considering what sort of problems are most often encountered by counsellors and psychotherapists.

Seeking help

What sorts of problems do counsellors and psychotherapists commonly see? In one survey it was found that the most common problems people bring to counselling and psychotherapy are, firstly, anxiety and depression, followed by interpersonal difficulties, marital problems, school difficulties, physical complaints, job-related difficulties, substance abuse, psychotic conditions, and finally, learning difficulties (VandenBos and Stapp, 1983). Psychiatrists and psychologists, on the other hand, are more likely to work with people with more severe and chronic conditions, such as psychotic conditions and learning difficulties. Of course, the types of problems seen by counsellors and psychotherapists will vary depending on a number of factors. Some counsellors and psychotherapists will specialise in seeing clients with particular difficulties. In recent years the range of client difficulties seen by counsellors has greatly diversified as more counsellors and psychotherapists work in psychiatric settings, primary care settings such as General Practitioners surgeries, workplaces, and agencies specialising in crisis counselling (see Woolfe and Dryden, 1996). Indeed, it is now estimated that over 50 per cent of GP practices in Britain offer some form of counselling service. Also, it is becoming increasingly common for counsellors and psychotherapists to work with clients who would traditionally have been seen by psychiatrists and psychologists.

Counsellors and psychotherapists will usually work with someone who has not been able to find the help that they need from family or friends, or who is reluctant to approach others in their life, or whose problems go beyond the help that can be provided by family and friends. Of course, often when we are troubled in some way our first port of call will actually be friends or family and not a professional therapist. Friends and family can provide very important resources for us in times of need. Before going on to look at the roles of counsellors and psychotherapists, I'd like to say a little more about this and what makes social support from family and friends different from what professional therapists do.

Social support

In times of crisis we will often turn to our family and friends for help. Barker, Pistrang, Shapiro, and Shaw (1990) carried out a survey of over 1,000 adults representative of the UK population with respect to age, sex, and social class. They asked: if you had a personal problem, whom would you talk to about it? The most frequent answer was partner (68 per cent), followed by a close relative (54 per cent), a friend or neighbour (43 per cent), the family doctor (41 per cent), a workmate (20 per cent), and finally, the priest (17 per cent). Some interesting differences were found between men and women. Men were more likely to seek help from their partner (71 per cent) compared to women (64 per cent). Women were more likely to seek help from a close relative (61 per cent) compared to men (45 per cent), and more likely to seek help from a friend or neighbour (52 per cent) compared to men (34 per cent). Men were more likely to seek help from a workmate (23 per cent) compared to women (18 per cent). But can social support from our friends and family really help?

Depending on the relationship between the people involved and the nature of the problem, social support from family or friends might indeed be sufficient in helping a person overcome their difficulties. Certainly, there is now a substantial body of research showing that people who have high levels of social support from friends and family are psychologically healthier than those who have low levels of social support. By social support, what is meant is the provision of emotional or practical aid to a person from others in their social network. Family and friends who are able to provide emotional reassurance, who can help us see things differently, help us feel valued and esteemed, who are able to provide a loan of money if needed, and who are able to offer advice on how to deal with a situation can help us cope with the most upsetting and stressful experiences in life. We know this, not only from accounts of what people tell us, but also from the numerous research studies that have been carried out. In these studies, the researchers have found ways of measuring social support and psychological health, through the use of questionnaires, interviews, or observing interactions between people. They then go on to test statistically whether or not there is an association between social support and psychological health. What the results of the numerous studies show is that greater levels of social support are associated with lower levels of psychological distress (see Cohen and Wills, 1985; Sarason, Sarason, and Pierce, 1990).

Indeed, social support from family and friends has even been shown to be associated with better adjustment following the most horrific and traumatic events (e.g., Cook and Bickman, 1990; Flannery, 1990). In a series of investigations that my colleagues and I carried out we found that social support from family and friends in a time of crisis is one important determinant of adjustment. Following the *Herald of Free Enterprise* disaster, the ferry capsize which took place off the coast of Zeebrugge in 1987, we found that those survivors who reported having higher levels of social support in the immediate aftermath of the disaster subsequently fared better than those who reported having lower levels of social support (Joseph, Andrews, Williams, and Yule, 1992; Joseph, Yule, Williams, and Andrews, 1993; Dalgleish, Joseph, Thrasher, Tranah, and Yule, 1996). So, if social support from family and friends is so important, why should we need counsellors and psychotherapists? What is it that counsellors and psychotherapists are able to provide that our family and friends can't?

When our friends and family are not enough

Alex feels that he has alienated his friends through his aggressive behaviour and that he has no one that he can turn to for support. Helen has withdrawn from her family and friends who although they want to help feel shut out by her. Furthermore, family and friends are often unable to provide us with the support we need. They might not have the emotional or practical resources themselves to help us deal with our problems. Matt's family and friends would like to be able to help, but they just don't know what to do.

Not everyone has people around him or her to provide support. This is most evident, for example, in the case of someone who has lost a loved one. Not only have they been bereaved and in need of social support to help them cope with their grief, but they have also lost their main source of social support. In this case, bereavement counselling might provide a very valuable emotional resource which will help the person to work through and accept their loss and find ways of dealing with their painful feelings. But most counselling and psychotherapy is not about providing a substitute for family and friends.

Furthermore, family and friends might offer us support that we actually find unhelpful. For example, family and friends might offer us advice when all we want is to be listened to. They might encourage us to talk when all we want to do is sit in silence. They might try to stop us crying when all we want to do is cry. Family and friends in their attempts to be supportive will often do things that we find unhelpful. Most of us will be able to find examples of when we have found the attempts of others to be supportive to be unhelpful or even harmful.

Psychologists have investigated this and one very interesting study set out to investigate what types of social support are helpful and unhelpful in people with cancer. Dakof and Taylor (1990) asked their sample of people diagnosed with cancer to state the particular acts that others carry out that are helpful or harmful. Based on the assumption that the ties of kinship, marriage, or friendship all create different obligations and constraints, Dakof and Taylor asked respondents about seven other people:

1.   spouse
2.   other family members
3.   friends
4.   support group members
5.   doctors
6.   nurses
7.   acquaintances.

For each of these people, respondents were asked:

1.   what is the most helpful thing?
2.   what have they said or done to make you angry?
3.   what have they done that nobody else could have?
4.   what have you wished they did?

Dakof and Taylor then analysed the answers to these questions dividing helpful and unhelpful actions into three types of social support, which they called:

1. esteem support, i.e., support in which the person was made to feel cared for, valued, and esteemed
2. information support, i.e., support in which the person was provided with advice, guidance, and information
3. instrumental support, i.e., support in which the person was offered practical help of some kind.

Relating these types of support to their providers, Dakof and Taylor found that 70 per cent of the cancer patients said that their spouse, family or friends were most helpful with regard to esteem support and their inappropriate attempts at esteem support were the most unhelpful. Other cancer patients and doctors were seen as the most helpful regarding information support and the lack of this from them was seen as the most unhelpful. More specifically, partners were seen as helpful for expressing concern and affection and for being accepting of the illness. Partners who were seen as critical of the person's response to cancer were seen as particularly unhelpful, as was their failure to express concern. Other family members were most appreciated for expressing concern, being there and providing practical assistance such as transport. However, criticising and minimising the impact of the cancer was seen as most unhelpful. So, sometimes friends and family, despite their best intentions, can be unhelpful in the way that they provide support. Indeed, other research with men with HIV found that having a partner was associated with poorer social adjustment (Packenham, Dadds and Terry, 1994). Pakenham and colleagues suggested that having a partner may have encouraged dependency and adherence to a sick role and, as a consequence, fostered ill health and impaired social functioning.

The nature of counselling and psychotherapy

For a variety of reasons, friends and family are not always able to be supportive in the way that would help us deal with our problems and so sometimes it might be appropriate for a person to visit a counsellor or psychotherapist. Counsellors and psychotherapists are not simply substitutes for friends and family. Instead, they are trained in using particular skills derived from complex theoretical understandings of what causes psychopathology. The help counsellors and psychotherapists offer is of a very different nature to that offered by family and friends. So, how can we define *counselling* and *psychotherapy*? The British Association for Counselling (1996) states that:

> The overall aim of counselling is to provide an opportunity for the client to work towards living in a more satisfying and resourceful way. The term 'counselling' includes work with individuals, pairs or groups of people often, but not always, referred to as 'clients'. The objectives of particular counselling relationships will vary according to the client's needs. Counselling may be concerned with developmental issues, addressing and resolving specific problems, making decisions, coping with crisis, developing personal insight and knowledge, working through feelings of inner conflict or improving relationships with others. The counsellor's role is to facilitate the client's work in ways that respect the client's values, personal resources and capacity for self-determination. (British Association for Counselling, 1996)

For some, psychotherapy and counselling are understood to be different. For others, counselling and psychotherapy are interchangeable terms. For the purposes here, unless specified, the latter view will be adopted and these two terms will be used interchangeably with the words therapy and therapist. However, a useful definition of psychotherapy is that provided by Norcross (1990):

> Psychotherapy is the informed and intentional application of clinical methods and interpersonal stances derived from established psychological principles for the purpose of assisting people to modify their behaviours, cognitions, emotions, and/or other personal characteristics in directions that the participants deem desirable (Norcross, 1990, p. 218)

Is there a difference between counselling and psychotherapy?

Although for many the above definition would apply equally well to counselling as well as psychotherapy, there are those who would argue that counselling and psychotherapy are different activities requiring separate definitions. Given that distinctions have been drawn between counselling and psychotherapy, it might be useful to look at this issue in a little more detail before proceeding further. Counselling has been seen by some as a short-term activity, lasting only weeks or months, whereas psychotherapy is seen as a longer-term activity lasting up to several years in some cases. Also, some would argue that counselling tends to operate at a relatively superficial level of human experience whereas psychotherapy operates at much deeper levels of human experience. These two points, duration and depth, are the ones most often used to make a distinction between counselling and psychotherapy. Also counselling has sometimes been associated with the humanistic approach whereas psychotherapy has been associated with the psychodynamic approach, as it is believed by some that the humanistic approach operates on a more superficial level than the psychodynamic approach. More will be said of these approaches in later chapters. However, for the moment it is sufficient to say that in practice the distinction between counselling and psychotherapy is not clear cut. Nevertheless this remains a controversial question and not everyone will agree with these opinions; and the definition of therapy remains a topic for debate. As Emmy van Deurzen (1998) writes:

> As soon as one tries to reach an agreed definition there is immediately disagreement about whether psychotherapy is to be seen as a form of treatment or as a form of personal development. There is still no agreement about whether psychotherapy is primarily a medical, a psychological, an educational or a spiritual activity . . . Psychotherapy for some is about priesthood, for some about parenting, for some about education, for some about healing, for some about friendship, for some about mental or moral exercise. (Deurzen, 1998, pp. 4–5)

This quote sets the scene very much for this book and I hope that the reader will come to understand the nature of these disagreements and to begin to reach their own view of the nature of therapy. However, having looked at the differences between counselling and psychotherapy, it is also important to look at the similarities. One important aspect of the above definition by Norcross (1990) that applies equally well to both counselling and psychotherapy is that the person seeking help, the client or patient, has control over the direction the therapy takes, that people are assisted in making changes that they themselves deem to be desirable. This is an important distinction and sets counselling and psychotherapy apart from the more medically oriented professions in which people can be sectioned within the Mental Health Act and treated against their will. In such cases the treatment is likely to be drug-based therapy rather than some form of psychological therapy. Most of the therapies employed by counsellors and psychotherapists are derived from some psychological theory. The aim of this book is to look at some of these psychological theories. But, first, having defined the terms counselling and psychotherapy, we might now ask who exactly carries out therapy.

The different mental health professionals

Although this book is primarily written with trainee therapists in mind, I have included the following section with the consumer of therapy also in mind as I am aware that much confusion still exists surrounding the different mental health professions.

Having decided to seek professional help, the first port of call is often the General Practitioner or family doctor. The person might recognise their need for psychological help and approach their GP for help and advice. Alternatively, the person might visit their GP seeking help, but be unaware that their problem is of a psychological rather than a physical nature. One of the most frequent complaints of people visiting their GP is that they are 'tired all of the time'. This can mean a number of things, from being indicative of some underlying physical illness to being indicative that the person is suffering from stress, for example. The task of the GP is to understand the nature of the problem and to treat the person appropriately or to refer the person on to some other specialist service. In the case of psychological problems GPs are able to prescribe medication that might be appropriate and in some cases will be able to offer some form of psychological help. However, although he or she might sometimes be able to offer appropriate psychological help, GPs are not usually trained in the delivery of psychological therapies. More often they will refer the person to one of the many health professionals who are specifically trained to provide psychological help: a counsellor, a psychiatrist, a community psychiatric nurse, a psychologist, or a psychotherapist. For many people the differences between these professional groups is unclear. When referred on by their GP for professional help many people will not give much thought to the type of health professional they have been referred to. After all we expect our doctor to make decisions in our best interest. But perhaps we should be more concerned about the referral process and to whom we get referred. What happens to the person next is very much influenced by the type of health professional they turn to.

Each of the professional groups differ in their training, the services they offer, and in their assumptions about the causes of psychological suffering and how it should best be treated. In this book I want to discuss the underlying assumptions of each of these groups of mental health professionals and how they understand psychopathology. There is no doubt that there has been, and still is, much rivalry between these professional groups.

In North America and in the United Kingdom, psychiatrists are medically qualified doctors and certified to prescribe medication. Following their medical training they have gone on to postgraduate training in the treatment of emotional and mental disturbances and will have received some training in psychotherapy. Psychologists have trained for several years in academic psychology and have gone on to take a specialist postgraduate degree in some branch of applied psychology. There are several branches of applied psychology in North America and in the United Kingdom, including clinical psychology, counselling psychology, and health psychology. Although the training programmes differ slightly in North America and the United Kingdom, there are some broad similarities. Clinical psychologists tend to work with people with more severe and chronic conditions such as psychosis, learning difficulties, and suicidal depression, and are most often employed in the Health Service. Counselling psychologists tend to work with people facing life transitions, less severe forms of depression and anxiety, and personal growth issues and tend to work more in private practice. Health psychologists work with people with severe and chronic physical health complaints, and deal with issues of stress and coping, as well as helping people to maintain healthier lifestyles. Of course, these are generalisations and there is also considerable overlap between what people in each of these branches of applied psychology actually do. Many psychologists will also work in university settings, carrying out teaching and research. Indeed, this is one of the defining features of the psychologist, the fact that they are scientists as well as practitioners. Psychologists endeavour to apply those methods of treatment that science has shown to be most effective. Psychologists have played an important role in the development of Evidence-based Practice (EBP). More will be said of this later. At present, psychologists are not entitled to prescribe medication. In North America, although not in the United Kingdom, clinical psychologists are pursuing the right to prescribe medication. In other countries this right already exists. In South Africa, for example, psychologists are registered with the Medical and Dental Council and entitled to prescribe medication without the supervision of a psychiatrist. Although it is possible that psychologists will eventually gain this privilege in North America, in the United Kingdom psychologists have not expressed the same degree of interest in achieving prescription rights.

Counsellors and psychotherapists have intensive training in one or more of the different forms of psychological therapy available. Unlike psychologists or psychiatrists, a major focus of their training will often have been on their own personal development, and it is usually a requirement of their training that they undergo personal therapy themselves. Indeed, depending on the nature of the training, this can be at least weekly for several years. It is currently a requirement for those seeking accreditation with the British Association for Counselling and Psychotherapy (BACP) that they have had some experience of personal therapy themselves, although many people who qualified before this regulation was introduced will not have had such experience. Also, some forms of counselling and psychotherapy, notably the humanistic and psychodynamic, are more likely to emphasise the importance of personal therapy as part of the training programme. Personal therapy is not always viewed as important in the more behavioural and cognitive forms of counselling and psychotherapy.

Of course, these are generalisations and there will be many exceptions, with some individuals having training in more than one of the professions for example. Furthermore, the roles of the different groups are constantly changing over time. Nevertheless, it gives a broad idea of some of the differences existing between these groups, at least within the United Kingdom.

Professional bodies

Therapists can belong to a variety of different professional bodies. Psychiatrists will be members of the Royal College of Psychiatrists, psychologists will usually be members of the British Psychological

Society (BPS), counsellors and psychotherapists will usually be members of the British Association for Counselling and Psychotherapy (BACP) or the United Kingdom Council for Psychotherapy (UKCP).

The BACP was formerly the British Association for Counselling (BAC), having changed its name in 2000 in an attempt to unite the profession.

People seeking help are often advised to seek out someone who is recognised by one or more of these bodies to offer the help they claim to be able to provide. This is sound advice, as it remains legally possible for someone without the appropriate training to simply advertise himself or herself as a counsellor or psychotherapist. Selecting a therapist randomly from the yellow pages is not advisable and someone seeking a therapist would be best advised to ask for advice from one of the professional bodies. At the time of writing, however, there are moves to pass a parliamentary bill to produce a register of therapists which should go some way towards resolving this chaotic situation. Of course, there are also therapists who are well trained and who do not belong to one of these professional bodies. Although some organisations will require the employees to be members of an appropriate professional body, not all organisations do, and some therapists will simply choose not to be members of a professional body.

Some, for example, may disagree with what they see as increasing bureaucracy and hierarchical political structure in the field of therapy. In recent years, there has been the development of the Independent Practitioners Network, an organisation whose members share such concerns. There are also a number of other smaller associations that some therapists will belong to. The British Association of Behavioural and Cognitive Psychotherapy, for example, is one body whose membership spans the different professional groups, containing a mix of psychiatrists, nurse therapists, psychologists, psychotherapists, counsellors, simply all those who share a common interest in the cognitive and behavioural forms of therapy. Similarly, for those who share an interest in the treatment of posttraumatic stress there is the International Society for Traumatic Stress Studies whose membership body covers a wide range of mental health professionals.

As we have seen, a wide variety of health professionals with very different training backgrounds carry out counselling and psychotherapy, and despite differences in title the work being carried out is often much the same. However, there is no standard single qualification entitling someone to work as a counsellor or psychotherapist, and no single professional body accrediting psychological therapists. It is not surprising therefore that clients looking for counselling and psychotherapy can often be confused. The situation is exacerbated by the fact that there is much professional rivalry and political struggle between the various professional groups for the ownership rights to the field of therapy. Mahrer (1998) explained it as follows:

> Picture a gathering of all the psychotherapy-related professions and someone asking, 'who has a justified right to train psychotherapists?' Psychologists would raise their collective hand. So would social workers, nurses, and educators. The school of medicine would raise its hand. So would schools and departments of pastoral studies, human relations, rehabilitation, guidance, child development, family studies, philosophy, and many others. (Mahrer, 1998, p. 20)

Nevertheless, all of these professionals, be they called counsellors, psychologists, nurse therapists, social workers, psychiatrists, or psychotherapists, will have some form of expertise and skills in helping which are derived from some theory about how people develop psychological problems. Despite their differences in training, all claim to be committed to the alleviation of human suffering and therefore strive to offer help on the basis of what they believe is the best way to do so. But what is the best way to offer help?

Models of psychopathology

Theories about the causes of psychopathology are concerned with understanding the mechanisms which lead one person and not another to develop psychological problems. Historically, psychopathology has been understood in many ways – the result of supernatural forces, the wrath of gods, demonic possession, the influence of the moon, for example – and at different times, psychopathology has attracted ridicule, fear, pity, anger, and been variously treated, from attempts to exorcise demons to taking cold baths. Today, there are seven major ways in which we can understand psychopathology. These are:

- the biomedical model
- the psychodynamic model
- the behavioural model
- the cognitive model
- the humanistic model
- the transpersonal model
- the sociocultural model.

By model, what is meant is a particular set of shared assumptions underlying how we see the world. A model provides us with the boundaries of inquiry, a way of looking at the world, a shared set of assumptions about reality which allow us to communicate with each other. Another word which is often used instead of model in this context is paradigm. Each of these seven models, or paradigms, has a consistent view of human nature, how it can go awry and lead to psychopathology, and how the resultant psychopathology can be prevented and treated. In each of the successive chapters I will say a little more about the main ideas behind each model. I have tried to treat each model sympathetically. It is my understanding that each model can tell us something important about human experience, and many of the disputes between theorists have been compared to the well-known fable about philosophers who were sent by the wise king into the pitch-dark barn where there was an elephant. Never before had they encountered an elephant and each one on touching a part of the elephant assumed that they now had the key to understanding the whole animal. One of them, reaching out and touching the elephant's trunk, exclaims: 'I understand the nature of this animal, it is like a snake.' Another, touching a leg of the elephant, cries out in reply: 'No, it is like a tree.' Different versions of the fable abound, but the point is, of course, to remind us of the folly in drawing conclusions on the basis of limited evidence and to remind us to question our own beliefs. When we try to understand the nature of psychological suffering we are sometimes like these philosophers standing in the dark around the elephant. The idea is that although truth exists, our knowledge is limited and we can never fully know that truth. But before I say more about this, let me first say a little about each of the models and their underlying assumptions.

A brief look at the models

The biomedical model suggests that psychological problems are the result of physical dysfunction; the psychodynamic model suggests that psychological problems are caused by conflict between unconscious forces; the behavioural model suggests that psychological problems are a result of maladaptive learning; the cognitive model suggests that psychological problems are caused by irrational or distorted thinking; the humanistic model suggests that psychological problems are caused by a failure to know oneself and accept oneself; the transpersonal model is concerned with spirituality; and the sociocultural model suggests that psychological problems result from social factors. Of course, these are superficial generalisations of what each model is about and more detailed accounts of each model will be provided in subsequent chapters. Each chapter will begin by outlining each of the models of psychopathology followed by a description of some of the therapeutic approaches associated with that tradition. In the final chapter, current perspectives on models, the role of evidence-based practice, and eclectic and integrative approaches to therapy will be considered. For the moment, however, the point is simply to show how each model contains assumptions about the driving forces behind human behaviour and how psychological problems develop and how people can be helped to overcome those problems (see Table 1.1).

The biological and sociocultural models are not usually considered in books about counselling and psychotherapy. Neither model forms the basis for a psychological therapeutic approach, the sociocultural model emphasising instead the need to change social structures and to rethink how we perceive psychological suffering, and the biological model emphasising anatomical structures and the need for physical treatment. Nevertheless, each of these two models promises to tell us something about human experience and how psychopathology might develop, and should therefore also be of interest to counsellors and psychotherapists. We are biological beings who live in a social world and the importance of both biology and society should not be dismissed. Counsellors and psychotherapists tend to work using ideas developed within either the psychodynamic, behavioural, cognitive, humanistic, or transpersonal models, and consequently emphasise the psycho-

Table 1.1   Models of psychopathology

	Psychological problems are caused by:	People can be helped with:
Biological	biochemical imbalances, genetic factors, brain defects	medication, electric shock therapy, surgery
Psychodynamic	internal psychological conflict between unconscious forces	therapist interpretations which help to bring unconscious conflicts into consciousness
Behavioural	maladaptive learning	learning of new behaviours to replace old behaviours
Cognitive	dysfunctional attitudes about the self and the world	techniques which modify existing attitudes, schemas, thoughts
Humanistic	thwarted personal growth	therapeutic relationship
Transpersonal	lack of touch with spirituality, the divine, God	meditation, spiritual experience
Sociocultural	adverse social and environmental factors, maladaptive communication patterns	changing the nature of society, family and community psychology

logical or spiritual aspects of human nature, sometimes with the danger of overlooking the possibility that distress can have biological or social causes. We live our lives within confines dictated by biology and society.

Today, we also see a resurgence of interest in other paradigms, most notably the transpersonal model, which its adherents might argue reflects the developments over the last century in quantum physics which have made us stop and think about the very nature of the universe and its relationship with consciousness. Transpersonal psychology is concerned with those experiences which transcend, or go beyond, the individual, and therapists working from within the transpersonal model are concerned with using mystical, spiritual, or psychic experiences to increase human potential. Some might argue that the popularity of these ideas within the general population reflects a need people have for a spiritual existence in their lives with the decline of traditional religious observation. Certainly, some of these ideas might seem bizarre and are not usually considered within texts on mental health, and often the exponents of transpersonal psychology are not taken seriously within the scientific community.

Eclectic and integrated approaches

A question that has occupied many people over the years is whether any one model is sufficient to explain all the different ways in which psychopathology is expressed. For example, can all psychological problems be attributed to sociocultural factors, or are all psychological problems a result of biological factors? Most mental health professionals today, of whatever persuasion, would probably agree that human experience is so diverse that no one model is able to offer the full explanation for all psychological problems for all of the people all of the time. For example, research suggests that people who are depressed have both lower levels of social resources (evidence for the sociocultural model), and lower levels of the neurotransmitter serotonin (evidence for the biological model) than people not suffering from depression. For this reason, many therapists working today do so in an *eclectic* way, that is to say, drawing on the techniques and interventions associated with one therapeutic approach when they see it as appropriate and then drawing on the ideas of another model when that seems appropriate. Also, many therapists describe themselves as *integrative*, meaning that they have adopted and blended one or more of the models that they see as being consistent with each other. Surveys suggest that at least one third of therapists describe themselves as either eclectic or integrative (see Prochaska and Norcross, 1999). I will say more about the different ways of working of psychiatrists, psychologists, and counsellors later, but for the moment I want to say a little more about what it means when therapists say that they work in an integrative way.

Those working in an integrative way endeavour to work in a more circumscribed and theoretically consistent way, drawing on the ideas from models that they see as reconcilable. Indeed, trying to find a reconciliatory path, one that is able to integrate the different paradigms, has been one of the greatest challenges of recent years for the professions of counselling and psychotherapy. Perhaps the most successful attempts at therapy integration has been the merging of ideas from the cognitive and the behavioural models to produce what is known as the cognitive-behavioural approach, and in more recent years, the merging of ideas from the psychodynamic and the cognitive models to produce what is known as the cognitive-analytic approach (Ryle, 1990). In the final chapter, views on integration will be discussed. However, most counsellors and psychotherapists undergo extensive training in the ideas and way of working associated with one of the psychological models, that is the behavioural, cognitive, humanistic, or psychodynamic models. Although there are advantages to having a detailed and thorough training in one model of therapy – and traditionally counselling and psychotherapy training in the UK has been of this nature – what it means is that counselling and psychotherapy graduates often lack a common language.

Although humanistic therapists might be well versed in the language and ideas of Rogers and Maslow, psychodynamic therapists in the ideas and language of Freud and Klein, and cognitive therapists in the language and ideas of Ellis and Beck, for example, each is not well versed in each other's language and ideas. Furthermore, traditional counselling and psychotherapy training has not left its graduates well versed in the language and ideas of psychologists and psychiatrists. This is unfortunate as it is increasingly common for counsellors and psychotherapists to work alongside these other professionals as part of a multidisciplinary team within the National Health Service (NHS).

At present the biomedical model is the dominant one in the NHS and reflects our understanding of ourselves as organisms shaped through millions of years of evolution. Certainly the biomedical model is the dominant force in psychiatry, where practitioners are medically qualified. Within the professions of counselling and psychotherapy, it is probably true to say that the humanistic and psychodynamic paradigms are the dominant ways of looking at psychological problems, and within the profession of psychology, the behavioural and cognitive paradigms are probably the most dominant ways of looking at psychological problems. Of course, there will be many that do not fit these generalisations, but overall, the different mental health professions are fairly entrenched in these different theoretical camps.

But does it make a difference what the therapist believes? I think it does. Let me give an example to explain what I mean. Let us suppose that a person goes along to a friend and says that they have problems with alcohol. The friend, who is well meaning, suggests that they get in touch with Alcoholics Anonymous (AA). That would seem to be good advice and probably fairly typical of what many of us might do in that situation. But how many of us are aware of the underlying assumptions, or model, of the AA programme. The essence of AA's underlying philosophy is contained in its Serenity Prayer: 'God grant me the serenity to accept the things I cannot change, courage to change the things I can, and wisdom to know the difference.' Although there is undoubtedly much wisdom contained in this statement, it also suggests that the ability to make these changes may depend on forces external to the person rather than internal to the person. The AA have what they call the 12-step programme (see Table 1.2).

The philosophy underlying the AA programme seems to be that the person should accept that they are powerless over their behaviour, at least in regard to alcohol. The alcoholic's life is under the control and direction of powerful forces that may, depending on their understanding of God, reside outside of themselves. This belief system represents a way of looking at the world that is in direct contradiction to that held by many counsellors and psychotherapists, at least in Western culture. It is probably true to say that most counsellors and psychotherapists in Western society operate from the basic, and secular, assumption that positive therapeutic change will be evident when the client is able to take control of their life. Personal responsibility is fundamental to counselling and psychotherapy in Western culture (Nelson-Jones, 1984). This is not to say that a therapist would challenge such belief systems as those expressed in the AA programme. The British Association for Counselling (1996) notes that counsellors are responsible for working in ways which promote the client's control over his or her life, and respect the client's ability to make decisions and change in the light of his or her own beliefs and values.

Table 1.2   The 12-step programme of Alcoholics Anonymous

1. We admitted we were powerless over alcohol – that our lives had become unmanageable.
2. Came to believe that a power greater than ourselves could restore us to sanity.
3. Made a decision to turn our will and our lives over to the care of God, *as we understood Him*.
4. Made a searching and fearless moral inventory of ourselves.
5. Admitted to God, to ourselves, and to another human being the exact nature of our wrongs.
6. Were entirely ready to have God remove all these defects of character.
7. Humbly asked Him to remove our shortcomings.
8. Made a list of all persons we had harmed, and became willing to make amends to them all.
9. Made direct amends to such people whenever possible, except when to do so would injure them or others.
10. Continued to take personal inventory and when we were wrong promptly admitted it.
11. Sought through prayer and meditation to improve our conscious contact with God *as we understood Him*, praying only for knowledge of His will for us and the power to carry that out.
12. Having had a spiritual awakening as the result of these steps, we tried to carry this message to alcoholics, and to practice these principles in all our affairs.

The point here is not to criticize the AA programme (as we shall see later there are many other therapeutic approaches with a spiritual element), but simply to make explicit the idea that every therapeutic approach rests on some basic assumptions about human nature.

Introducing evidence-based practice

How we make sense of the world around us and what we believe about human nature is fundamental to how we practise as counsellors and psychotherapists. For this reason as counsellors and psychotherapists we have a duty to reflect upon our own beliefs and to monitor the effectiveness of what we do. Let us suppose that a person develops an illness and goes to the doctor, who says that there are two different treatments available. One of the treatments has been shown from scientific studies to cure 60 per cent of the people with this illness; the other has been shown to cure 20 per cent of the people with this illness. There is no difference in the possible side effects of the two treatments. Most people would choose the treatment with the best cure rate. Proponents of evidence-based practice would argue that the practice of counselling and psychotherapy should be no different. If a client comes suffering from depression, for example, then they should be offered the treatment that has been shown to be most effective.

National Institute for Clinical Excellence

Within the NHS, the National Institute for Clinical Excellence (NICE) is attempting to produce guidelines by which treatments should be adopted. The approach consists of six stages. First, identification of health interventions, either potentially new and important treatments or existing treatments which may no longer be justifiable; second, research to assess the clinical and cost effectiveness of these health interventions; third, consideration of the implications for clinical practice of this evidence and production of guidance for the NHS; fourth, dissemination of guidance; fifth, implementation of guidance; and sixth, monitoring the impact of health interventions. Those interventions which do not have a research base to support their effectiveness will not be adopted in the NHS. Traditionally, research training has not formed a large part of training in counselling and psychotherapy, although it is the foundation stone of the disciplines of psychiatry and psychology, which have developed a range of methodological and statistical techniques (see e.g., Barker, Pistrang, and Elliott, 1994; Robson, 1993). However, it might be argued that the future development of counselling and psychotherapy as health professions will now also be shaped by their inevitable movement towards evidence-based practice.

Although more will be said about the role of evidence-based practice in later chapters, for the moment I want to say a little more about why it is thought to be important. What the traditional scientific method supposedly allows us to do is to check up on the validity of what we think is true. To illustrate, there is a well-documented area of psychological inquiry which shows that people may remember things or report events in a way that has been shown to be false. People will often make the wrong connections between events and distort evidence to make it fit their beliefs. Sutherland (1992) argues that the need to hold on to our expected ways of seeing the world is powerful and can often mislead us. For example, read the following three lines:

PARIS

IN THE

THE SPRING

This is a well known example used by Sutherland (1992) to illustrate how we cling to what we think to be true and, unless you have encountered this before, you might have read it incorrectly as 'Paris in the spring'. We see what we expect. If we are working within a particular model of counselling or psychotherapy which we believe to be effective and we are not recording data on our clients' outcomes in a systematic way which is amenable to scientific scrutiny, we will, the argument suggests, see what we expect. Although the term evidence-based practice is a relatively recent one, the idea that we should use the methods of science to check up on what we think we know is not a new one. Rogers (1961), the originator of the person-centred approach to counselling, made the following statement:

Scientific research needs to be seen for what it truly is; a way of preventing me from deceiving myself in regard to my creatively formed subjective hunches which have developed out of the relationship between me and my material. (Rogers, 1961)

The point is simply that we can be irrational in our thinking (see Sutherland, 1992) and according to Rogers (1961) we might be best advised to adhere to the principles of scientific investigation if we want to avoid deceiving ourselves. For example, when it comes to therapies themselves, psychoanalysis, as we shall see in Chapter 3, has been much attacked over the years as an example of self-deception by its practitioners. For example, Sutherland, one of the critics of psychoanalysis, asks why it is that psychoanalysis is still with us despite the fact that the available evidence shows that its techniques have not proved effective. He says that when controlled scientific studies have been carried out comparing the effects of psychoanalysis with placebo treatments, psychoanalysis does not fare any better than the placebo treatment. Sutherland suggests several reasons why psychoanalysts continue to 'peddle their wares'. For example, the therapist has been through a lengthy and expensive training and rather than admit that it was a waste of money they come to believe that some good has come out of it. Also, it is the case that patients often get 'better' anyway and the non scientifically trained therapist, he argues, is more likely to attribute this to his or her intervention, and anyway if the patient does not get better it is because of their own failure to co-operate. Sutherland is not positive in his views on psychoanalysis and he has written about his own experiences as a patient very scathingly. He argues that there is no evidence from scientific studies to support the effectiveness of psychoanalysis and the only possible reason anyone would continue with it is because they discount the evidence, or are simply not aware of it, and base their decisions on the belief that it is effective. Although there is little compelling scientific evidence for psychoanalysis as Sutherland says, as we shall see in Chapter 3, there is growing evidence to support the effectiveness of psychodynamically oriented therapies.

This is a compelling argument in favour of evidence-based practice. Also, it is an argument in favour of the use of traditional scientific methods in the evaluation of the effectiveness of the different therapeutic approaches. But can we always trust the scientific evidence? Not according to some exponents of the sociocultural paradigm who, as we shall see in Chapter 6, point towards the misuse of statistical techniques by some and implicit political agendas of others. Also, scientists, like anyone else, are not immune to getting things wrong, to deceiving themselves, and finding it difficult to relinquish what they think is true. It is important therefore that counsellors and psychotherapists are able to evaluate the scientific literature for themselves. This is a topic however that trainee counsellors and psychotherapists are often uninterested in or even fearful of. Nevertheless it is an important area as, following the recent NHS Plan, more and more therapists are expected to be employed in National Health contexts which demand evidence-based procedures. There is no doubt that the next generation of therapists will have to take these issues more seriously. Although I will return to the topic of traditional scientific research throughout this book to try to illustrate some of the basic issues, this is not a text on the scientific method per se and what I have to say is largely confined to understanding the experimental method.

Conclusion

An aim of this chapter was to define the term psychopathology and introduce some of the difficulties in drawing a clear distinction between what might be considered as normal and abnormal behaviours. Broadly speaking, psychopathology refers to those thoughts, feelings, and behaviours that are distressing to the person, are perhaps dangerous to the person or to others, or unusual in some way for that person or for the society in which they live. A range of health professionals are involved in trying to understand psychopathology, counsellors, psychotherapists, psychologists, and psychiatrists, and a second aim was to describe some of the differences between these professional groups. An aim was also to describe what it is that therapists do that is different from the social support we receive from family and friends. Therapists mainly derive their ways of working from complex theoretical models about the nature of psychopathology. Several models were briefly introduced: the biomedical model; the psychodynamic model; the cognitive model; the behavioural model; the humanistic model; the transpersonal model; and the sociocultural model. The role of traditional scientific research was introduced as a way of preventing ourselves from engaging in self-deception regarding our beliefs.

Summary points

● Psychopathology is a term that refers to the branch of psychology concerned with abnormal workings of the mind. It is a term also used to refer to abnormal psychological conditions.

● Deviance, distress, dysfunction, and dangerousness are useful concepts for thinking about what constitutes an abnormal psychological condition, although it is difficult to draw a clear boundary between abnormality and normality.

● Considerations of what is normal and what is abnormal are not value free and consequently these are terms which are disliked and disowned by the professions of counselling and psychotherapy.

● Definitions of counselling and psychotherapy vary with some viewing these as interchangeable terms, and others seeing counselling and psychotherapy as distinct activities.

● A broad definition of counselling and psychotherapy is that they are activities concerned with assisting people to modify their behaviours, cognitions, emotions, and other personal characteristics in directions that the participants deem desirable using methods derived from psychological principles.

● There is no one agreed set of principles for how to assist people to change and there is disagreement among the various professional groups involved in counselling and psychotherapy as to what constitutes counselling and psychotherapy.

● Several approaches to therapy exist, from biologically based treatments through various psychological and spiritual interventions, to considerations of the social forces acting on a person.

● In order to establish what approach to therapy is most helpful the scientific method can be used to establish evidence-based practice.

2

Biomedical and Medical Approaches

Introduction

Anyone who has ever had a few alcoholic drinks will recognise that human behaviour can be profoundly affected by biochemistry. As counsellors and psychotherapists we must be aware of the possibility that some forms of psychopathology are actually caused by abnormal workings of the brain and are best treated by practitioners who can address the problem biomedically rather than psychologically. The biomedical approach has had a profound influence on how mental health professionals think about the nature of psychopathology. In this chapter I will introduce some historical background to the biomedical understanding of psychopathology, consider the scientific basis which underpins psychiatry, and introduce the reader to the *Diagnostic and Statistical Manual of Mental Disorders*.

Within the biomedical model it is recognised that a person's behaviour and experience may change if there are physical or chemical changes in the brain and nervous system. For example, we know that a severe injury to the brain can have a profound effect on behaviour. There may be problems in concentration and memory and the personality of someone who sustains a severe head injury can change dramatically. For example, someone who was once outgoing and sociable can become shy and solitary. We also know the effects on behaviour that result from taking alcohol. People are more likely to act aggressively, to lose their inhibitions, to slur their speech, and so on. So, it is not unreasonable to suggest that psychological problems might reflect disturbances in the physical make-up of the brain or in the chemistry of the brain. The aim of the biomedical model is to understand the relationship between psychopathology and physiological processes. So, for example, if it can be shown that a certain way of behaving is related to a certain aspect of brain chemistry, then it might be possible to help that person change or control their behaviour through some form of chemical intervention. This way of looking at human problems is the dominant one among psychiatrists who are medically qualified and allowed to prescribe drugs.

History of the biomedical model

Prior to the biomedical model, people held beliefs about supernatural causes of psychopathology and there are accounts of the casting out of demons in people who today would be seen as suffering from some form of psychological problem. Beliefs in demonological possession were widely held in the Middle Ages; thousands of people were accused of being witches and many executed for their supposed crimes. Fortunately, few people still hold these particular beliefs today in Western society. It was in the late eighteenth century and early nineteenth century that the biomedical model replaced the demonological model. This was the age of enlightenment in which it was argued that psychopathology was not the result of supernatural forces but rather the result of physical illness. This was the time of scientific medicine, with its emphasis on an experimental approach to understanding human behaviour. Consequently, psychopathology could be treated like any other illness using biomedical techniques.

The biomedical model has a long history dating back to the father of modern medicine, the Greek physician, Hippocrates (hence, the 'Hippocratic Oath' taken by medical practitioners). In the fourth century BC when most people believed that psychological problems were caused by supernatural forces, Hippocrates, wrote this about epilepsy:

> If you cut open the head, you will find the brain humid, full of sweat and smelling badly. And in this way you may see that it is not a god which injured the body, but disease. (Quoted in Zilboorg and Henry, 1941)

What Hippocrates believed was that psychopathology resulted from bodily disturbances. He distinguished between various forms of 'madness' which resulted from various disturbances in the brain. The brain's healthy functioning was, he thought, dependent on a balance of four bodily fluids, or humours as they were called. The four humours were blood, black bile, yellow bile, and phlegm. Each of these four humours corresponded to the basic elements of earth, air, fire, and water, all of which must be in a state of balance within the universe. Illness was thought to be caused by an imbalance of the humours within the body. Someone with too much blood was moody, someone with too much black bile was melancholic, someone with too much yellow bile was anxious, and someone with too much phlegm was sluggish. Treatment therefore consisted of attempts to achieve a balance in the four humours. Such views persisted into the nineteenth century when treatments for physical and mental illnesses included blood letting, abstinence from sexual activity, and immersion in cold water – all attempts to restore the balance of the humours (see Starr, 1982). Hence the phrase that someone is in good humour! So, the idea that psychological problems are caused by biological disturbances is not a new one – it can be dated back to Hippocrates, and the biomedical paradigm has, in one way or another, dominated the way we think about psychological problems in the Western world.

The biomedical paradigm suggests that physical illnesses, brain dysfunction, and biological abnormalities of one sort or another cause psychological problems. Much of modern psychiatry adopts this perspective, looking to biology, and more recently neurochemistry, to explain psychological problems. One early example, which helps to illustrate the biomedical model, is the story of a man called Phineas Gage. Phineas Gage suffered damage to his brain when, whilst working on the railways at the end of the nineteenth century, a piece of metal almost four feet long was propelled into his skull by an explosion. The metal went into his left cheek and exited through the top of his skull. Luckily for Phineas Gage he survived and his cognitive abilities, intellectual functioning and so on, remained relatively unimpaired. However, his behaviour changed remarkably. He became much less restrained, more impulsive and less patient (see Harlow, 1868). Although the case of Phineas Gage is an unusual one, what it illustrates clearly is that disturbances in the brain can affect psychological functioning.

Today, most psychiatrists and psychologists would agree that at least some psychological problems are caused by biological factors. With increased technological advancements, more recent research, has allowed us to look at neurochemical and genetic factors as possible causes of psychological problems. But, as we will see in Chapter 6, not everyone has accepted the biomedical model view of psychological problems, and criticisms of the biomedical model as applied to psychopathology have been made. However, the biomedical model has remained dominant within the profession of psychiatry, and today the fact that psychological problems can be shown to be associated with physiological changes is not controversial. There are plenty of research studies showing links between various behaviour patterns and various aspects of brain chemistry (see e.g., Heston, 1992). However, central to the biomedical paradigm is the more controversial assumption that psychological problems are caused by biological disturbances and therefore psychological problems are indicative that something has gone wrong with the normal biological processes.

Scientific method

In Chapter 1 the idea of evidence-based practice was introduced. Here I want to say a little more about the role of the scientific method. The biomedical paradigm is grounded in scientific research and it is useful for therapists in training to understand the principles of scientific research if they are to appreciate the complexity of this model. One example, which is often used to illustrate the workings of the biomedical paradigm, is the story of general paresis. Most people today will not have heard of this condition and might be surprised to learn that a century ago about a quarter of people admitted to mental hospitals were diagnosed with general paresis (Dale, 1980). The symptoms included memory problems, impaired intellectual functioning, delusions of grandeur, and paralysis, generally leading to death within two to five years. But despite the fact that general paresis was so common, the cause was not known. It was found to be more common in men, in those who used alcohol, and among sailors, prompting suggestions that it was caused by something to do with being a man, using alcohol, or going to sea. Some suggested, it may have had something to do with sexual behaviour. Following this line of thought it was then suggested that general paresis was caused by untreated syphilis. In order to test this hypothesis, in 1897 Richard von Kraft-Ebing injected pus from syphilitic sores into nine patients who had general paresis. What he reasoned was that, because people who have already contracted syphilis cannot do so again, then, if general paresis was caused by untreated syphilis then the nine patients should be immune and would not develop syphilis in response to his injection. None of his patients went on to develop syphilis, confirming that all had previously had syphilis.

This study was important in showing an association between untreated syphilis and general paresis. Although such a study is ethically questionable by today's standards of medical research, it provided the first evidence that eventually led to the successful treatment of this condition. Once the cause of general paresis was identified as syphilis bacteria infecting the cerebral cortex of the brain, medical practitioners were able to develop a test to diagnose the presence of the bacteria and treat it in the same way as any other infection. Today general paresis has all but vanished from the psychiatric textbooks except as an historical illustration that problems which seem to be of a psychological nature can turn out to be of a medical nature. The story of general paresis also illustrates the process of scientific thinking as applied to psychological problems. The general idea is that the scientist observes some phenomenon, attempts to explain its occurrence, and then finds ways to test out the validity of the explanation. More will be said about the scientific method and how scientists go about this process of testing out their hypotheses in Chapter 3 when we look at the psychodynamic model.

The story of general paresis illustrates the beginnings of the scientific method with its emphasis on experimentation. It also helps to illustrate how some psychological conditions have their roots in biology. Current research suggests that some psychological conditions like schizophrenia might also have their basis in biological functioning. We shall return to this shortly, but first it is necessary to understand the role of classification in scientific enquiry.

Psychiatric classification

One consequence of adopting the biomedical model is that it encourages the use of classification. In the same way that physical disorders can be classified, so too can mental disorders. We recognise, for example, that a sore throat is a different condition from a skin rash. Both have different causes and consequently different treatments are appropriate for each. So if a person goes to their doctor with a throat infection they might expect treatment with an antibiotic, whereas if they had a skin rash they might expect treatment with hydrocortisone cream. If doctors did not distinguish between a throat infection and a skin rash and their different causes they would not be able to provide differential treatment. What use would it be if you went to the doctor and were given indigestion tablets for a broken leg?

We expect medical practitioners to provide us with whatever treatment is most suitable for our illness or injury. This is the logic that the biomedical model applies to psychological problems and so the first step must be to understand all of the different psychological problems. When we adopt the same view, even when we are not dealing with biological causes, this is referred to as the medical model.

Diagnostic and Statistical Manual of Mental Disorders

In an attempt to classify the different 'abnormal' psychological conditions, the American Psychiatric Association have produced what is called the *Diagnostic and Statistical Manual of Mental Disorders* (DSM). The roots of this system go back to the turn of the century and a German doctor called Kraepelin who, in the late nineteenth century, observed that some symptoms tended to occur together leading him to develop early classifications of mental disease.

DSM was first introduced in 1952 (DSM-I), followed by revised editions in 1968 (DSM-II), 1980 (DSM-III), 1987 (DSM-III-R), and is now in its fourth edition (DSM-IV) (American Psychiatric Association, 1994). The DSM-IV is a voluminous work running to many hundreds of pages. Although earlier editions of the DSM attempted to relate psychiatric disorders to their supposed *aetiology*, or causes, the more recent editions have not done this. Now each disorder, with a few exceptions such as post-traumatic stress disorder and puerperal psychosis, is now defined in terms of its observable signs and symptoms.

Axis of functioning

Psychiatrists use DSM to assess people on five different axes (areas of functioning). Axis I is a list of clinical syndromes from which a person might be suffering. Axis II is a list of life-long, deeply ingrained and maladaptive personality patterns. Axis III is a list of medical conditions. Axis IV is a list of psychosocial and environmental problems. Axis V is a global assessment of functioning on a 100-point scale extending from 1 (persistent violence, suicidal behaviour or inability to maintain personal hygiene) to 100 (symptom free, with superior functioning across a wide range of activities). So, for example, a person might be diagnosed with an anxiety disorder on Axis I, as having an obsessive-compulsive personality disorder on Axis II, no related physical disorders on Axis III, as having occupational problems on Axis IV, and as having functioned over the past year at a general level of 40 on the Axis V global scale. The purpose of having these five axes of functioning is to provide a comprehensive description of the client's difficulties.

It should be noted that there is another system of classification in use as well as DSM: the *International Classification of Diseases* (ICD) produced by the World Health Organisation (WHO) which is now in its tenth edition (WHO, 1992) and which serves a similar function. Much of what will be said here about the use of the DSM system also applies to the WHO system.

DSM is the reference work used by psychiatrists as a basis for their diagnoses of psychiatric disorders. DSM-IV lists almost 300 separate disorders defined in terms of their observable symptoms. The disorders are further grouped into several major categories. It is beyond the scope of this book to go into detail on all of the separate disorders, but to illustrate the system a little further it might be useful to look at each of these major categories listed on Axis I. On Axis I, psychological problems are classified into several major classes of psychiatric disorder (see Table 2.1).

Table 2.1   DSM-IV classes of disorder

- **Disorders usually first diagnosed in infancy, childhood, or adolescence.** *For example, conduct disorder and infantile autism.* This category includes emotional, intellectual, and behavioural disorders which occur before adulthood although they often persist into adulthood.

- **Delerium, dementia, amnestic, and other cognitive disorders.** Problems associated with impairment of brain by injury or illness.

- **Substance-related disorders.** These disorders are identified by substance, for example alcohol, and are conditions in which there is psychological distress or physical damage.

- **Schizophrenia and other psychotic disorders.** Disorders in which the person has lost contact with reality; there may be delusions and hallucinations, as well as deterioration in social functioning. The person might become severely withdrawn from others.

- **Mood disorders.** Depression or bipolar mood disorder in which the person alternates between periods of severe depression and mania, i.e., increased excitement and activity.

- **Anxiety disorders.** For example, phobia, panic disorder, obsessive-compulsive disorder, and posttraumatic stress disorder.

- **Somatoform disorders.** For example, problems with physical symptoms but no organic cause. A person might suffer from paralysis without there being any clear organic cause.

- **Factitious disorders.** Physical or psychological problems that are deliberately produced or faked.

- **Dissociative disorders.** Problems in which there is a splitting of consciousness, memory, e.g., multiple personality disorder.

- **Sexual and gender identity disorders.** Problems involving sexuality, ability to perform sexually, inappropriate sexual orientation, cross-gender identification.

- **Eating disorders.** Problems involving unusual patterns of food consumption, e.g., anorexia nervosa and bulimia nervosa. Anorexia nervosa involves a preoccupation with being thin accompanied by extreme weight loss. Bulimia nervosa involves periods of binge eating followed by purging through vomiting, use of laxatives.

Table 2.1 *Continued*

- **Sleep disorders.** Problems in which normal pattern of sleep is interrupted. For example, sleep terrors in which the person wakes up confused and in a state of panic.

- **Impulse control disorders.** Problems in which there is an inability to refrain from harmful behaviours, e.g., kleptomania (stealing), pyromania (fire-starting), and compulsive gambling.

- **Adjustment disorders.** Problems in which there is a maladaptive and excessive response to an identifiable stressor.

Scientific use of DSM

Although a full discussion of the DSM-IV system is beyond the scope of this book, I want to emphasise why psychiatrists have adopted this system. In the same way as there is a need to distinguish between different physical illnesses, it is believed by those who adopt the medical model that we must be able to distinguish between the different psychological conditions. By observation of all the symptoms people experience, what symptoms always seem to occur together, what symptoms do not seem to occur together, we should be able to sort all the symptoms into different categories. So, we are then able to say, in this category, we have, for example, loss of sexual interest, loss of appetite, and loss of interest in other people, and these 'symptoms' are usually seen together, that is they co-occur. In this other category, we have, for example, hallucinations, apathy, and lack of pleasure and motivation, and these 'symptoms' usually co-occur. Once this has been achieved labels are given to each of the categories. The examples above are symptoms from the psychiatric disorders of depression and schizophrenia respectively.

The point of doing this is that it facilitates communication between mental health professionals and this in turn enables effective research programmes to be carried out into the causes of these different conditions and what therapeutic interventions work with particular client groups. If different psychological problems are caused by different factors then it is important for researchers not to throw all psychological problems together but rather to look at separate psychological problems in relation to the different factors. For example, from your own experiences you would probably agree that when you describe yourself or someone else as being depressed that you mean something very different from when you describe yourself or someone else as being anxious. By depressed you probably mean the person is sluggish, tearful, sad, and down in the mouth, whereas by anxious you probably mean the person is nervous, excited, scared, and worried. The question is whether or not feeling anxious and feeling depressed are somehow different in the same way that you might say that a sore throat is different from a stomach upset. If they are different then a coherent research programme, which is trying to look at, for example, the treatment of depression and anxiety, must treat them as such.

Experimental method
One of the functions of classification, therefore, is to drive scientific enquiry by providing a common language among mental health researchers and clear operational definitions of the phenomena under investigation. For example, if you suspect that a particular drug will help to alleviate depression, you might plan an experimental research programme in which a group of people who you thought were depressed were given the drug and another group of people who you thought were equally depressed were given a placebo drug (i.e., an inactive substance which resembles the real drug so that those taking part in the study don't know whether they are being given the active or inactive substance). The allocation of the participant to the active substance or inactive substance group would be determined by chance. This is called random allocation and serves to make sure that there is as little bias as possible in the way that people are allocated to the groups.

To avoid the expectations of the researcher affecting the results, he or she will also not know if the participant in the experiment is being given the active or inactive substance. Then when the drug is thought to have worked the researcher looks again to see if the people given the drug are now less depressed than those given the placebo. If they are, it can be concluded that the research has provided evidence that the drug alleviates depression. This method is known as a randomised control trial (RCT) and is commonly used to test out new drugs as well as the efficacy of other forms of therapy. The above is a very simple example of an RCT and experimental designs can be much more complex than this, involving perhaps several groups for comparison. Perhaps, the researcher is also interested in whether the drug was even more effective when it was coupled with psychotherapy; he or she might also want to include for comparison a depressed group who were given the drug and psychotherapy. Although it is difficult and expensive to carry out such studies (Seligman, 1995), the results can be very useful in guiding practice.

In order to carry out this type of research you must be able to define exactly what you mean by the term depression (or whatever the target problem is that has been identified for treatment), and be able to measure depression. The researcher needs to be able to say that the people in the group given the drug were equal in their level of depression to the people given the placebo at the beginning of the study, and that the level of depression in the group given the drug decreased while the level of depression in the placebo group did not.

Also, the researcher needs to be able to communicate to his or her colleagues exactly what was done so that others can do the same and confirm the results. The nature of good scientific practice is that experiments should be replicable. It is only when an experiment has been replicated by different researchers in different parts of the world that we can say with confidence that the evidence is robust enough for us to accept. So, we must be able to define very precisely the phenomenon under investigation, to be able to measure it, and observe changes in it over time. Thus, it is important that we are able to translate our psychological concepts into numerical scores so that we are able to conduct the relevant statistical tests.

This is a very brief account of the experimental method in the context of the medical model. First the researcher must be able to clearly define the phenomenon under investigation and measure it in some way. Second, some intervention is carried out in such a way so that any changes are directly attributable to the intervention. This is ostensibly the scientific purpose of psychiatric classification. There are of course criticisms of the scientific method and of psychiatric classification which we will consider shortly. But first it is useful, given the above discussion, to look in more detail at two of the most common psychiatric disorders, depression and generalised anxiety disorder and how they are defined in DSM-IV.

Measurement

Classification serves to provide the scientific community with a common language; DSM-IV (American Psychiatric Association, 1994) lists hundreds of psychiatric disorders. It is beyond the scope of this book to summarise all of these here, but to give a flavour of the nature of the DSM-IV, the symptoms listed in Table 2.2 are those for major depressive episode. Note that nine 'symptoms' are listed and to be diagnosed with major depressive episode, a person must be seen to have experienced at least five of the 'symptoms'.

So, when two psychiatrists are talking about a patient who is diagnosed with major depressive episode, they both have a clear understanding of what this means. Similarly, someone who is diagnosed with what is known as generalised anxiety disorder (GAD) would have to meet the following criteria which are also outlined in DSM-IV (American Psychiatric Association, 1994) (see Table 2.3).

The *Diagnostic and Statistical Manual* provides psychiatrists, as well as others who use the manual, with a shared frame of reference, a common language, and a fundamental tool for scientific enquiry. Based on DSM, psychiatrists and psychologists have developed a number of interview and questionnaire methods for measuring psychological problems such as depression and anxiety. These are used in such a way so as to give numerical scores which can then be used in research to show changes over time.

Some criticisms of DSM

The authors of the current DSM-IV system have tried to achieve greater reliability by focusing as much as possible on observable behaviours. Nevertheless, subjective factors still play a role in clinicians' evaluations. Consider, for example, the diagnostic cri-

Table 2.2   Symptoms listed in DSM-IV for the diagnosis of major depressive episode

---

A. Five (or more) of the following symptoms have been present during the same two-week period and represent a change from previous functioning; at least one of the symptoms is either 1. depressed mood, or 2. loss of interest or pleasure. *Note:* Do not include symptoms that are clearly due to a general medical condition, or mood incongruent delusions or hallucinations.

  1. Depressed mood most of the day, nearly every day, as indicated either by subjective reports (e.g., feels sad or empty) or observation made by others (e.g., appears tearful). *Note:* In children and adolescents can be irritable mood.
  2. Markedly diminished interest or pleasure in all, or almost all, activities most of the day, nearly every day (as indicated by subjective account or observation by others).
  3. Significant weight loss when not dieting or weight gain (e.g., a change of more than 5 per cent of body weight in a month), or decrease or increase in appetite nearly every day. *Note:* In children, consider failure to make expected weight gains.
  4. Insomnia or hypersomnia nearly every day.
  5. Psychomotor agitation or retardation nearly every day (observable by others, not merely subjective feelings of restlessness or being slowed down).
  6. Fatigue or loss of energy nearly every day.
  7. Feelings of worthlessness or excessive or inappropriate guilt (which may be delusional) nearly every day (not merely self-reproach or guilt about being sick).
  8. Diminished ability to think or concentrate, or indecisiveness, nearly every day (either by subjective accounts or as observed by others).
  9. Recurrent thoughts of death (not just fear of dying), recurrent suicidal ideation without a specific plan, or a suicide attempt or a specific plan for committing suicide.

B. The symptoms do not meet criteria for a mixed episode (see DSM-IV, p. 165).

C. The symptoms cause clinically significant distress or impairment in social, occupational, or other important areas of functioning.

D. The symptoms are not due to the direct physiological effects of a substance (e.g., a drug of abuse, a medication) or a general medical condition (e.g., hypothyroidism).

E. The symptoms are not better accounted for by bereavement, i.e., after the loss of a loved one, the symptoms persist for longer than two months or are characterised by marked functional impairment, morbid preoccupation with worthlessness, suicidal ideation, psychotic symptoms, or psychomotor retardation.

Table 2.3   Symptoms listed in DSM-IV for the diagnosis of
generalised anxiety disorder

A. Excessive anxiety and worry (apprehensive expectation), occuring more days than not for at least six months, about a number of events or activities (such as work or school performance).
B. The person finds it difficult to control the worry.

C. The anxiety and worry are associated with three (or more) of the following six symptoms (with at least some symptoms present for more days than not for the past six months). *Note:* Only one item is required in children.
   1. restlessness or feeling keyed up or on edge
   2. being easily fatigued
   3. difficulty concentrating or mind going blank
   4. irritability
   5. muscle tension
   6. sleep disturbance (difficulty falling or staying asleep, or restless unsatisfying sleep)

D. The focus of the anxiety and worry is not confined to features of an Axis I disorder, e.g., the anxiety or worry is not about having a panic attack (as in panic disorder), being embarrassed in public (as in social phobia), being contaminated (as in obsessive-compulsive disorder), being away from home or close relatives (as in separation anxiety disorder), gaining weight (as in anorexia nervosa), having multiple physical complaints (as in somatization disorder), or having a serious illness (as in hypochondriasis), and the anxiety and worry do not occur exclusively during post-traumatic stress disorder.
E. The anxiety, worry, or physical symptoms cause clinically significant distress or impairment in social, occupational, or other important areas of functioning.
F. The disturbance is not due to the direct physiological effects of a substance (e.g., a drug of abuse, a medication) or a general medical condition (e.g., hyperthyroidism) and does not occur exclusively during a mood disorder, a psychotic disorder, or a pervasive developmental disorder.

teria for major depressive episode or generalised anxiety disorder. What exactly does it mean to say that there is a markedly diminished interest or pleasure in activities? What level of anxiety and worry must there be for us to consider it excessive? The current state of knowledge about the classification of psychopathology is not set in stone. In one hundred years' time people may look back and see our current knowledge as relatively primitive, as we do today when we look back to the turn of the century and the work of the phrenologists who studied personality through bumps and indentations on the head. One of the problems with the current system may be seen when we look at the criteria for depression and anxiety. Although the goal is to describe discrete categories of psychological disturbance, often it is not clear where one category ends and another begins, and where the boundaries between different disorders should be drawn. For example, both the diagnostic categories of depression and anxiety include symptoms of sleep disturbance, fatigue, and difficulty concentrating. What this means is that diagnosis can be an unreliable procedure. It is possible that a person with these symptoms would be diagnosed with depression by one psychiatrist and with anxiety by another. Criticisms about the reliability of the diagnostic system have been made for many years, with agreement between psychiatrists for some disorders being less than 50 per cent (Zigler and Phillips, 1961; Williams *et al.*, 1992). One of the tasks of each revision of DSM has been to try and achieve a more reliable system and, although not perfect, most would agree that the present system seems to be more reliable than the previous one.

Others have criticised the validity of the diagnostic system. Validity here refers to the extent to which the diagnostic category measures what it was designed to measure. Perhaps one way in which current systems will come to be seen as primitive is the way in which they are categorical, i.e., someone either has or has not a particular disorder. Hans Eysenck, arguably the most influential British psychologist in the twentieth century, made this criticism suggesting that we would be better to view psychological functioning continuously, ranging from one extreme to another, with most people somewhere in the middle (Eysenck, 1986). Although this is an interesting suggestion and might better reflect the reality of at least some conditions, the fact that the biomedical paradigm is based on the idea of a dichotomous split between 'normality' and 'abnormality' means that psychological disorders continue to be viewed in an all or nothing way, i.e., a person either has the disorder or they don't. This way of thinking is implicit in the idea that mental disorders are an illness. Eysenck's views are interesting and perhaps his suggestion will eventually lead to a better classification system.

However, although Eysenck is not criticising classification and diagnosis per se, over the years there have been and still are many critics of the medical model of psychopathology and the role of classification and diagnosis. Advances in evolutionary psychology also promise to lead us to a better understanding of the nature of psychopathology, a topic that will be returned to in Chapter 7, but for now I want to discuss some research that has been conducted in recent years. How well has the biomedical approach fared? One avenue of research, which has attracted much attention, is the investigation of the association between psychological functioning and biochemical imbalances.

Biochemical imbalances

A first assumption of the biological perspective is that biochemical imbalances in the brain result in abnormal behaviour. The brain is composed of a complex network of neurons (nerve cells) which communicate with each other by electrical impulses. The electrical impulses are transmitted using chemicals which are called neurotransmitter substances. If there is an excess or deficit of a neurotransmitter substance, or the transfer of a neurotransmitter substance between neurons is blocked in some way, then the normal processes for which these neurotransmitters are responsible will go awry. Different types of neurotransmitter serve different regions of the brain. Researchers working within the biological model have attempted to study the relationship between the different neurotransmitters and the different psychological problems (as defined using the DSM system). For example, researchers have investigated the relationship between one subset of neurotransmitter substances called monoamines and the psychiatric diagnosis of depression, finding that people who are severely depressed and suicidal often have low levels of monoamines called serotonin and norepinephrine (e.g., Coppen and Doogan, 1988; Korpi *et al.*,

1986; McNeal and Cimbolic, 1986). The case for associations between biochemical and psychological functioning is good. There would seem to be little reason to doubt that our biochemical functioning is associated with our psychological functioning. However, although we can say that biochemical functioning is associated with psychological functioning, the evidence that biochemical imbalances cause psychological problems is not so clear. Biochemical functioning is equally likely to be caused by psychological functioning. Other researchers, trying to pin down the biological cause of certain psychological problems more securely, have investigated genetic deficits.

Genetic factors

A second assumption of the biomedical model is that biochemical processes are affected by genetic factors. Research in developmental genetics has shown that abnormalities in the structure or number of chromosomes (the structures within cells that contain the genes) are associated with a range of malformations such as Downs syndrome. There is no doubt that Downs syndrome has a genetic cause. At locations on the chromosome there are long molecules of deoxyribonucleic acid (DNA) which are the genes (if the chromosome is the necklace then the genes are the beads on that necklace). We know that genes determine physical characteristics such as eye colour, but the relationship between genes and behaviour is less direct and also depends on the environment. A person's genetic endowment is known as their genotype and the characteristics that result from an interaction between genes and environment is their phenotype. Thus, two people might have a genetic predisposition to a particular behaviour (i.e., the same genotype) but whereas one person goes on to develop that behaviour the other one may not (i.e., they exhibit different phenotypes).

The complexity of gene–environment interaction is such that it is only with a few conditions that scientists have identified faulty genes. For example, Huntington's disease is thought to affect about one person in 15,000 and to be caused by a single gene (Gusella *et al.*, 1983). This is a disorder in which a person's limbs and facial muscles undergo irregular spasms, there is impaired speech, difficulty swallowing, failing memory, attention difficulties, and progressive dementia, leading to death after about 10–20 years. Other disorders of which we think we now largely understand the biological basis, include Parkinson's disease, multiple sclerosis, Alzheimer's disease, Tourette's syndrome, AIDS dementia complex, and Korsakoff's syndrome (see Table 2.4). The biomedical paradigm is extremely useful in investigating organic disorders. What problems now thought to be of a psychological nature might be included within a list of organic disorders in the future? As already mentioned there is evidence that biological factors are associated with a range of psychological problems, but the direction of causality remains uncertain in most cases. A possible exception to this, it might be argued, is the so-

Table 2.4   Organic disorders

Huntington's disease	a progressive dementia, with movement difficulties, caused by degeneration of brain cells
Parkinson's disease	loss of intellectual functioning, accompanied by tremors, caused by dopamine deficiency
Multiple sclerosis	loss of intellectual functioning, accompanied by weakness and unsteadiness and spasticity of legs, caused by Myelin loss
Alzheimer's disease	a progressive dementia caused by loss of neurons in hippocampus
Multi-infarct dementia	dementia caused by series of strokes
Brain injury	intellectual, cognitive, personality changes caused by blow to the brain
Tourette's syndrome	multiple tics caused by neurochemical (acetylcholine/dopamine) imbalance
AIDS dementia	cognitive impairment caused by AIDS
Korsakoff's syndrome	memory and attention problems caused by damage to thalmus as a result of alcohol use and nutritional deficiencies

called disorder of schizophrenia. Contrary to what many people think, if a person is diagnosed with schizophrenia it does not mean that they have a split personality, but rather that there is a split between thoughts and emotions. DSM-IV outlines the symptoms that must be present before a diagnosis of schizophrenia can be made:

1. psychotic symptoms lasting at least one month
2. a marked deterioration in such areas as work, social relations, and self-care
3. signs of some sort of disturbance for at least six months.

Twin studies

If schizophrenia has a genetic cause then one would expect that twins are both likely to be diagnosed as schizophrenic. This is indeed what the evidence shows. The most famous study was carried out by Gottesman and Shields (1972) who, from the histories of 45,000 people treated at two hospitals in London between 1948 and 1964, contacted 57 schizophrenics with twins who agreed to be studied. What they found was that 42 per cent of the identical twins had schizophrenia and 9 per cent of the non-identical twins had schizophrenia. The prevalence of schizophrenia in the general population is about 1 per cent and so these results suggest that the closer two individuals are in biological relatedness, the more likely it is that if one has schizophrenia, then so too does the other. Since the study by Gottesman and Shields there has been a number of such studies and a similar pattern is consistently reported (Heston, 1970; 1992). Of course, those who are biologically related are usually brought up together and so share similar environments. Consequently, it is not always clear in such studies that the high rate of concordance is attributable solely to genetic factors. But where investigators have tried to rule out environmental factors by comparing twins brought up together against those brought up apart, it is found that the high rate of concordance holds even for twins who have been separated early in life (Gottesman, 1991). It is now generally accepted by most psychologists and psychiatrists that schizophrenia has a biological underpinning, although the nature of that underpinning, i.e., the precise role of genetic and neurochemical factors, is not yet certain. But this is not to say that genes cause schizophrenia. What the studies suggest is that if one twin has schizophrenia then there is about a 50 per cent chance that the other twin has too. What this also means is that if one twin has schizophrenia there is around a 50 per cent chance that the other one does not! This fact suggests that although there may be a genetic vulnerability to the so-called disorder of schizophrenia, other factors seem to be equally important in determining whether or not a person goes on to develop this condition. The question of how factors interact in this way will be revisited in Chapter 7 when we will consider what is known as the diathesis-stress model. But are we able to identify which genes identify those individuals at risk of schizophrenia?

Although there have been some studies published which provoked speculation that a gene for schizophrenia had been found (e.g., Bassett, McGillivray, Jones, and Pantzar, 1988), other studies have not been able to confirm this (e.g., Owen, Craufurd, and St. Clair, 1990). So, although there may be a genetic component to schizophrenia, scientists have not yet been able to pinpoint an exact gene in the way that Huntingdon's disease has been linked to one single gene. Also, we don't know precisely how genes influence behaviour, although there is much speculation and research on how genes might influence the neurochemistry of the brain. Interestingly, other recent thinking has led to alternative explanations for schizophrenia such as the possibility that during pregnancy viral infections such as chicken pox or measles affect the development of the child at a time when the brain is forming (see e.g., O'Callaghan *et al.*, 1991; 1993) and so the causes of schizophrenia remain a focus for debate.

Bipolar disorder, or what used to be called manic-depression, is a condition in which individuals experience mania, often alternating with periods of depression. Mania consists of an elevated and expansive mood, perhaps with inflated self-esteem and self-grandiosity, decreased need for sleep, increased talkativeness, racing thoughts and flights of ideas. About 1 per cent of adults have this condition at some point in their lives and it seems to be equally prevalent among men and women, and across social class. If one twin has this, the other has around a 50 per cent chance that they too will have it (McGuffin and Katz, 1989). However, as with schizophrenia, at present medical scientists do not know which or how many genes are involved or what the mechanisms are, assuming that there is a genetic predisposition.

The evidence seems to suggest that biological factors are necessary in the development of some psychological problems. In particular, the psychiatric diagnoses of schizophrenia and bipolar disorder appear to be, at least in part, biologically based. However, it is much less certain for other psychological problems whether biological factors are a cause or are themselves a product of the psychological problem. Psychiatrists and psychologists will be interested in obtaining a history of the client and will enquire into their family background and whether there is a history of psychological problems in the family, particularly for those patients like Matt, for whom there is the possibility of a genetic loading (see Box 2.1).

Therapies based on the medical model

The biomedical model views psychopathology as resulting from physical factors. According to the model, treatment needs to focus on changing the physical state of the person. Three types of therapy will be discussed:

- drug therapy
- electroconvulsive therapy
- psychosurgery.

Drug therapy

We probably know more about depression than any other so-called psychiatric disorder. The reason for this is that it is one of the most common of all psychiatric problems and consequently has been the focus of much research interest. Antidepressants were first introduced in the 1950s and heralded the beginnings of psychiatry as we know it today. Drug therapy is now widespread in the National Health Service and millions of prescriptions for drugs to treat psychological conditions are issued every year.

It has already been mentioned that there is evidence showing that depression is associated with low levels of the monoamines serotonin and noradrenaline. Consequently, drugs have been

Box 2.1

Matt was referred to a psychiatrist through his GP. From reading the referral notes the psychiatrist quickly came to the conclusion that it was possible that Matt was suffering from some form of psychotic illness, possibly a form of schizophrenia or bipolar disorder, with a genetic component. Following a detailed interview with Matt the psychiatrist ascertained that Matt did indeed meet the necessary symptom criteria for a diagnosis of schizophrenia. Most prominent were Matt's grandiose and paranoid delusions that he was doing work which was vital to the safety and security of the world. Matt believed that there were governmental and alien forces operating to prevent him from telling the world the truth about the conspiracy between alien beings and the Western governments. Matt found it hard to trust the psychiatrist, suspecting that he was in on the conspiracy and part of the plot to silence him. The psychiatrist took a detailed history of Matt's immediate context, finding out about his living arrangements, his relationships with other people, his experiences at school, as well as asking about difficulties that other members of Matt's family had experienced. From careful and systematic questioning of Matt and his parents it turned out that Matt's elder sister had dropped out of university because of problems with her nerves and that an uncle of Matt's had also been hospitalised with a diagnosis of schizophrenia 20 years previously when he was around the same age as Matt. These details helped to confirm in the psychiatrist's mind that Matt was suffering from some form of psychotic illness to which he was genetically susceptible.

manufactured which act to increase serotonin and noradrenaline activity. This is what the monoamine oxidase inhibitors (e.g., 'Nardil') and tricyclic antidepressants (e.g., 'Tofranil') do. However these drugs have a variety of side effects because, as well as influencing the level of serotonin and noradrenaline in the nervous system, they also influence the activity of other neurotransmitters which are not thought to be connected to depression. Side effects include cardiac arrhythmias and heart block, dry mouth, blurred vision, and urinary retention. For this reason, researchers have been interested in developing drugs that simply influence the level of serotonin and noradrenaline. These more recent antidepressant drugs are called *selective serotonin re-uptake inhibitors* (SSRIs) and *selective serotonin and noradrenaline re-uptake inhibitors* (SNRIs). The best known of these new antidepressants is Prozac, which was first introduced in 1987. Around 15 million people worldwide now take this drug. But do antidepressants work? Certainly they do seem to be effective in the short term with people suffering from severe depression, but there are concerns about their long-term use and research does not always suggest that antidepressants are more effective than psychotherapy. Some evidence suggests that antidepressants are effective in about two-thirds of patients (Dinan, 1995) although other evidence suggests that once people come off drugs their symptoms often return (in about 50 per cent of cases) (Evans *et al.*, 1992). Antidepressant medication has also been found to be helpful in some cases with those suffering from problems of an obsessive-compulsive nature (e.g., Marks and O'Sullivan, 1988).

Also, for those people diagnosed as suffering from bipolar disorder (manic-depression), lithium carbonate, a naturally occurring salt, seems to be able to control the symptoms if it is taken continuously (O'Connell *et al.*, 1991). Another neurotransmitter, dopamine, has been implicated in schizophrenia. It has been found that drugs which increase the level of dopamine in the brain produce symptoms similar to those found in individuals diagnosed as schizophrenic (e.g., Lieberman, Kinon, and Loebel, 1990) and antischizophrenic drugs which decrease the level of dopamine reduce the symptoms of schizophrenia (e.g., Kleinman *et al.*, 1984). But even though the dopamine hypothesis has attracted much research support, the exact relationship between dopamine levels and schizophrenia remains uncertain. Drug therapies do seem to be effective in alleviating the symptoms of some so-called disorders, albeit often accompanied by side effects, and the antischizophrenic drugs are a cornerstone of modern psychiatry.

One of the concerns about drug-based treatments is that underlying problems can remain. For example, someone with a fear of flying might take a tranquilliser before the flight enabling him or her to cope successfully with the journey. However, the effects of the drug will wear off and the fear of flying will remain (O'Sullivan and Marks, 1988; 1991). A full discussion of drug therapies is well beyond the scope of this book and interested readers might consult O'Mahony and Lucey (1998) for a fuller introduction.

For people suffering from a psychotic disorder some form of antischizophrenic medication would usually be prescribed. Matt was referred by his GP to psychiatric services where he was prescribed a course of neuroleptic medication. Helen's GP prescribed a course of Prozac for her (see Box 2.2). One of the disturbing things about drug therapies for forms of psychopathology is that they are often prescribed by people such as GPs who, although medically trained, have not trained in psychology or psychiatry and are not qualified as psychological therapists. People who present to the GP and who are put on a course of drugs might sometimes benefit at least as much from counselling and psychotherapy. However, fortunately, this situation seems to be slowly changing as more and more psychological therapists are being employed in community health centres and general practices.

Electroconvulsive therapy

The research discussed above has attempted to understand the cause of psychological problems with the aim of introducing treatments to alleviate the cause. However, other treatments are used to alleviate the symptoms without an understanding of the cause. Electroconvulsive therapy (ECT) involves passing electricity through the brain in order to induce seizure and was originally introduced in 1938 by Ugo Cerletti and Lucio Bini. The rationale for this was that it had been observed that epilepsy was rare among schizophrenics and thus, the reasoning went, epileptic seizures might prevent schizophrenia. We now know that epilepsy is not as rare among schizophrenics as first thought, and that the rationale for this treatment was therefore mistaken. As a treatment for schizophrenia, ECT has been ineffective. But, ECT continues to be used today for severe depression, either bilateral ECT in which electrodes are placed on both left and right temples, and electric-

Box 2.2

Helen has recently broken up with her partner after a long-standing relationship of seven years and her GP determines that this event has played a major role in the onset of her depression. Although a short course of antidepressant medication is offered to Helen to help her cope better while she rebuilds her life, her GP also considers that Helen's problems are related to low self-esteem and the way she has appraised the break-up with her partner as proving that she is worthless and unattractive. In the longer term it is thought that she might benefit considerably from counselling and her GP also refers her to the practice counsellor. In the short term, however, Helen finds that Prozac helps her to feel better and more able to function on a day to day basis. She is able to continue with work and the GP recommends that she continues taking Prozac for the following six months during which time she also enters into counselling with a therapist at the GP's practice. The GP, in consultation with the counsellor, recommends at the end of the six month period that she reduces the dosage and gradually comes off Prozac. Meanwhile the counsellor is helping Helen understand how her self-esteem is tied to her perception of how other people perceive her and how much she succeeds in living up to their expectations of her.

ity is passed through both sides of the brain, or unilateral ECT, where electricity is passed through only one side of the brain. Initially ECT was a very dangerous treatment with patients suffering spasms leading to physical injury. However, during ECT as it used today, the patient is administered muscle relaxant to prevent the dangerous jerking body movements that occur during convulsion (Weiner and Krystal, 1994). Although there are those who claim that ECT has been of great benefit to them, and there is supportive research evidence, ECT has received a great deal of criticism.

Notably, it has been criticised for its lack of scientific basis. It has been likened to hitting the television set when you can't get a clear picture. It has also been criticised for the side effects, for example that it causes memory loss. Furthermore, it has been criticised as being a barbaric and inhumane treatment. But, those who use ECT say that in cases of severe and chronic depression in which other treatments have failed, it is often an effective last resort. Most psychiatrists would probably agree that ECT is highly effective in the treatment of severe and suicidal depression and unlike other treatments whose effects take time to work, particularly psychotherapy, the effects of ECT are immediate, and in that respect can save lives.

Psychosurgery

As well as drug therapy and ECT, in extreme circumstances psychosurgery might be deemed appropriate. Psychosurgery involves the deliberate destruction of a small part of the brain. Although psychosurgery was once a fairly widespread treatment for psychiatric disorders, it is rarely carried out today (Snaith, 1994). Modern technology means that the surgery is more precise than before, although not surprisingly it remains a controversial treatment which can lead to irreversible and negative side effects.

Treatment-aetiology fallacy

One of the issues that all therapists need to be aware of is the *treatment-aetiology fallacy*. It is easy to conclude that just because a treatment works that this tells us about the cause of the problem. Although this applies to all therapies, it is perhaps easier to see it in relation to medical approaches; even if ECT or drug therapies are effective, this does not mean that the cause of the problem was biochemical.

Conclusion

In summary, the biomedical model suggests that psychopathology is the result of physical imbalances, and that psychological problems represent some underlying disease process. Forms of treatment considered under the biomedical model are drug therapy, ECT, and psychosurgery. But despite the growing evidence for the role of biological factors in the origins of several so-called psychiatric disorders, there is a saying that anatomy is not destiny. It is important to understand that although there might be biological factors important in the causes and treatment of at least some psychological problems, this does not lead us to adopt an attitude of extreme biological determinism. Certainly, there are some who do seem to overemphasise the role of biological factors, but most theorists and researchers understand that it is only through an interaction of biological and environmental factors that psychological difficulties arise. This is a topic that we will return to in Chapter 7 when we go on to look at the biopsychosocial model, and in particular the diathesis-stress point of view. The biomedical paradigm is the foundation block for the profession of psychiatry, although many of the assumptions will also be shared by other mental health professionals such as psychologists. Although psychologists do not often take a wholly biological approach to understanding psychopathology, they will often adopt a medical approach; that is to say they might share the same assumptions about scientific practice and the need for diagnosis in order to formulate an appropriate form of treatment. The *Diagnostic and Statistical Manual* might be used in this respect as an aid in understanding the client's problems.

However, the system of psychiatric classification is not without criticism. For example, there are questions about its reliability and validity, i.e., the extent to which different clinicians can reach agreement about what disorder a person is suffering from and exactly what the disorder consists of. As we shall see in Chapter 6, there are those like Szasz who claim that the medical approach to psychological problems also has other more covert social and political aims. One final issue worth considering in the context of medical treatments for psychological problems is the fact that there remains much stigma attached to mental health problems and for some people it is easier to perceive themselves as suffering from a physical problem than from a mental problem. Consequently, for those people, it will be easier to go along to a doctor for biomedical treatment than to a psychological therapist.

Summary points

- The biomedical model emphasises psychopathology as resulting from biological abnormalities or neurochemical imbalance in the brain.

- The biomedical model adopts a medical perspective to psychopathology by attempting to classify the different forms of psychopathology that people may experience. The most widely used classification system is the *Diagnostic and Statistical Manual of Mental Disorders* (DSM) published by the American Psychiatric Association.

- Using DSM, people are assessed on five different axes (areas of functioning): clinical syndromes; life-long personality patterns; medical conditions; psychosocial and environmental problems; and a global assessment of functioning.

- Classification is the fundamental tool of scientific enquiry and the biomedical model has a rich history of experimental investigation. The main tool of scientific enquiry is the randomised control trial (RCT) which is the way to test for the efficacy of new treatments.

- Much research evidence exists to support the idea that biological functioning is associated with psychological functioning. There is evidence that biochemical imbalances are associated with so-called psychiatric disorders such as depression, anxiety, schizophrenia, and bipolar disorder. However, the causal relationship between biochemical factors and psychological problems is less clear.

- There is also evidence from twin studies suggesting that there may be a genetic vulnerability for some people to develop psychiatric disorders, although it is emphasised that scientists do not know exactly how genes are involved in the development of schizophrenia or other so-called disorders.

- Therapies based on the biomedical model are most often drug-based therapies which aim to redress the neurochemical imbalance in the brain. Evidence shows that drug therapies can be effective in alleviating symptoms and in helping people cope, but symptoms can return once the person is no longer taking the drug and underlying problems are not addressed.

- Other therapies include electroconvulsive therapy (ECT) and psychosurgery. These are more controversial treatments involving passing electric shocks through the brain and surgery to the brain, respectively, and are less commonly used today.

3

Psychoanalytic and Psychodynamic Approaches

Introduction

Like the biomedical model, it is an assumption of the psychodynamic model that psychological problems have causes internal to the person. But rather than emphasising biological causes, the psychodynamic model emphasises psychological causes. In this respect it is similar to the humanistic, cognitive, and behavioural models. The psychodynamic model is the oldest and the best known of these four psychological models. Psychodynamic theorists believe that unconscious dynamic forces largely determine behaviour, and that psychopathology is the result of conflict between these forces. Such conflicts, it is believed, have their roots in early life experiences and the relationship with the caregiver in the first years of life. One survey of psychologists found that around one fifth described themselves as psychodynamic (Norcross, Prochaska, and Farber, 1993). Sigmund Freud has been called the grandfather of the psychodynamic approach and it is his ideas which chiefly concern us here. What Freud did which was so important was that he was able to show that the chaos of psychopathology had meaning and pattern which could be understood by an observer.

Sigmund Freud and the psychoanalytic model

The psychodynamic model was introduced around one hundred years ago in Vienna by Sigmund Freud (1856–1939). Freud first introduced this idea as a way of explaining *hysteria*, a condition in which physical symptoms are experienced but no organic cause can be found. For example, someone who suddenly can't see or can't hear but yet there seems to be no physical explanation for these symptoms. In such a case, Freud would have said that the cause was psychological, perhaps the person is trying to block out something that is distressing to them, something that they can't bear to confront and to acknowledge.

Very few people will not have heard of Freud and few people would disagree that his ideas have changed how we think about human nature, and at least in this respect he deserves to be credited as one of the most influential thinkers of all time. But this is not to say that everyone would agree that the model he developed to explain human behaviour is correct, and in the past one hundred years some theorists have proposed reformulations of the psychodynamic model and others have rejected it outright. One of those who has rejected it is Sutherland (1998) who writes:

> One must ask what is the standing of Freudian theory and practice today: I write 'theory and practice' advisedly, since it is important to separate the two. It could be that Freud's theories about human motives and the development of the personality are correct while the therapy has no value: It is also possible that his theories are nonsense while the therapy works – neurotics might, just possibly, be helped by being presented with mythical stories about the origins of their feelings and actions. (Sutherland, 1998, p. 139)

As with all of the models presented in this book, each of us must make our own decision as to what to think about Freudian theory and psychoanalytical practice. So, first, let us look at psychoanalytical theory and the work of Freud.

Psychoanalytical theory

In 1885 Freud studied hypnosis in Paris with the neurologist Jean Charcot, then returned to Vienna to work with Josef Breuer (1842–1925). Breuer, at that time, was conducting experiments on hypnosis and what was then called hysterical illness, i.e., physical complaints which seemed to have no biological cause. In one of the most famous studies of all time, Breuer had been treating a woman called 'Anna O' and it was through this case that psycho-analysis was born.

The case of Anna O

Anna O was a young educated woman who suffered from various symptoms including physical weakness, paralysis and deafness. She had fallen ill while caring for her father, who was severely ill. Over time she developed a dual personality, one personality spoke German and the other English. She would fall into a hypnotic trance during which her symptoms disappeared and she talked of past traumatic experiences, and was able to express strong emotions, which, Breuer argued, was therapeutic in her recovery. This was the important discovery that Breuer made, that physical symptoms could be removed through the verbal expression of feelings and ideas. An example of this was Anna O's difficulty in swallowing water, which reportedly disappeared after she recounted to Breuer her disgust at seeing a dog drinking water from a glass. Anna O called this her 'talking cure' and this method became known as the 'cathartic method', a term derived from the Greek word *katharsis* meaning purgation. Also, what was important was that these observations implied that psychological problems had meaning which was determined by principles of cause and effect.

Breuer and Freud went on to investigate a number of other cases and together proposed that hysterical illnesses are caused by psychological conflicts outside of conscious awareness and which had their roots in traumatic experiences which were most often sexual in nature. By bringing these conflicts into conscious awareness, Breuer and Freud argued, the symptoms of hysterical illness would diminish. Although Breuer and Freud later went on to disagree over these ideas, they provided the foundation stone for Freud's later work and he continued to explore the nature of the unconscious mind and the role of early experiences for the rest of his life.

Through his work with Breuer, Freud initially developed an interest in hypnosis, seeing it as a tool through which people could recall forgotten traumatic memories. However, fairly early on in his career Freud dropped hypnosis as a method of treatment, although he continued having patients lie on a couch, and focused on developing ways in which he could help patients bring to consciousness their previously unconscious conflicts. Over time, Freud came to see hypnosis as unnecessary in the recall of forgotten traumatic memories developing other methods to accomplish this task. What Freud discovered was that people actively resisted remembering traumatic and unpleasant events. People 'repressed' their memories. It was in 1896 that Freud first used the term psychoanalysis to describe his methods and in 1900 he published what is perhaps the most well known of all his works, *The Interpretation of Dreams*, which was followed the subsequent year by *The Psychopathology of Everyday Life*. During the rest of his life, Freud published voraciously on psychoanalysis with his last book, *An Outline of Psychoanalysis*, being published in 1940. The method of treatment he developed was known as psychoanalysis. Thus, Freud can be credited with introducing the first psychological theory of abnormal behaviour, a theory that drew attention to the role of early childhood experiences and unconscious mental forces within the person. Such an approach was a dramatic shift in perspective from the biological treatments that were dominant at the time.

Many would argue that the importance of what Freud did was to draw attention to the unconscious and how this part of the human mind influenced behaviour. Within the unconscious, Freud argued, are instinctual elements which are inaccessible to the conscious mind along with other material which has been censored or repressed but which affects consciousness indirectly. Today, therapists of all persuasions find this or some similar distinction very useful. Freud distinguished the unconscious from the conscious and the preconscious. The conscious is what we are aware of at any given moment and the preconscious is material that we are not consciously aware of but which is accessible to conscious introspection. Thus, the essence of psychoanalysis is that psychopathology is a result of unconscious conflicts between different parts of the personality. Freud viewed personality as being divided into three parts, what he called the id, ego, and the superego.

The id, the ego, and the superego

Freud believed that human personality is composed of three structures – the *id*, the *ego*, and the *superego* – and that behaviour is the product of interaction between these structures. The id is that part of personality that we are born with and which consisted of basic biological, instinctual, urges towards sex, food, warmth, elimination; urges that are unconscious. Freud described the id as a 'cauldron of seething excitement' (Freud, 1933, pp. 103–04). The id was further divided into two basic instincts, an instinct towards life which Freud called *Eros*, and an instinct towards death which Freud called *Thanatos*. However, it was Eros that Freud was chiefly concerned with and he viewed this force towards life as mainly consisting of sexual energy which he called the *libido*. It was only later in his career that Freud began to explore Thanatos. The id seeks immediate gratification and operates on what Freud called the *pleasure principle* (i.e., always seeking gratification). Gratification is achieved, Freud thought, through reflex activity such as when an infant receives milk from the mother's breast. However, if immediate gratification is not forthcoming, then gratification is obtained through generating fantasies of what is desired (i.e., the generation of an image or a memory of the desired object, in this case the mother's breast) through what Freud called *primary process* thinking. Gratification of id impulses through primary process thinking is known as wish fulfilment. Thus, the id is a deep reservoir of basic sexual and aggressive impulses and desires that reside in the unconscious.

In contrast to the id, which operates at the unconscious level, the ego resides in preconscious and in part of conscious awareness and begins to develop, Freud thought, out of the id at around six months after birth. The infant comes to recognise that not all instinctual needs are met. For example, the mother is not always there to provide for the infant. So, part of the id becomes differentiated into the ego which also seeks gratification. However, the function of the ego is to confront reality through *secondary processes* of planning and decision making. The ego operates on the basis of what Freud called the *reality principle* as it strives to meet the demands of what gratification is obtainable and the demands of the id.

Freud called the third part of personality the superego which is concerned with social and moral standards. The superego consists of introjections from caregivers and operates within the unconscious, preconscious, and, to a greater extent than the ego, within the conscious. The superego develops out of the ego and has two parts. First, the conscience which reminds us that certain thoughts, feelings, or behaviours are right or wrong, good or bad. The second is the *ego ideal* which is a composite of all the values acquired and an image of the type of person we are striving to become. The ego-ideal part of the superego rewards moral or ethical behaviour with feelings of pride.

Thus, Freud viewed psychopathology as resulting from intra-psychic conflict between these different parts of personality which formed a closed energy system with the three parts battling for their share of the id's energy. When we use the term psycho-dynamic today what we are referring to is the interplay of these forces. For example, imagine the hypothetical conversation between the id, ego, and superego of a boy standing in a sweet shop:

Id 'I'll put the sweets in my pocket and just walk out of the shop.'
Ego 'I could do that, but tomorrow I get my pocket money and I could come back then.'
Superego 'And I know that it isn't right to just take things that don't belong to you.'

The conflict, Freud believed, was always there between the forces. It is when these forces are balanced in this way that psychological health is present. The idea of balance between these instinctual forces is reminiscent of Hippocrates humoural theory discussed in Chapter 2.

Whenever id impulses demand gratification and the ego cannot allow these impulses to surface into consciousness, the ego experiences intense anxiety. The superego in turn can attempt to control id impulses by flooding the personality with guilt feelings. As well as producing psychological discomfort, unconscious processes can produce physical complaints. Most notably, Freud discussed what he called *conversion disorder*, which is a physical symptom, such as blindness, that has no biological cause but instead is the conversion of unconscious psychological conflict.

Psychosexual development

Freud also viewed personality as being formed through four separate stages of *psychosexual development*. In the first to second year of life, the principal erogenous zone, Freud argued, was the mouth.

Thus, the first stage is the *oral* stage during the first year when the infant derives most gratification through id impulses of sucking and feeding. Between the second and third years of life, Freud argued, the anal area provides the major source of pleasurable stimulation. Thus, the second stage is the *anal* stage during the second to third year when pleasure moves to the retention and elimination of faeces. The third stage is the *phallic* stage which takes place between age three to six when pleasure comes mostly from genital self-manipulation and children notice that the genitals of boys and girls are different. At around five to six years, the child's sexual motivations, Freud argued, begin to recede in importance. It is as if the child's sexual drive has become inactive. Now the child is preoccupied with developing skills and engaging in new activities. The *latency* stage, as it is called, continues until around the age of 12 and the onset of puberty. After puberty, Freud argued, comes the *genital* stage during which adult sexuality emerges and most pleasure is derived from heterosexual relationships (see Table 3.1).

Healthy psychological functioning, Freud believed, was the result of successful and normal progress through each of these stages. Adult personality is determined by this process of development. So, for example, the age of toilet training will be related to later personality. If a child is toilet trained too early he or she will develop what are termed anal personality characteristics, i.e., being overly tidy, orderly, mean, and obstinate. Likewise, early weaning

Table 3.1 Freudian psychosexual stages of development

Age	Stage	Source of libidinal pleasure
0–2	Oral	sucking
2–3	Anal	retention and elimination of faeces
3–6	Phallic	self-manipulation of genitals
6–12	Latency	sexual motivations recede
12–	Genital	adult sexuality begins to develop

is associated with what are termed oral personality characteristics, i.e., a love of eating and drinking, pessimism, guilt, and dependence. Certainly, these are intriguing suggestions as to why some people seem to possess more of certain characteristics than others. Some researchers have developed questionnaires to assess these two personality types, the oral and the anal, and tried to test whether it is in fact the case that people with more of one characteristic do indeed have different childhood experiences. But the findings are mixed, with some studies providing evidence in support of Freud's ideas, other studies showing no associations, and yet other studies showing the complete opposite to what Freud claimed. So, there is no compelling scientific evidence to support these ideas.

The most difficult stage to move through, Freud believed, was the phallic stage. During the phallic stage, the child is filled with sexual desire for the opposite sex parent, a desire which is so threatening, because of fear of punishment from the same sex parent, that the child pushes the conflict into the unconscious. Freud referred to this conflict as the Oedipus complex when referring to boys and the Electra complex when referring to girls. As this element of Freud's theory is so central to psychoanalysis it is worth spending a little more time looking at it.

Oedipal dilemma

Boys at the phallic stage, Freud proposed, develop a sexual attachment to their mother and want to possess her sexually. The father is seen by the young boy as a sexual rival. This is what Freud called the *Oedipal dilemma*, after the Greek tragedy Oedipus Rex. Consequently, Freud suggested, the boy fears that his father wants to take vengeance on him, that the father will castrate him (the castration complex) and in turn the boy also wants to kill his father. But the father is too powerful and so the boy must either disguise this desire by identifying with the father or by identifying with the mother. Identification with the father allows the boy to sleep with his mother in fantasy and so he obtains vicarious gratification. When the boy gives up his desire for his mother and instead starts to identify with his father, the conflict is resolved. If the conflict is not resolved, Freud suggested, the foundations for psychopathology in adulthood are laid. The other way of resolving the conflict, identification with the mother, leads the boy to sleep with his father in fantasy. Although this disguises his jealousy of his father, the boy in giving free rein to his homosexual tendencies, which Freud believed we all had, would lead to later disturbances. The unconscious forces can be so distressing to the person that, Freud argued, there are a variety of defence mechanisms that are called into play to protect the person. Some of these will be discussed below.

Defence mechanisms

Neurotic anxiety, according to Freud, was a result of such repressed conflicts as those discussed above and the fear of the consequences if a punished id impulse was to be expressed. Neurotic anxiety was to be distinguished from objective anxiety, i.e., the ego's reaction to realistic danger, and moral anxiety, i.e., fear of the superego's punishment for transgressing moral standards. Freud went on to describe how neurotic anxiety and guilt was dealt with using unconscious distortions of reality through the use of various *defence mechanisms* such as *repression, projection,* and *displacement.* The most important defence mechanism discussed by Freud was that of repression, keeping unacceptable impulses unconscious. But the repressed wish still exists and so can cause neurosis. Other defence mechanisms are therefore used to allow the repressed wishes to be released in a way in which they are not recognised. For example, projection might involve thinking that someone else wants to sleep with their mother. A range of other defence mechanisms have been discussed (see Table 3.2). But whether or not they have their roots in childhood experiences and represent the conflict between the unconscious forces discussed earlier remains uncertain and perhaps even unlikely in some cases.

Freud and psychopathology

In the previous chapter, the psychiatric disorder of schizophrenia was described and the biomedical explanation discussed. So, how can Freudian theory explain the so-called psychiatric disorder of schizophrenia? One possibility is that when the ego becomes

Table 3.2 Some ego-defence mechanisms

Denial: Refusing to face reality, behaving in a way as to suggest that the person is unaware of something he or she might be expected to know, e.g., refusing to accept that smoking is related to cancer, blocking a painful experience from memory.

Repression: Prevention of painful, unacceptable, and dangerous thoughts and emotions from entering consciousness, e.g., a person who has been assaulted cannot remember what happened; or a man failing to recognise his attraction for his daughter-in-law.

Projection: Attributing one's own unacceptable negative thoughts and feelings to another, e.g., an employee who is angry at his boss being convinced that it is his boss who is angry at him, or a teacher who is attracted to her student perceiving the student as attracted to her.

Reaction formation: Preventing the awareness of unacceptable desires by the adoption of the opposite behaviour, e.g., someone who is sexually attracted to another person acting towards them in a cold and hostile way; or someone who is strongly attracted to homosexual behaviour expressing strong homophobic attitudes.

Displacement: Venting feelings on less dangerous substitute people or objects, e.g., feeling angry with a colleague at work and then coming home to shout at the children, or smashing a plate during an argument with one's spouse.

Intellectualisation: Cutting off from emotional awareness, e.g., a person talking about a life-threatening situation in a cold and calm way.

Regression: Reverting to an earlier developmental level in which behaviour is less mature, e.g., sulking like a child during an argument, or having a temper tantrum when things do not go the way we want them too.

Identification: Affiliating oneself with a group or another person often perceived to be of high standing, e.g., an insecure young man emulating a movie idol who is known for a particular style of dress.

Sublimation: Channelling frustrated energy into socially acceptable activities, e.g., an aggressive and conflictual woman who becomes a police officer.

Rationalisation: Making socially acceptable explanations that serve to justify behaviour that are based on unacceptable motives or to conceal disappointment, e.g., after being sexually rejected deciding that the other person was unattractive anyway, or after failing to get offered a job deciding that you didn't really want it anyway.

overwhelmed by the demands of the id or is besieged by over-whelming guilt from the superego, the person regresses to an earlier developmental stage, the oral stage of psychosexual development. Remember that this is the stage in which the child has not yet learned to separate itself from the world around it. At this stage, the infant is the centre of experience, and so the adult regressed to this stage might manifest what we would see as delusions of self-importance. Fantasy and reality become confused, which might manifest as unusual perceptual experiences, paranoid ideation, and magical thinking. We also saw that the biomedical model proposes that depression is caused by an imbalance of certain neurotransmitters in the brain. How would Freudian theory explain depression? Freud (1917) noted that there was a similarity between grieving and depression and argued that depression was a grief process in relation to a real or imagined loss that is reminiscent of losses incurred in childhood. In summary, Freud suggested that psychological suffering was due to inner conflicts that the person is not consciously aware of because of various defence mechanisms. Conflicts often date back to childhood and early sexual experience and through psychoanalysis a person can become aware of these conflicts. Freud's view of psychopathology therefore was a psychological one. Freud's focus was primarily on the energy of the id and how this energy was either channelled or transformed.

Given the sexually repressive society that existed in Victorian times, we can see just how radical Freud's ideas were. However, Freud's ideas have since become part of the Western world's cultural heritage and inform the way we think about the nature of human personality and psychological suffering. But, as we saw in Chapter 1 his ideas have also been subject to much criticism over the years, including that by Sutherland (1998). The main criticism is that, contrary to Freud's own claims, his ideas are generally not scientific contributions.

Popper and the concept of falsification

A little was said in the previous chapter about the role of scientific enquiry and how traditional research requires the processes that are hypothesised to occur be measurable in some way. But this is not the whole story. The work of Freud provides an opportunity to say a little more about the nature of scientific hypothesis testing. What Freud did was to observe patients within a clinical setting, then develop theoretical ideas about how unconscious forces operated to produce disturbances, and then through a series of further observations of patients who seemed to fit the expected pattern concluded that there was support for his theories. But there is a major problem with this method: it has no logical basis. If you observe something to happen ten times, it does not follow that it will happen again on the eleventh time. What that means is that it is not logically possible to verify the theory.

Modern science is instead based on the concept of falsification developed by Popper (1959). What Popper argued was that hypotheses should be formulated in a way that they are capable of refutation. Popper argued that science needs to consist of making a clear conjecture that can be shown to be false. An example of this would be if someone claimed that all swans are white. It doesn't matter how many white swans they find; it only takes one black swan to falsify the claim. What scientists endeavour to do is to find the black swan and what Freud did was to find lots of white swans. This is what critics of Freud mean when they say that his work was not scientific.

However, some of Freud's conjectures can be tested scientifically. For example, Freud hypothesises a relationship between toilet training practices and personality development, such that children who are weaned early go on to develop more obsessive personalities. Overall, however, most of his theoretical formulations are complex and do not easily lend themselves to the process of falsification discussed by Popper (1959). Another criticism of Freud is that although his theoretical formulations were thought to tell us about human nature, his observations themselves were largely restricted to middle class Viennese women between the ages of 20 and 44. Should we therefore dismiss Freud's ideas altogether?

Much of Freudian thinking cannot be easily put to the test of scientific investigation (Fisher and Greenberg, 1996). Sutherland (1998) says that Freud's ideas are generally 'so flexible and imprecise that it is difficult to have faith in any of his detailed interpretations' (Sutherland, 1998, p. 140) and perhaps this is most evident when we look at movement through the phallic stage described by Freud. Clearly, it is not possible to test out these ideas using scientific methodology, and we can see why some might refer to such ideas as nothing but mythical stories. But does it seem so unlikely that a child could have such complex ideas about sexuality? Just because an idea can't be tested scientifically doesn't mean that it isn't true, only that it isn't possible to provide evidence in support of it. Freud's own evidence was from the dreams and free associations of his patients. But although sometimes seemingly convincing we must remember that this is not scientific evidence and, as Sutherland (1998) notes, 'with sufficient ingenuity any chain of associations or any dream can be interpreted in any way one wants' (Sutherland, 1998, p. 135).

However, in defence of Freudian psychoanalysis it must be said that although Freud did attempt to outline some broad inductive principles that apply universally to human behaviour, his work was chiefly concerned with the complex and very personal experiences that do not lend themselves to experimental enquiry. To dismiss Freud because his work falls short of fulfilling standards of enquiry derived from the more inductive physical sciences is to misunderstand Freud and the importance of his approach.

Psychoanalysis

Turning now to practice, Freud's view was that the psychoanalyst's role was to uncover the unconscious conflicts that cause psychological distress, to bring formerly unconscious material into conscious awareness, and to achieve the reintegration of the previously repressed material into the total structure of the personality. Simply treating the symptom, as would happen in behaviour therapy, is not sufficient to lead to cure. Unless the underlying conflict is resolved, another symptom will appear. This is referred to as *symptom substitution*. The client, or analysand in psychoanalytic terms, must achieve insight. To do this, Freud reasoned, the psychoanalyst must encourage free and open expression, and the analysand must express whatever comes to mind. The conventions of ordinary conversation are set aside and the analysand is asked to be completely candid and to tell the analyst whatever comes to mind.

Free association

Free association is the name given to the technique through which the analysand says whatever comes to mind, any thoughts, feelings, images that come to mind, no matter if they seem unimportant, trivial, or offensive. The psychoanalyst listens for clues to what is going on within the person. In response, the psychoanalyst has three main tools, *confrontation, interpretation*, and *reconstruction*. Using these techniques, the analysand is directed by the psychoanalyst, in a safe and secure setting, to re-experience repressed unconscious feelings and wishes which were frustrated in childhood. Confrontation is when the psychoanalyst mirrors what the analysand is revealing through what they say, e.g., 'you are denying your anger'. Interpretation is when the psychoanalyst explains the unconscious motives behind the behaviour, motives that often relate to past experience, e.g., 'you are denying you are angry because I remind you of your father and if you express your anger you are scared that you will lose the love of your father that you so desperately seek'. Reconstruction uncovers those past experiences, e.g., 'when you felt angry as a child your father would turn away from you'.

Resistance and transference

Using these tools of confrontation, interpretation and reconstruction, the psychoanalyst looks for *resistance* of the analysand. Resistance is when the analysand encounters a block in their free association, perhaps changing the subject of their dialogue to avoid a painful topic. For example, the analysand might be talking about their childhood when suddenly they change the topic to some trivial event that happened at work the previous day.

The psychoanalyst is also on the look out for *transference*. This is when the analysand acts or feels towards the psychoanalyst as if he or she was an important figure from their childhood. Thus, in classical psychoanalysis, the psychoanalyst often sits behind the analysand while he or she lies on a couch. The psychoanalyst uses this to maintain neutrality, an uninvolved stance, a blank screen, in which the analysand is most able to freely express whatever comes to mind. Importantly, this also encourages transference, a process in which the analysand transfers the feelings they have towards some key figure in their lives onto the psychoanalyst, who in turn promotes insight into the transference. The idea is that the psychoanalyst, a shadowy figure traditionally sitting behind the analysand, becomes a focus for the analysand to transfer thoughts and feelings onto. For example, someone who has been brought up with parents who are rejecting and demanding will relate to the psychoanalyst as if she or he is rejecting and demanding. The psychoanalyst in seeing this negative transference will encourage it and explore it with the analysand. It is generally recognised that transference does occur in the psychotherapy setting, as in other contexts too, but it is only within the psychodynamic way of working that it is actively encouraged and made a focus for exploration.

Another method employed by psychoanalysts is the examination of what are known as Freudian slips, or *parapraxes*. Unconscious material sometimes slips out, and according to the psychoanalysts such slips of the tongue can tell us something about our unconscious desires.

Dreams

Another, and perhaps the most important, aspect of psychoanalytic work is the emphasis on dreams. Freud believed that during dreams the defence mechanisms, such as those described above, were less in operation and so dreams could be used to reveal more about the workings of the unconscious. Importantly, Freud distinguished between the *manifest content* and the *latent content* of a dream. The manifest content was that which was consciously recalled whereas the latent content was the symbolic meaning. It was through understanding the latent content rather than the manifest content, Freud argued, that insight could be achieved.

Unconscious wishes, Freud thought, were expressed in dreams, but often these unconscious wishes are too distressing for the person to confront and so they are expressed in symbolic form. Freud described dreams as the royal road to the unconscious and psychoanalysts, as well as psychodynamic therapists, operate on the assumption that through our dreams we are able to catch glimmers of our unconscious and repressed fears and wishes. A large part of psychoanalysis is concerned with the interpretation of dreams. Free association is one technique used to uncover the latent content of dreams. Clients are encouraged to say whatever comes to mind, no matter how irrelevant or irrational it seems. The idea is that nothing is censored and through free association we are able to glimpse into the unconscious processes at work.

However, classical psychoanalysis is a lengthy and time consuming process and psychoanalysts would argue that several sessions are required every week for several years for deep changes in personality to occur. For this reason, classical psychoanalysis is often impractical and overly expensive for most people. Nevertheless some of the concepts derived from psychoanalytical ideas remain popular among therapists of different orientations. Understanding the client's use of defence mechanisms will, for example, be a focus for therapists from a wide variety of therapeutic orientations. But perhaps the psychoanalytic concept which enjoys most attention is transference. Although not all therapists will use the term, all recognise that the past has a way of repeating itself in the present (see Box 3.1).

Neo-Freudian psychodynamic models

Jung and analytical psychology

It was in 1907 that Freud and Jung first met and the two men quickly became close friends and collaborators in developing the psychoanalytic movement. Freud saw Jung as his successor as leader of the psychoanalytical movement and Jung became the first ever president of the International Psychoanalytical Society. However, Jung saw Freud as holding entrenched ideas and resisted the idea that he should become a successor to Freud, simply going on to promote Freud's ideas. Jung had his own ideas and in 1914 the collaboration and friendship ended. Jung resigned as the president of the International Psychoanalytical Society. The split was due, among various reasons, to a major point of disagreement on the nature of libidinal energy and infantile sexuality as the cause of neurosis. Whereas Freud saw the libido as essentially sexual in

Box 3.1

Alex began to realise that he had to change if he was to keep his friends and job, and after seeking advice from his GP he consulted a local psychotherapist. The psychotherapist worked with Alex for the next two years helping him to understand how his early experiences were related to his current behaviour. Alex's parents separated when he was a small boy and he continued living with his father. Alex lost contact with his mother and his father remained hostile to his mother, always criticising her in front of Alex. Alex found growing up painful and in therapy he struggled to recollect his childhood. He described how his father would drink heavily, coming back drunk at the weekends when he would often shout at Alex and belittle him. Sometimes his father behaved violently and he lived in fear of his father. Alex's marriage of several years had been very tempestuous and had ended one night after a heavy drinking episode when he returned home to accuse his wife of sleeping with another man. In the ensuing argument Alex had put his fist through the window and threatened his wife. She left the following day. At first he found it difficult to commit himself to regular therapy sessions, often phoning up to cancel the day before. He would often accuse the therapist of thinking belittling thoughts about him. The therapist was aware of how Alex was behaving towards him, as if he, the therapist, possessed the same characteristics as Alex's father. Through exploring this transference reaction, Alex began to understand how he often did this with people who reminded him of his father, how he expected to be belittled and teased and would react defensively to other people. In therapy, Alex began to understand how he dealt with this situation as a child through repressing his feelings, how he had used alcohol to help him regulate his emotions, and how as an adult his aggression was a way of displacing the feelings that would rise up in him. Through exploring his childhood, Alex began to understand how his feelings of rage were connected to his experiences of childhood, his anger with his mother for leaving and his fear of his father.

nature, Jung saw the libido as essentially spiritual. Also, whereas Freud saw libidinal energy as the primary motivating force, Jung saw libidinal energy as only one of several forces operating in the person. For Freud, this was heresy.

Jung also proposed the existence of what he called a collective unconscious, a record of human experience which is revealed in the myths that each culture creates, containing universal symbols, narrative themes, or archetypes, that occur time and again in art, religion, and literature. Much of this material, Jung argued, did not come through personal experience but rather through our psychological heritage. In the same way that the body has been shaped by evolution, so too, Jung believed, was the mind.

Also, whereas Freud was concerned with the development of the child, Jung was also concerned with the development of the person across the life-span. Jung introduced the concept of *individuation*, a process which began at around the age of 40 and involved the person beginning to develop those archetypes within him or her self which up to that point had remained primitive. Individuation was the force for personal growth and the development of the self. The repressed unconscious conflicts discussed by Freud are no longer the central forces for development as they were in adolescence. Jung also wrote extensively about personality and introduced the idea that people differ in personality, some people being more concerned with the internal world, *introverts*, and others being more concerned with the external world, *extroverts*. After the split from Freud and psychoanalysis, Jung went on to develop his own ideas and formulated new techniques of psychotherapy which he called *analytical psychology*.

Alfred Adler and individual psychology

Another early collaborator of Freud and a president of the Vienna Psychoanalytical Society was Alfred Adler (1870–1937). As with Jung, Freud and Adler developed conflicts over theory, with Adler also criticising Freud's emphasis on sexuality, while Freud criticised Adler's emphasis on the role of conscious processes. Adler emphasised the role of the person's striving for control and power in their life, maintaining that early experiences of powerlessness in childhood can lead to later feelings of inferiority in adulthood. The way the person deals with their feelings of inferiority, Adler believed, could result in psychopathology. For example, a person might over-compensate for their sense of inferiority by becoming withdrawn from others. Alternatively, they may be abusive and bullying (see Box 3.2).

Adler and Freud parted company, splitting the membership of the Vienna Psychoanalytical Society, and Adler (1931; 1964) went on to develop a system of therapy which he called *individual psychology*. In individual psychology the core motive of human personality development is a striving for superiority, by which Adler meant that we all create goals for ourselves in life, which give us purpose and which we then strive to attain. We all create an ideal self which represents the perfect person we strive to become, feelings of inferiority in relation to our perfect self are normal and the drive to overcome the sense of inferiority is the stimulus for our striving towards superiority. Adler discussed how women are in an inferior social position to men and how they strive for status, how someone who felt intellectually inferior as a child may strive as an adult to be intellectually superior, perhaps becoming a university

Box 3.2

The sense of powerlessness experienced by Alex while he was growing up with his father seemed to have played an important role in shaping his adult personality. As a child Alex was often belittled by his father and sometimes was hit quite violently. Alex grew up feeling powerless and inferior. As a child he could not understand his father's behaviour and made the assumption that in some way he must deserve to be treated in this way. Although he is able to look back and say that his father treated him violently for reasons that were nothing to do with Alex himself, even as an adult he still feels inferior to those around him. At work he feels that other people are more competent than him and that what he does is never good enough. Often he will feel criticised even if no criticism is intended, and will react aggressively and defensively to others.

professor. Adler also discussed how the position in one's family – birth order – influences lifestyle. Adler emphasised the social nature of human beings and how interpersonal relations and the social context into which we are born, shape the personal goals we choose to strive towards. Psychopathology was the result of becoming discouraged from being able to attain the sense of superiority. For example, families characterised by mistrust, resentment, neglect, and abuse produced children who would strive for perfection using pathological selfish goals such as attention seeking, power seeking, and revenge seeking.

Adlerian therapy involves the patient becoming aware of his or her destructive goals, through consciousness raising. The therapist endeavours to help the patient to become aware of how their behaviour works to make real the fictional goals created early on in life. This is done using a lifestyle analysis which consists of understanding the patient's family background, his or her position in relation to siblings, and how the patient came to construct a view of the world. This aspect is similar in some ways to that of the cognitive approach of Ellis and Beck, whose work we will consider in more detail in Chapter 4. Furthermore, many of the ideas of Adler have been highly influential in current psychological theories (Ellenberger, 1970).

Melanie Klein and object relations

But although Freud was chiefly concerned with the id and how control over id processes was the core organising principle for personality and psychopathology, later psychoanalytical theorists became more concerned with projective and introjective mechanisms. This became known as the *object-relations* school of thought. Object relations is mostly associated with the work of Melanie Klein (1882–1960) who published *The Psychoanalysis of Children* in 1932 detailing the developmental process through which children introject (incorporate) the values and images of important caregivers who were viewed with strong emotional attachment. These object representations (introjected people) become incorporated within the child's ego leading people to respond to the environment through the perspective of people from their past. Klein (1932) viewed infants as having a need to relate to others, first as part objects (e.g., the breast) and later as whole objects (e.g., the mother). Behaviour is a result of fantasies about these objects. Although several strands of object-relations theory have been developed, all share the idea that early relationships are central to personality and the development of psychopathology (e.g., Fairburn, 1952; Kernberg, 1976; Kohut, 1971).

Splitting

Early childhood experiences involving, for example, inconsistent messages from parental figures (perhaps being warm and loving inconsistently), lead children to develop insecure egos. The person is unable to incorporate the object representation fully and as a protective mechanism the person uses the defence of *splitting*, in which the person views objects as all good or all bad. For example, a teacher is seen as wise, caring and all good until she later fails the student who reacts furiously that the teacher is incompetent, cold and all bad. Therapy involves attempts to strengthen the weakened ego and help the client understand how he or she uses such defences as splitting to regulate their emotions (see Box 3.3).

Box 3.3

Splitting is characteristic of Alex's behaviour. The friend that Alex attacked on the evening out had been a close companion of his at work for the last year since he joined the company. At first, they had got on well together and Alex had thought that his companion, John, was a great guy, loyal, trustworthy, one of the best. But after John had been promoted to a position which involved him commenting on Alex's work, Alex had come to see him as critical, harsh, and someone who just could not be trusted. This was typical of Alex's relationships with other people.

Attachment theory

Psychodynamic approaches to personality and psychopathology have continued to develop since Freud, and theoretical developments have tended to shift away from an emphasis on innate drives toward an emphasis on relationships. Perhaps most influential of all is the work of Bowlby (1969; 1973; 1980) whose attachment theory emphasised the importance of early relationships, and the way in which the child forms attachments to others, and how these early attachments shape experiences in later life and can result in the development of psychopathology. Bowlby emphasised how parenting involved a delicate balance between neglect and overprotection so that the child was able to undertake appropriate exploratory behaviour and develop a sense of security in the world.

Erik Erikson and ego psychology

Whereas Freud outlined a stage theory of psychosexual development (see Table 3.1), Erik Erikson (1902–1994) offered a psychosocial stage theory of development which emphasised the social tasks and their associated conflicts throughout the lifespan (Erikson, 1963) (see Table 3.3). Each of Erikson's stages is dependent on the development of the preceding stage and the unfolding of each stage is based on two underlying basic assumptions. The first is that

> the human personality in principle develops according to steps predetermined in the growing person's readiness to be driven forward, to be aware of, and to interact with a widening social radius. (Erikson, 1963, p. 270)

The second is that

> society, in principle, tends to be so constituted as to meet and invite the succession of potentialities for interaction and attempts to safeguard and to encourage the proper rate and the proper sequence of their unfolding. (Erikson, 1963, p. 270)

The first stage, *basic trust vs. mistrust,* is one in which the infant develops a sense of trust in the self and the world dependent on

Table 3.3   Erikson's psychosocial eight-stage theory

Age	Stage	Virtue
Infancy	Basic trust vs. mistrust	Hope
Early childhood	Autonomy vs. shame and doubt	Will
Play age	Initiative vs. guilt	Purpose
School age	Industry vs. inferiority	Competence
Adolescence	Identity vs. identity confusion	Fidelity
Young adulthood	Intimacy vs. isolation	Love
Adulthood	Generativity vs. stagnation	Care
Old age	Integrity vs. despair	Wisdom

the quality of care received. If the caregiver is sensitive and responsive to the needs of the infant, who at this stage of life is helpless and dependent on the caregiver, the infant learns to trust in the self and the world. The virtue that results is hope. In the second stage, *autonomy vs. shame and doubt*, the child begins to interact with the world and develops a sense of autonomy and acquires the virtue of will. In the third stage, *initiative vs. guilt*, the virtue of purpose develops. In the fourth stage, *industry vs. inferiority*, there is a shift from play to work, practical skills are developed and the virtue of competence achieved. In the fifth stage, *identity vs. identity confusion*, there are questions about the real self as the person faces up to making choices about their values and goals, and the virtue of fidelity is achieved. In the sixth stage, *intimacy vs. isolation*, a sense of independence and adult responsibility develops and the virtue which is established is love. In the seventh stage, *generativity vs. stagnation*, there are concerns with productivity and creativity and the virtue which is established is care. In the eighth stage, *integrity vs. despair*, a perspective on life is sought with wisdom as the resultant virtue.

Identity

As well as going through the psychosexual stages outlined by Freud, the child also, Erikson suggested, goes through these psychosocial and ego-development stages. Also, in contrast to Freud's stage theory, Erikson's stage theory was concerned with the complete life-span of the person. Furthermore, at each stage, Erikson suggested that there can be positive or negative outcomes. Erikson discussed the crises that occur in development, i.e., turning points in a person's life where the person is between progression and regression. Successful resolution of the crisis, Erikson suggested, promotes the particular virtue, or strength, at each stage. Erikson coined the term 'identity crisis' to describe the experiences of the soldiers he was working with in San Francisco in the 1940s (Erikson, 1968). He described them as not knowing who they were and as having lost their shock-absorbing capacities and as suffering from a range of psychological and physical problems which today sound similar to what psychiatrists and psychologists would describe as posttraumatic stress disorder (American Psychiatric Association, 1994). *Identity* was a central concept composed of four facets: a conscious sense of one's existence as a distinct entity; continuity between what one has been and what one will be; a sense of wholeness; and a sense of meaning in relation to others (Evans, 1969).

Like the humanistic psychologists, whom we shall consider in Chapter 5, Erikson recognised that the therapist should facilitate the growth and development of the client rather than impose his or her own views. Also, like the humanistic psychologists, Erikson has also been criticised by some for the lack of empirical data supporting his observations. Is it really the case that everyone in all parts of the world progresses through the eight psychosocial stages? Erikson's approach is known as ego psychology. Whereas Freud's approach emphasised the role of the id (instincts and conflicts are seen as central in shaping personality and psychopathology), ego psychology assumes that the ego functions not only as a defence against the workings of the id, but also that the ego strives for mastery of the environment and produces a separate and conflict-free driving force towards adaptation to reality. Perhaps this is most clearly illustrated by considering the Freudian latency period. Whereas Freud did not view the latency period as important in shaping personality, Erikson viewed the latency period as one in which the person strives to develop a sense of industry, the failure of which led to a sense of inferiority. Failure and success at developing a sense of industry was largely determined, Erikson believed, by cultural forces, i.e., through discrimination of race, sex, religion, some individuals grow up lacking the sense of industry (Erikson, 1963). There are therefore parallels with the sociocultural theorists, whom we shall consider in Chapter 6. Other theorists who were important in developing ego psychology were Hartmann (1958) and Rapaport (1958), but Erikson is probably the best known of the ego psychologists.

However, returning to the central theme of this chapter on psychodynamic approaches to psychopathology, we are left with the question of whether or not the therapeutic techniques which have grown out of this model are indeed effective for clients in distress.

Does psychodynamic therapy work?

As we have seen, the psychodynamic approach has been mostly criticised for its lack of scientific rigour. Notable critics are Sutherland (1992) and the behavioural psychologist, Hans Eysenck who argued that Freud's theories are not only sufficiently vague to make them scientifically untestable, but also based on the study of a limited number of people from whom it is not possible to generalise to all human beings (see Eysenck and Wilson, 1973). These are well-worn criticisms familiar to several generations of psychologists and, as we have seen, there is at least some validity to their arguments. However, even if the theories themselves are scientifically difficult to test, we can still ask, using the scientific method, whether psychodynamic therapy works? The answer to this seems to be a hesitant yes.

In more recent years there have been a number of studies which provide some evidence for the efficacy of brief psychodynamic therapies (e.g., Anderson and Lambert, 1995; Crits-Christoph, 1992; Piper, Azim, McCallum, and Joyce, 1990). This applies to different population groups, for example, the elderly (Thompson, Gallagher, and Breckenridge, 1987), people diagnosed with personality disorders (Winston *et al.*, 1991), and methadone patients (Woody, Luborsky, McLellan, and O'Brien, 1990). However, it must be cautioned that the evidence does not suggest that psychodynamic therapy is superior to other psychotherapies (see Svartberg and Stiles, 1991). For psychodynamic therapists, this is indeed encouraging evidence, although it should be noted that well-controlled research studies into the effectiveness of traditional psychoanalysis itself remain to be conducted (Grawe, Donati, and Bernauer, 1998). Taken together, it might be concluded that short-term psychodynamic therapy is more effective than no therapy at all, although how it compares with other therapies remains uncertain (see Prochaska and Norcross, 1999 for a review).

Conclusion

It might be argued that what was important about the psychodynamic perspective introduced by Freud was that it showed that psychological processes rather than biological processes can result in psychopathology. The legacy of Freud is that we have an understanding that unconscious motives and defence mechanisms influence behaviour and that early childhood experiences influence adult personality adjustment. Psychopathology, Freud argued, is the result of fixation at early developmental stages, excessive use of defence mechanisms, and that through psychoanalysis, repressed wishes and feelings can be brought to the surface and dealt with in a more mature way. Although Freud's ideas have attracted much attention, much of this has been critical. In particular, the idea that sexual and aggressive impulses are the basis for human behaviour has been questioned. Several subsequent writers in the psychodynamic tradition have offered competing theoretical approaches which emphasise other impulses. Furthermore, it has been suggested that any theory must be falsifiable, otherwise it is scientifically of little value. Much of Freud's work does not lend itself to testing. For example, how are we to test whether there is the hypothesised psychic structure of id, ego, and superego? Others have suggested that the weakness of Freud's work was that he based his ideas on a small number of women living in what was then a sexually repressive society. Many feminist theorists have been outraged at some of Freud's ideas, which they have seen as sexist. Nevertheless, today many therapists would describe themselves as psychodynamic and there are a variety of different training courses available for people who are interested in working professionally in this area. Although training as a psychoanalyst is lengthy and requires one to undergo years of personal therapy, many therapists use psychodynamic techniques in their work. The concept of transference in particular remains a useful one to therapists from all orientations. Also, despite the various criticisms that are made of psychoanalysis, and psychodynamic approaches in general, there is no doubt that they can provide those of us interested in human behaviour with a rich source of ideas.

Summary points

- Like the biomedical model, the psychodynamic model assumes that the causes of psychopathology are internal to the person. The psychodynamic model suggests that psychopathology is the result of conflict between unconscious forces.

- Freud introduced the psychodynamic model. He suggested that the human personality is composed of three structures, the id, the ego, and the superego. Psychopathology resulted from conflict between these three forces.

- Freud also described stages of psychosexual development and how psychopathology resulted if a person did not progress successfully through these stages. Many problems in adult life are thought to have their roots in the phallic stage of a child's life.

- Freud also discussed how people use defence mechanisms such as repression which involves a person keeping unacceptable impulses or painful memories from entering consciousness.

- Freud's ideas have attracted many followers as well as harsh criticism from scientific psychologists who are concerned that Freud's ideas are not capable of refutation, which is the foundation of the scientific method.

- Freud also introduced psychoanalysis, a form of intensive long-term therapy which aims to bring unconscious material into conscious awareness through the use of such techniques as free association and the exploration of the transference relationship between therapist and client.

- Although psychoanalysis in the form described by Freud is rare today, many therapists work using similar techniques and ideas drawn from psychoanalytical thinking, such as transference, and would describe themselves as psychodynamic therapists.
- Psychodynamic therapists are not only influenced by Freud, but by many other theorists subsequent to Freud such as Jung, Adler, Klein, and Erikson.
- Although many of the ideas generated by psychodynamic theorists lack scientific support, evidence suggests that psychodynamic therapy can be helpful.

4

Behavioural and Cognitive Approaches

Introduction

In this chapter the behavioural and the cognitive models will be introduced. In contrast to the psychodynamic model, which as we have seen in the previous chapter, emphasises unconscious forces, the behavioural model emphasises the observable behaviour of people. The reason for this shift in emphasis, as I shall go on to describe in more detail, was that the behavioural model was in part a response to the early criticisms of psychoanalysis. The founders of behavioural psychology were concerned that their approach should be grounded securely in scientific thinking, and that their theories would be amenable to measurement and scientific testing. However, over time many began to think that the behavioural model was limited in its explanatory power and so cognitive determinants of behaviour began to be introduced resulting in a synthesis of the two approaches – what is known as the cognitive-behavioural model. Although the behavioural model was a reaction in some ways to psychoanalysis, both the psychodynamic and behavioural models present a deterministic view of human functioning. In the behavioural model environmental factors are thought to shape our behaviour and our behaviour is the sum of all we have learned. As we shall also see in the following chapter, the deterministic approach to human behaviour advocated by the psychodynamic and behavioural models stands in some contrast to the humanistic model, which emphasises free will and choice.

Behavioural model

The behavioural model has its roots in academic psychology. Understanding the processes through which learning took place increasingly became a main concern of psychologists in the first half of the twentieth century. As we have seen, the argument that there was a need for research into the effectiveness of psychotherapy and counselling came about in part because of the criticisms by Eysenck of the psychodynamic model for its unscientific nature and lack of effectiveness as a therapeutic approach (Eysenck, 1952; 1965). In response to Eysenck's criticisms of psychoanalysis, psychologists began to apply the principles of learning that had been discovered in the laboratory to clinical practice. In contrast to psychoanalysis which focuses on the internal processes of the person, the behavioural model focuses on the environmental conditions that shape our behaviour. Theorists in the behavioural tradition have emphasised two types of conditioning, classical conditioning and operant conditioning.

Pavlov and classical conditioning

Ivan Pavlov (1849–1936), a Russian physiologist, is credited with the discovery of a process called *classical conditioning* (sometimes called *Pavlovian conditioning*). Essentially, this is a process of learning by temporal association. Simply, what this means is that if two events occur in close succession they become associated and eventually we come to respond to one as we do to the other. Pavlov (1928) came across this phenomenon while he was studying the digestive process in dogs. As part of his research, the dogs were given a meat powder and what Pavlov noticed was that after a while the dogs began to salivate when the researchers were about to feed the dogs. After another while, it was noticed that the dogs began to salivate when they heard the footsteps of the researchers coming to feed them. Pavlov went on to experimentally test this observation out by ringing a bell before the food was brought finding that the dogs came to associate the sound of the bell with the food and would begin to salivate.

In the language of classical conditioning theory, an unconditional stimulus (UCS) (e.g., food) is a stimulus that automatically

Preconditioning	UCS (food) —— UCR (salivation)
Conditioning	CS (bell) ——— UCS (food) ——— CR (salivation)
Postconditioning	CS (bell) ——— CR (salivation)

Figure 4.1   The process of classical conditioning

produces the unconditional response (UCR) (e.g., salivation). The conditioned stimulus (CS) (e.g., bell) which when paired with the UCS (e.g., food) comes to produce a conditioned response (CR) (e.g., salivation) (see Figure 4.1). Although seemingly a simple process, it is one which has far-reaching implications for understanding some forms of psychopathology and therapeutic intervention.

The behavioural model suggests that psychopathology can develop as a result of classical conditioning and that through modifying environmental stimuli, psychopathology can be extinguished. Classical conditioning has been put forward as an explanation for a number of psychological problems, and is now generally accepted by many as an explanation as to why some people develop phobias. The earliest study to demonstrate this was carried out by J. B. Watson (1878–1958) who is today credited with recognising, in his study of Little Albert, the importance of classical conditioning as an explanation for psychological problems.

The Little Albert study

In the most famous study to illustrate how classical conditioning might lead to the development of phobias, Watson and Rayner (1920) introduced an eleven-month-old boy called Little Albert to a tame white rat. At first, Albert showed no signs of fear and would reach out and touch the rat. However, what Watson and Rayner did was to then startle Albert with a loud noise made by striking a hammer upon a steel bar when he reached out to touch the white rat. This procedure was carried out over several days, with Watson and Rayner introducing the rat to the boy and observing his reactions. After a while, Albert showed fear of the white rat and would no longer reach out to touch it. Furthermore, Albert's fear spread to include a white rabbit, cotton wool, a fur coat and other objects similar to the white rat. Although this study showed that classical conditioning could be used to induce fear, can classical conditioning explain all our fears? Wolpe and Rachman (1960) answer:

> Any neutral stimulus, simple or complex, that happens to make an impact on an individual at about the same time a fear reaction is evoked, acquires the ability to evoke fear subsequently . . . there will be a generalisation of fear reactions to stimuli resembling the conditioned stimulus. (Wolpe and Rachman, 1960)

Psychology as the behaviourist views it
Although by today's standards the study of Little Albert might be seen as ethically questionable and methodologically weak, it was an important study and drew importance to the role of conditioning. Later work has not always found it possible to replicate the Little Albert study and it has been suggested that early writers on conditioning tended to ignore these data in their attempt to replace psychoanalysis with a science of behaviour (Samelson, 1980). As Watson and Rayner state, somewhat scathingly, towards the end of their paper on conditioned emotional reactions in Little Albert:

> Freudians, 20 years from now, if they come to analyse Albert at that age, will probably tease from him the recital of a dream which will be interpreted as showing that Albert, at three years old, tried to play with his mother's pubic hair and was scolded violently for it. Albert may be fully convinced of the truth of this interpretation of his fear if the analyst has the authority and personality to put it over convincingly. (Watson and Rayner, 1920, p. 13)

Watson went on to revolutionise the field of psychology through his emphasis on the study of behaviour and subsequent generations of psychologists have been taught to be scathing of psychoanalysis. Watson's best-known paper today was one he published in 1913 entitled 'Psychology as the behaviourist views it'. In this paper, Watson argued that the science of psychology could only progress if it was concerned with observable behaviour. In making the focus of study observable behaviour, psychology could aspire to become a science. Mistakenly, however, behaviourism is sometimes seen as a school of thought in which its adherents believe that there is no such thing as mental experience. Rather, Watson's argument was that mental concepts were not observable and therefore were not properly the focus of scientific inquiry. This approach to the study of psychology was, of course, in direct opposition to the study of psychoanalysis. Behavioural approaches assumed that it was not necessary to be aware of one's behaviour or the factors controlling it in order to function effectively (Skinner, 1971). Many psychologists today would still adhere to the view that psychology should be concerned with observable behaviours that can be reliably measured, and although it is also now common for psychologists to speculate on the unobservable processes of the mind, the influence of Watson in shaping modern psychology as a scientific discipline was great. Unlike psychodynamic therapies, the behaviourist is committed to providing scientific evidence for the effectiveness of the therapy. Other influences, aside from Pavlov and Watson, on the development of behavioural psychology were the important work of Thorndike and Skinner.

Skinner and operant conditioning

Whereas classical conditioning is concerned with the pairings of an unconditional stimulus with a conditional stimulus to produce behaviour, *operant conditioning* (sometimes called *instrumental conditioning*) is a process that is concerned with how that behaviour is maintained. Edward Thorndike, an American psychologist, noted that when something positive happens to us we tend to repeat what it was we were doing, and when something negative happens to us we tend not to repeat what we were doing. What Thorndike did to demonstrate this process was to place a cat in a box that was carefully designed so that the cat had to press a certain lever to escape from the box. The cat was then deprived of food and a piece of fish was placed just outside the box where the cat could see it. Thorndike observed how, although at first the cat's behaviour was erratic as it tried to find a way out of the box, the cat would eventually press the lever, escape, and get the fish. The next time the cat was placed in the box, the time it took to press the lever was shorter. The next time, shorter still. Eventually, the cat would, on entering the box, very quickly press the lever and escape. Thorndike reasoned that when responses lead to positive consequences, in this case getting the fish, those responses are strengthened and are more likely to occur in the future. However, when responses lead to negative consequences the responses are not strengthened and are less likely to occur in the future. This was called by Thorndike the *law of effect* and became a further theoretical cornerstone of behavioural psychology.

B. F. Skinner (1904–1990) took up the work of Thorndike and went on to describe in more detail the relationship between instrumental behaviour and its consequences. Skinner (1953) coined the term *operant conditioning* to describe the process outlined by Thorndike. The idea is that operant behaviour is controllable and voluntary behaviour and that this behaviour can become conditioned by what he termed *reinforcers*. Reinforcers are those environmental situations that increase the frequency and strength of behaviours. There are two types of reinforcement: positive reinforcement and negative reinforcement. Positive reinforcement comes about when the behaviour is followed by the occurrence of a positive event, and negative reinforcement comes about when the behaviour is followed by the omission of a negative event. These two forms of reinforcement are distinguished from punishment, which occurs when the behaviour is followed by the occurrence of a negative event, and which aims to decrease the strength and frequency of a behaviour. Various psychological problems have been approached from the behavioural perspective and operant conditioning helps to explain the persistence of maladaptive behaviours. Learning contingencies operate over time so that complex behaviour patterns are slowly shaped from childhood onwards (Gewirtz and Pelaez-Nogueras, 1992).

Mowrer's two-factor theory

So, operant conditioning explains the persistence of maladaptive behaviour and classical conditioning explains the formation of the behaviour in the first place. Mowrer (1947) proposed the *two-factor* model of fear and avoidance, in which fear was acquired through classical conditioning (first factor) and maintained through operant conditioning via negative reinforcement (second factor) as the person avoids their fear. We can see therefore how these processes can be applied to understanding how psychopathology occurs. Importantly, operant conditioning and classical conditioning also provide a theoretical framework for developing therapeutic interventions.

Behaviour therapy

The terms behaviour therapy and behaviour modification are sometimes used to refer to treatments based on classical conditioning and operant conditioning, respectively. Historically, the term behaviour therapy was employed by British therapists and behaviour modification by American therapists, reflecting the different emphasis given to the two forms of conditioning in the two countries. Here, for simplicity, I have used the term behaviour therapy to refer to all forms of therapy based on principles of learning. In behaviour therapy there is seen to be no need to uncover unconscious forces as in the psychoanalytic approach, rather, the task of the therapist is simply to eliminate those unwanted behaviours which are the result of learning. Behaviour therapy is concerned with: first, removing specific symptoms; second, developing new adaptive behaviours; and third, changing environmental reinforcement contingencies.

Behavioural analysis

The first task of the behaviour therapist is to conduct a *behavioural analysis*. The therapist endeavours to describe the client's maladaptive responses in objective terms and to generate hypotheses about the behavioural and environmental factors that are controlling and maintaining those behaviours. On the basis of the behavioural analysis, the therapist proceeds to design a treatment programme which will consist of manipulating the controlling and maintaining factors in such a way as to modify the maladaptive responses. In classical conditioning, as we have seen, behaviours are controlled by stimuli that come before the response and in operant conditioning behaviours are controlled by stimuli which come after the response. Based on these theories, behaviourists have attempted to explain a variety of psychological problems.

A classical example of behaviour therapy is that used by Mowrer and Mowrer (1938) to treat children with bed-wetting problems. Using the principles of classical conditioning, Mowrer and Mowrer developed the 'bell and pad' method to treat nocturnal enuresis. It was hypothesised that nocturnal enuresis resulted from not associating a full bladder with waking up, so what Mowrer and Mowrer did was to develop a moisture sensitive blanket which triggers an alarm bell when urination takes place. Thus, over time, the person comes to associate having a full bladder with waking up.

As we will see, however, behaviour therapies seem most applicable to anxiety-related problems. First, let us look at some of the specific therapeutic techniques which have been developed on the basis of learning theory. Notably, systematic desensitisation, flooding, aversion, and modelling. These techniques are based on the principle of classical conditioning. The principle of exposure to the feared or threatening situation, either in imagination or in reality, is the theme that runs throughout these behavioural approaches.

Wolpe and systematic desensitisation

Joseph Wolpe was a South African psychiatrist who developed a technique called *systematic desensitisatun*. Wolpe viewed neurotic behaviour as consisting of persistent habits of conditioned behaviour, acquired in anxiety-generating situations. Systematic desensitisation is based on the principles of classical conditioning. Recall the case of Little Albert, the child whom Watson and Rayner (1920) used to show that a fear of white rats could be conditioned. Shortly afterwards another study was published by Jones (1925) regarding a boy called Little Peter, showing that once fears had been conditioned, they could also be alleviated using the principles of classical conditioning – for example, by pairing the feared object with a desirable response such as food. Following this line of enquiry, Wolpe (1958) assumed that fears could be unlearned and set out to devise a technique, which he called systematic desensitisation, to help people unlearn their fears. Systematic desensitisation has three stages:

1. Relaxation training
2. Construction of a fear hierarchy
3. Learning process.

The idea behind systematic desensitisation is that feeling anxious is incompatible with feeling relaxed, so the client is first taught to use relaxation techniques. Once this has been learned, the client is helped to develop his or her own hierarchy of fear. So, for example, a person with agoraphobia is asked to construct a list of things they find fearful, starting with the thing that they are most fearful of and ending with the thing of which they are least fearful. An example of a fear hierarchy is shown in Table 4.1 for a person who is fearful of social situations.

The learning process requires the person to maintain their state of relaxation and imagine the least fearful event. When this has been accomplished successfully, the client moves on and repeats the process, imagining the next most fearful event while in a state of relaxation. Eventually, the client learns to maintain their relaxed

Table 4.1   Systematic desensitisation hierarchy

	Degree of fear experienced
Saying hello to someone you know on the way to the shops	very low
Stopping to have a five-minute conversation with someone	low
Giving a short and informal talk to some colleagues at work	moderate
Attending a job interview	high
Giving a talk to a large group of people you don't know	very high

state even when imagining the most fearful event in their hierarchy. When desensitisation is carried out this way it is called *imaginal desensitisation* which is in contrast to *in-vivo desensitisation* which involves the person gradually being exposed to real-life fears. For example, someone with a fear of going outside (agoraphobia) might, with the therapist's help, start off by opening the front door, progress through taking a few steps outside, right up to going on a trip to the shops. Many studies have been carried out to assess the effectiveness of this treatment for different fears and phobias, and the evidence suggests that it does indeed seem to work (e.g., Kazdin and Wilcoxin, 1976), although research has shown that the relaxation component of the treatment may not always be necessary (Wolpe, 1990). It is the element of exposure to the feared or unwanted situation that seems to be most effective in helping people overcome their difficulties and which, as we shall see, has come to be an important element running though behavioural procedures.

Flooding

Another treatment based on classical conditioning is that of *flooding*. Like systematic desensitisation, flooding involves exposure to the feared object, but in contrast to systematic desensitisation, flooding does not involve gradual exposure to the feared object, but instead involves exposure to the feared stimulus at full intensity without relaxation. The rationale is that this eliminates anxiety through the process of extinction, that is to say, the conditioned stimulus is repeatedly presented without avoidance until the unconditioned response is no longer produced (Wolpe, 1990). Usually, when we have a fear of something, we avoid it and so extinction does not take place. Flooding can be extremely anxiety provoking and for some a form of graded exposure can be used to avoid the intense anxiety. Graded exposure is essentially the same as flooding except that exposure to the threatening or feared object is carried out in a series of small steps. This is similar to the process used in systematic desensitisation except that relaxation is not used and whereas systematic desensitisation is usually conducted in vivo, graded exposure is conducted in real-life settings. Such exposure techniques have been used successfully with people suffering from phobias (e.g., Mattick, Andrews, Hadzi-Pavlovic, and Christensen, 1990; Menzies and Clarke, 1993; Marks, 1990), posttraumatic stress (e.g., Foa, Rothbaum, Riggs, and Murdock, 1991), and obsessive-compulsive problems (e.g., Marks and O'Sullivan, 1988).

Aversion therapy

Classical conditioning theory is also employed in *aversion therapy*. Here, very simply, the idea is to take an unwanted behaviour and pair it with an unpleasant consequence so that the unwanted behaviour becomes associated with the unpleasant consequence and thus becomes less frequent. Aversion therapy was first used by Kantorovich (1930) with people with alcohol problems. Electric shocks were administered accompanied by the smell, sight, and taste of alcohol. Similarly, aversion therapy might be used to help someone to stop smoking. Someone who wants to stop smoking might be required to take a pill which makes them feel nauseous (an emetic). Once they feel nauseous they would then be required to smoke. Smoking becomes associated with feeling nauseous and so the frequency of smoking decreases. Although aversion therapy has been subject to ethical objections, and the evidence for its effectiveness is not consistently strong, there are occasions when it can be very beneficial. Classic studies were carried out by Bucher and Lovaas (1967) who used electric shocks to decrease self-destructive behaviour in an autistic boy, and by Lang and Melamed (1969) who used electric shocks to the legs of an infant to successfully decrease persistent life-threatening vomiting behaviour. Aversion therapy has also been used with some success with people with so-called sexual disorders (e.g., Marks, Gelder, and Bancroft, 1970). However such approaches are less widely used today and clinicians would recommend the use of non-punitive forms of treatments where possible (e.g., Russo, Carr, and Lovaas, 1980).

Modelling

Albert Bandura described the process of *modelling*. This involves learning behaviour through watching others, i.e., learning by imitation (Bandura and Walters, 1963; Bandura, 1969). Interestingly, Freud (1940/1969) had also discussed the process of learning through identification and how children usually come to identify with the same sex parent. For example, Alex may have learned through modelling of his father to control his emotions through alcohol. In a series of famous studies conducted by Bandura, children watched adults behaving either in an aggressive or non-aggressive way. Then, children were allowed to play and it was found than those children who had watched the aggressive adults were more likely to play in an aggressive way than those children who had watched the adults behaving non-aggressively. Modelling can be used to help clients with a variety of anxiety-related problems. Essentially, the client watches the therapist model the appropriate behaviour and through doing so learns to do it for himself or herself. Often, the modelling will be conducted using a graded hierarchy of increasingly aversive behavioural performances involving the feared object or situation. Bandura's approach, although a behavioural one in that it relies on social learning, also relies on cognitive processes. Bandura claimed that the technique worked because it increases the person's sense of *self-efficacy*, that is to say the confidence with which they are able to perform the task. However, self-efficacy is an internal construct not amenable to observation in the strict behavioural sense.

Exposure to the unwanted or feared object seems to be the effective therapeutic ingredient common to these techniques (Marks, 1990). Exposure-based therapies are now the treatment of choice for many anxiety-based problems. There seems little doubt that approaches based on exposure can be useful in the treatment of fears and phobias (e.g., Barlow, 1988), and that they are at least as effective as biomedical therapies for fear and phobias (e.g., Margraf, Barlow, Clark, and Telch, 1993), although their application to the wider arena of so-called psychiatric disorders is now seen to be fairly limited (see Davey, 1992). Therapeutic approaches which use exposure in one way or another remain popular and widely used among more eclectic therapists.

Reinforcement-based techniques

Other therapies are based on operant conditioning and use *reinforcement* schedules to shape behaviour. First, it is necessary to conduct a functional analysis in order to understand which conditions are responsible for maintaining the behaviour, why and when the behaviour occurs. Then, armed with this information, the therapist can intervene by changing the conditions in such a way as to modify reinforcement schedules to increase the frequency of desired behaviour and decrease the frequency of undesired behaviour. An example is the approach used by Lovaas (1977) to induce speech in autistic children.

The use of operant techniques was first demonstrated by Allyon and Azrin who observed eating problems on a ward of chronic psychotic patients and hypothesised that these problems were functionally related to the reinforcements provided by the staff. At mealtimes patients who had difficulties were approached and helped by staff. Allyon and Azrin hypothesised that this increased social attention was rewarding for the patients and served to maintain the maladaptive behaviour. Thus, they changed the reinforcement contingencies such that staff ignored the eating problems and instead allocated their attention to other more socially desirable and prosocial behaviours. Within days it was reported that much of the disruptive and maladaptive behaviour had been extinguished. Then Allyon and Azrin introduced a monetary token system which staff could use to reward the socially desirable behaviours of the patients, such as making their beds and washing. Tokens could also be fined for socially undesirable behaviours. Tokens could be exchanged for goods and privileges such as watching television or trips outside. This too had a positive effect on increasing adaptive behaviours (Allyon and Azrin, 1968).

In summary, the behavioural model was most strongly promoted by the psychologist Watson who, as we have seen, argued that observable behaviour was the only appropriate subject matter for the relatively new science of psychology. Thoughts and feelings, Watson argued, could not be measured objectively. In behaviour therapy, the focus of treatment is the behaviour itself and the therapist will endeavour to change that behaviour using a range of techniques such as aversion or flooding. Techniques drawn from behaviour therapy are used with a variety of client groups, those with eating disorders (e.g., Greenberg and Marks, 1982), neurotic problems (e.g., Stravynski, Marks, and Yule, 1982), phobias and obsessive-compulsive problems (e.g., O'Sullivan and Marks, 1991) and a wide variety of health professionals are now trained in the use of behaviour therapy techniques (e.g., Duggan, Marks, and Richards, 1993).

As already mentioned, the behavioural approach, because of its emphasis on observable behaviours, lends itself well to traditional scientific research. However, the behavioural approach has been criticised as being unable to grapple with the complexities of human behaviour. Much human behaviour, many would argue, is a product of unobservable thoughts and feelings. This can be seen in Bandura's approach. Behaviour therapy is not often used in its pure form today and many of the principles of learning have become incorporated with the cognitive approach, leading to what is known as cognitive-behavioural therapy. One reason for this is that behavioural techniques, although successful in the treatment of various anxiety problems, did not seem to lend themselves as well to the treatment of depressive problems. In contrast, the cognitive approach did seem to lend itself well to understanding depression as well as a wider range of other psychological problems. We will go on now to consider the cognitive model.

Cognitive model

The cognitive model emphasises how aspects of cognition, thinking and reasoning, contribute to psychopathology. The cognitive model is the most recent of all the psychological models, introduced in the 1950s by Albert Ellis and popularised in the 1970s by Aaron Beck, it has a long history: Epictetus, the Greek philosopher, is often quoted as saying that people are disturbed not by events, but by the views they take of these events. Similarly, Shakespeare's Hamlet says that 'there is nothing either good or bad but thinking makes it so' (*Hamlet*, Act II, Scene ii). So, the idea that our behaviour is shaped by the way we think about ourselves and the world is not a new idea, but it was not until the second half of the twentieth century that these ideas were promoted by Ellis and Beck, who introduced cognitive approaches to therapy. The popularity of these approaches to therapy was accompanied by a movement within academic psychology towards an adoption of the cognitive model. Researchers began to investigate humans as information processors, and how psychological problems can result when this process goes awry.

Within the cognitive model, for example, the symptoms of schizophrenia are seen as representing faults in the way that information is processed. We are constantly bombarded with information from the external environment and if we are to function appropriately in the world we must selectively attend to the information. While I'm writing this I am focused on the words on the page and I am able to ignore for the moment the sound of the traffic outside, the sound of voices somewhere, a radio playing, and so on. But a breakdown in a person's ability to selectively attend in this way would result in them being overwhelmed by information. It has been suggested that people diagnosed with schizophrenia suffer such a breakdown and that their symptoms reflect the subsequent internal confusion. Their withdrawal into themselves is their way of keeping the bombardment of sensory stimulation to a manageable level.

If maladaptive behaviour is the result of the way we process information and perceive ourselves, then there are clear implications for therapy. Simply, people can be helped to see themselves and the world around them differently.

Albert Ellis and rational emotive behaviour therapy (REBT)

A-B-C model

Ellis's approach was known as *rational-emotive therapy* (RET), which he later renamed *rational emotive behaviour therapy* (REBT), in recognition that it contained strong elements of behavioural training as well as cognitive elements. Ellis proposed that maladaptive behaviour is the result of irrational beliefs (Ellis, 1962). Some examples of the type of irrational beliefs discussed by Ellis are given in Table 4.2. Ellis argued that it is not what happens to us that causes psychological problems, but rather it is how we come to understand these events. It is, according to Ellis, our beliefs (B) about activating events (A) that determine the consequences (C). This is called the *A-B-C model.* For example, a student with a strong belief that they must succeed at everything they do (B) is likely to become depressed (C) on failing an exam (A). Irrational beliefs,

Table 4.2   Examples of irrational beliefs

It is a dire necessity for an adult human being to be loved or approved by virtually every significant person in his community.
One should be thoroughly competent, adequate, and achieving in all possible respects if one is to consider oneself worthwhile.
Certain people are bad, wicked, or villainous, and they should be severely blamed and punished for their villainy.
It is awful and catastrophic when things are not the way one would like them to be.
Human unhappiness is externally caused and people have little or no ability to control their sorrows and disturbance.
If something is or may be dangerous or fearsome one should be terribly concerned about it and should keep dwelling on the possibility of its occurring.
It is easier to avoid than to face certain life difficulties and self-responsibilities.
One should be dependent on others and need someone stronger than oneself on whom to rely.
One's past history is an all important determiner of one's present behaviour, and because something once affected one's life, it should indefinitely have a similar effect.
One should become quite upset over other people's problems and disturbance.
There is invariably a right, precise, and perfect solution to human problems, and it is catastrophic if this perfect solution is not found.

(Ellis, 1962)

such as those described above, lead to what Ellis has called a '*mustabatory ideology*', i.e., they have a strong 'must' quality that places heavy demands on people who hold such beliefs (see also Warren and Zgourides, 1991) (see Table 4.3).

Table 4.3 A-B-C model of Ellis

	Example
Activating event (A)	Achieve a poor exam mark
Irrational belief (B)	I must do everything well or I am a failure
Consequences (C)	Feel depressed

Disputing

Likewise, a person who holds a strong belief that they must be liked by everyone (B) is likely to become depressed (C) if someone doesn't like them (A). In Ellis's REBT, the therapist would endeavour to help the client modify his or her irrational beliefs and to replace them with new and more rational beliefs. For example, someone who has the need to be liked by everyone might come to adopt a new belief such as: 'It's good to be liked, but I can't expect everyone to appreciate me in the same way. Some people might not like me, and that's OK; it's not essential for me that everyone likes me.' The therapy is active, challenging, and directive. The basic idea behind Ellis's approach to therapy, therefore, is to challenge the client's irrational beliefs so that, in this case, the client no longer believes that they have to succeed at everything or be liked by everyone. The central technique in REBT is *disputing*. Ellis described the REBT therapist as employing

> a fairly rapid-fire active-directive-persuasive-philosophic methodology. In most instances, he quickly pins the client down to a few basic irrational ideas which motivate much of his disturbed behavior; he challenges the client to validate these ideas; he shows them that they are extralogical premises which cannot be validated; he logically analyses these ideas and makes mincemeat of them; he vigorously and vehemently shows why they can't work and will almost invariably lead to renewed disturbed symptomatology; he reduces these ideas to absurdity, sometimes in a highly humorous manner; he explains how they can be replaced with more rational, empirically based theses. (Ellis, 1973, p. 185)

Ellis also encourages the client to behaviourally check out their irrational cognitions. For example, much dysfunctional behaviour is thought to stem from feelings of shame and Ellis also encourages the use of shame-attacking exercises where the client is encouraged to engage in behaviours which provoke feelings of shame. Ellis describes the case of Myra, a client with a fear of appearing foolish. Ellis describes how he encouraged Myra to walk down the street with a banana on a dog leash. By doing this, she was able to learn that nothing bad happens even when she looks foolish.

Although Ellis's approach might seem harsh, it is not the client themselves or the values that the client holds that are attacked, but rather it is the 'mustabatory' element of those values. This is an important point. The aim of the therapy is not to diminish the client but to modify their irrational beliefs. Also, some people question the use of the term irrational, believing that people's beliefs, even if they are irrational, can sometimes be helpful to them and therefore it would be better to think of beliefs as maladaptive or as dysfunctional (e.g., Arnkoff and Glass, 1982).

Another prominent thinker within the cognitive approach is Aaron Beck who also suggested that psychological problems result from faulty thinking. Like Ellis's REBT, the aim of Beck's cognitive therapy is to change the way in which a person thinks about a situation and to challenge maladaptive ways of thinking which are thought to contribute to the development and maintenance of psychological problems.

Aaron Beck and cognitive therapy

Beck proposed that people begin to formulate rules for living early on in life. Originally writing about depression, Beck (1963; 1967; 1974) argued that depression has its roots in the way in which people think about themselves and the world they live in. Depressed people, Beck argued, possess illogical ways of thinking: he discussed the way people might magnify their difficulties and failures, minimise their accomplishments and successes, arrive at conclusions based only on a selection of evidence, arrive at conclusions despite the absence of supporting evidence, or arrive at conclusions based on a single and trivial event. For example, if someone you know who is usually friendly hurries past you on the street without saying hello, would you conclude that they probably

Table 4.4 Illogical ways of thinking described by Beck

Magnification, i.e., magnifying difficulties and failures
Minimisation, i.e., minimising accomplishments and successes
Selective abstraction, i.e., arriving at a conclusion based on a selection of the evidence only
Arbitrary inference, i.e., arriving at a conclusion despite the absence of supporting evidence
Over-generalisation, i.e., arriving at a conclusion based on a single and trivial event

haven't seen you or would you conclude that they had taken a dislike to you? Beck's theory says that it is the person who would reach the conclusion on the basis of such an event that they are disliked who is more prone to developing depression than the person who concludes that the other person just hadn't seen them. Some of the illogical ways of thinking discussed by Beck are shown in Table 4.4. Illogical ways of thinking are also characteristic of Helen (see Box 4.1).

Negative cognitive triad

Beck argued that illogical ways of thinking lead to a negative view of the self, of current experience, and of the future. These negative views constitute, what Beck called, a *negative cognitive triad* underlying depression. The negative cognitive triad is experienced by people as *negative automatic thoughts,* that is to say, pessimistic ways of thinking, thoughts that come to mind like 'I'm useless, life is bleak, nothing will change'. Briefly, Beck and Weishaar (1989) noted five steps to cognitive therapy:

1. learning to monitor negative, automatic thoughts
2. learning to recognise the connection between cognition, affect and behaviour

Box 4.1

Helen was referred by her GP to a counsellor who uses the cognitive-behavioural approach. In the first session the counsellor interviews Helen to find out more about her relationship, her family background, and in listening to Helen the counsellor soon picks up on the way Helen tends to arrive at selective conclusions and over-generalises from single episodes. Although Helen did well at school and university, and now has a successful career in a large media organisation, she tells the therapist of how she feels like a failure. Although she has had many successes in her life she tends to focus on her perceived failures. One of the episodes she dwells on is when a request the previous year for promotion had been turned down. On enquiry it turns out that the feedback Helen received from her line manager was actually extremely positive. She was told that the reason for not being awarded the promotion was due to budget constraints and that she was almost certain of promotion within the next year. It was after this episode that Helen began feeling tired all of the time, began to lose interest in things, and to feel depressed. Robert, her partner at the time, had been unable to provide Helen with the psychological support she needed and rows between them became increasingly frequent until they broke up. Helen says that there is something wrong with her and that she is not capable of being in a relationship, and that she can never see herself meeting anyone who could love her. Although Helen is an attractive woman with plenty of friends and admirers she sees herself as unattractive and unlikeable. Recently it was her birthday and although she received cards and presents from many friends and colleagues there was one friend who forgot her birthday and Helen dwells on this episode.

3. examining the evidence for and against distorted automatic thoughts
4. substituting more reality-oriented interpretations for these biased cognitions

Box 4.2

The counsellor helps Helen to monitor her thoughts that she is unloveable and unlikeable, to explore the connections between her thoughts, her feelings, and her behaviours, and to examine the evidence for those thoughts. What evidence is there that the friend does not like her? Is it possible that they forgot to send her a birthday card because of some other reason? Over the coming weeks, the counsellor helps Helen to understand how she interprets events in such a way as to leave her feeling depressed, and shows her ways in which she can monitor her depressive thinking.

5. learning to identify and alter the beliefs that predispose a person to distort their experiences.

The cognitive therapist attempts to help the client to become aware and challenge their negative automatic thoughts and eventually replace them with more realistic and adaptive ways of thinking (see Box 4.2).

Collaborative empiricism

Furthermore, the cognitive approach encourages a collaborative relationship between the therapist and the client in which they both approach the client's problem using *collaborative empiricism,* that is to say, both work together to identify the problem and to formulate hypotheses about how change might be brought about (Hollon and Beck, 1994). Although there are clear similarities between the approach of Ellis and that of Beck, Beck's approach to therapy is less directive and confrontational than Ellis'.

Cognitive therapy is now a well-established treatment for depression and studies testify that it seems to be effective (e.g., Dobson, 1989; Hollon and Beck, 1994). In the long term, evidence suggests that cognitive therapies are more effective than drug therapies (Evans *et al.*, 1992). But although cognitive therapy was originally developed in relation to depression, Beck's cognitive approach has since been applied to understanding a wide range of psychological problems. Indeed, one of the criticisms of the REBT approach of Ellis is that there has been less systematic investigation of how REBT works with different forms of psychopathology.

As we have already seen, psychologists and psychiatrists have generally adopted a medical model view that there are different forms of psychopathology and therefore attempt to determine which treatments work best with what problems using traditional scientific methods. Beck and his colleagues have since extended their thinking to, for example, anxiety disorders (Beck and Emery, 1985) and personality disorders (Beck and Freeman, 1990), and there is growing evidence for the cognitive approach with different forms of psychopathology. The cognitive approach has gained greatly in popularity over the years, particularly among psychologists.

However, as already noted, many therapists recognise that no one model of psychopathology can give us the full understanding of how psychopathology develops or how it should be treated. For this reason, many theorists have been interested in finding ways in which different models can be integrated. The best-known integration of models is the cognitive-behavioural model.

Cognitive-behavioural approaches

Therapists began to integrate these new cognitive ideas with the behavioural ideas resulting in what is now generally known as *cognitive-behavioural therapy* (CBT).

Meichenbaum's self-instructional training

One of the first CBT techniques was that of self-instructional training (SIT) developed by Meichenbaum (1977). This approach helps clients to focus on their thought processes and how these affect behaviour, with the aim of allowing clients to control their thoughts in such a way as to improve performance and decrease distress. In the same way that children use self-talk when they are learning new skills, Meichenbaum's SIT pays attention to internal dialogues and in therapy the client is encouraged to externalise his or her dialogues and to change the instructions they give themselves. For example, think about learning to drive and how a person uses self-instructions, either silently or out loud, to learn: 'Check behind in the mirrors, put the car into gear, check again in the mirrors.' In SIT the client is retrained in the way they talk to themselves; dysfunctional self-talk is decreased and adaptive self-talk is increased. Initially, the therapist may model the new self-talk to the client, the client practices the new self-talk aloud, and over time comes to talk silently to themselves in the new way. This continues until the new self-talk becomes habitual. As well as learning the new skills, the client is encouraged to practice using more positive self-statements, to reinforce themselves positively, and to cope with failure using self-talk (see Box 4.3).

Today, the term CBT covers a wide range of approaches, some of which are more behavioural and some of which are more cognitive in their emphasis. Drawing on the range of cognitive and behavioural techniques that have been developed, it is possible to develop particular CBT interventions for use with clients with particular psychological problems. For example, it would now be common among psychologists working with people with phobias to use exposure techniques coupled with cognitive techniques (e.g., Marks, 1987). So, although the behavioural and cognitive models have been treated separately in this chapter, the distinction is not clear-cut. In practise, a person suffering from panic attacks

---

Box 4.3

This is one of the techniques taught to Helen by her counsellor. Now, when something happens at work she is able to monitor her negative automatic thoughts. Recently, Helen's line manager called her into her office. Immediately Helen was aware of how she automatically thought that she must have done something wrong and was now able to use self-talk to calm herself down and to prevent herself going into a depressed mood: 'There I go again, blaming myself for things that haven't even happened, I'm not going to do that today.'

might be asked to engage in activities that lead to panic-like symptoms, for example exercise to stimulate cardiovascular symptoms, thus exposing themselves to panic symptoms in a safe environment. We have already seen how exposure can be useful. The therapist might also use the sessions to help the client identify their automatic thoughts as they experience panic symptoms, and using educational techniques show the client how to reinterpret their experiences as normal bodily processes.

The cognitive-behavioural approach is the dominant perspective today in psychology and it has become a popular approach within the self-help literature (e.g., Persaud, 1998). Such self-help books are useful to many clients in beginning to better understand how they can change the way they feel through changing the way they think about themselves and their roles and goals in life.

Does CBT work?

The cognitive-behavioural model is used most extensively by psychologists and because of their more long-standing interest in evidence-based methods, cognitive-behavioural forms of therapy have been subject to research more than any other of the psychological models. This research has usually been taken by psychologists to support its effectiveness. Although a comprehensive review of this literature is beyond the scope of this book, cognitive-behavioural approaches are now well established as a way of treating people for panic disorder (e.g., Barlow, Craske, Cerny, and Klosko, 1989), generalised anxiety disorder (e.g., Chambless and Gillis, 1993), obsessive-compulsive disorder (e.g., Salkovskis and Kirk, 1997), and have been used with people suffering from psychosis (e.g., Fowler, Garety, and Kuipers, 1995), as well as some physical health problems such as chronic pain (e.g., Keefe, Dunsmore, and Burnett, 1992) (see Roth and Fonagy, 1996).

One of the factors that has been important in the development of the cognitive-behavioural model is that psychologists have adopted the language of psychiatrists, that is to say the use of the American Psychiatric Association's *Diagnostic and Statistical Manual of Mental Disorders*, and have tested the techniques of cognitive-behavioural therapy in relation to the various categories of so-called disorder. This can be seen even in the research studies mentioned above. Psychologists' adoption of the medical model has been important in gaining respectability for these psychologically oriented therapies within the medical profession and the health service. However, as we shall see in Chapter 6 perhaps this has not been without some cost (Albee, 2000).

Criticisms of cognitive-behavioural approaches

Although the research evidence is generally taken to support the effectiveness of cognitive-behavioural approaches to therapy, there have been critics of this approach. Some question the extent to which the research findings can be generalised to routine clinical settings and say that the approach has been overhyped (White, 2000). Others are more critical. Smail (1996a), for example, writes:

> the ruling dogmas of clinical psychology, usually referred to loosely as 'cognitive behaviourism', embody an, in my view, extraordinarily simplistic collection of ideas about how people come to be the way they are and what they can be expected to be able to do about it . . . Such ideas, acceptable enough perhaps to undergraduate students learning the experimental ropes, ring particularly hollow when they come to be applied in the clinical setting, where people's difficulties are often complicated and intractable. (Smail, 1996, pp. 29–30)

Certainly, many psychodynamic and, as we shall see, humanistically oriented therapists would agree with Smail's comment. Other commentators might note that behaviour therapies have traditionally been neglectful of the social setting in which therapy takes place and of the relationship which develops between the therapist and the client, although more recent writers in the behavioural tradition have begun to recognise the importance of the therapeutic relationship, and to question the stereotype of the behaviour therapist as someone who is cold and mechanistic (Schaap, Bennun, Schinder, and Hoogduin, 1993).

But it is not just theorists from the humanistic and psychodynamic models who have been critical of the cognitive approach. Skinner (1990), writing from the behaviourists perspective, has argued that the cognitive model is a return to *unscientific mentalism*, i.e., speculating about unobservable and unmeasurable phenomena which are outside the domain of scientific enquiry. However, despite Skinner's reservations about models which speculate on internal processes, most theorists would agree that it is indeed useful to do so, although as we have seen there remains disagreement about the nature of those internal processes. For example, the different ways of looking at internal processes as described by psychodynamically oriented therapists as opposed to cognitively oriented therapists.

Conclusion

In this chapter the behavioural and the cognitive models were introduced. Behaviourism was introduced by its exponents following criticisms of the psychodynamic model for its lack of scientific rigour. Although successful in many respects, particularly it seems with anxiety problems, the behavioural model also became subject to criticism as theorists began again to emphasise the importance of internal cognitive processes. The cognitive model, which first became popular in the 1960s, has received the greatest amount of research support and is widely used today to provide the theoretical basis for a number of therapies which research suggests to be effective for a variety of psychological problems. However, the cognitive approach to therapy is itself subject to criticism. Some see it as an overly simplistic approach to understanding human problems, and others see it as a return to unscientific mentalism.

Summary points

- The behavioural model developed in response to criticisms of psychoanalysis in an attempt to provide an approach to behaviour that was scientific.
- Two principles of learning theory form the basis for the behavioural model – classical conditioning and operant conditioning. Based on these principles, several behaviour therapy techniques such as systematic desensitisation, flooding, and aversion have been developed.
- Exposure to an unwanted or feared object without escape seems to be the effective ingredient common to many behaviour therapy techniques and more recent exposure-based

therapies have been used successfully with clients suffering from a range of anxiety-based problems.

- Although successful in helping people with anxiety, the behavioural model did not seem to lend itself as well to understanding depression as the cognitive approaches to therapy which were introduced by Ellis and Beck.

- The cognitive approaches of Ellis and Beck emphasise not just what happens to us but rather how we appraise and make sense of what happens to us. People with particular ways of thinking, such as those who magnify their difficulties and minimise their successes, are thought to be more prone to depression.

- Ellis's approach to therapy involves disputing with the client and directing the client to newer and more rational ways of thinking. Beck's approach to therapy is less confrontational and the therapist works in a more collaborative way, helping the client to examine the evidence for and against their distorted thoughts.

- Modern cognitive approaches tend to combine elements of behaviour therapy resulting in what is known as cognitive-behavioural therapy (CBT).

- CBT has attracted much research and its supporters claim that it has a good evidence base for a variety of different so-called psychiatric disorders.

5

Humanistic and Transpersonal Approaches

Introduction

Humanistic psychology has been referred to as the third force in psychology, after psychoanalysis and behaviourism. It emerged in the middle of the twentieth century as a reaction against these previous ways of looking at human experience, which were seen as overly deterministic. Psychoanalysis was seen as painting a bleak and pessimistic view of human nature, in which people are basically selfish and driven by sexual and aggressive impulses which must be restrained. Behaviourism was seen as objectifying and dehumanising the person and emphasising environmental forces as determinants of behaviour. In contrast, the humanistic approach emphasises human nature as essentially positive. The humanistic model emphasises choices, values, and purpose in life and psychopathology is seen as resulting from not accepting personal responsibility for one's actions. Humanistic therapies therefore strive to enable people to accept responsibility for their actions, to become aware of their subjective experiences, and to fulfil their personal potential for personal growth. Therapeutic approaches in the humanistic tradition emphasise the choices made by the client and the client's inner resources for change, as opposed to the techniques of the therapist.

As Szasz says:

> People seeking help from psychotherapists can be divided into two groups: those who wish to confront their difficulties and shortcomings and change their lives by changing themselves; and those who wish to avoid the inevitable consequences of their life strategies through the

magical or tactical intervention of the therapist in their lives. Those in the former group may derive great benefit from therapy in a few weeks or months; those in the latter may stand still, or sink ever deeper into their self-created life morass, after meeting with psychotherapists for years, and even decades. (Szasz, 1974, pp. 108–9)

The most well-known name associated with humanistic psychology is that of Carl Rogers (1902–1987) and it is his work we will first consider.

Carl Rogers and the person-centred approach

Carl Rogers was a psychologist by training. One of his earliest achievements was to pioneer the recording of therapeutic sessions which he then used for research (Rogers, 1942). Throughout his life Rogers was a prolific writer, publishing numerous academic papers and books, many of which are still widely read today. In his book *Client-centred Therapy*, Rogers began to outline his model of psychopathology and approach to therapy (Rogers, 1951). He went on to describe his ideas in more detail in later papers as he elaborated on his theory of personality and therapy (Rogers, 1957, 1959). Over the years, Rogers began to apply his ideas derived from therapy in wider contexts, such as education, conflict resolution, and encounter groups (see Thorne 1992), and in order to recognise the broader applicability of his model the term *person-centred* came to replace the term *client-centred*. These terms are often used interchangeably, although some prefer to use the term client-centred when referring to therapeutic work and the term person-centred when referring to the broader applications. Sometimes client-centred therapy is referred to as Rogerian therapy. However, Rogers disliked the use of this term maintaining that he did not want to see a school of therapists who were modelling themselves on him but rather to see therapists who were able to find their own ways of working within the person-centred approach.

Actualising tendency

The foundation of Rogers' theory is that of what he called the *actualising tendency*, which Rogers argued was the one natural motivational force of human beings and which is always directed towards constructive growth:

> It is the urge which is evident in all organic and human life – to expand, extend, to become autonomous, develop, mature – the tendency to express and activate all the capacities of the organism, to the extent that such activation enhances the organism or the self. (Rogers, 1961, p. 35)

This tendency towards growth however, can become thwarted when the person receives conditional positive regard from his or her social environment and thus develops what Rogers referred to as conditional positive self-regard (Rogers, 1959). An example of conditional positive regard is someone who grows up introjecting from the adults around the belief that to be valued he or she must always please others. Such a person would then develop a conditional positive self-regard, that is to say, that they only find value for themselves to the extent that they live up to this belief. Rogers argued that psychopathology results from the tension between the person's own inner life force, the actualising tendency, and the conditional positive regard they receive from others around them. Healthy functioning results when conditional positive regard is minimum and the actualising tendency is the driving force toward growth. The fully functioning person is one who is

> synonymous with optimal psychological adjustment, optimal psychological maturity, complete congruence, complete openness to experience . . . since some of these terms sound somewhat static, as though such a person 'had arrived', it should be pointed out that all the characteristics of such a person are process characteristics. The fully functioning person would be a person-in-process, a person continually changing. (Rogers, 1959, p. 235)

In terms of therapeutic practice, it is the therapist's trust in the person's actualising tendency which makes the person-centred approach, and those other humanistic approaches which adopt this stance, so radically different from other therapeutic approaches (see Bozarth, 1998). What this means in practise is that the person-centred therapist works in such as way as to attempt to be a companion to their client on his or her journey to understand themselves. The therapist endeavours to provide a facilitative environment in which the client can become their real self. Rogers

(1957) writes of how in his experience he found that whatever the client's problem was, whether it was to do with distressing feelings or troubling interpersonal relations, all were struggling with the same existential question, of how to be themselves.

Necessary and sufficient conditions

Rogers described in detail the nature of the facilitative environment which, he believed, would allow the person to become their real self. When the client perceives the therapist to be congruent, empathic, and providing of unconditional positive regard, the process of actualisation is promoted and therapeutic personality change will take place. Thus, congruence, empathy, and unconditional positive regard are viewed as the core conditions for constructive therapeutic personality change (Rogers, 1959). Given unconditional positive regard from significant others, the person increasingly develops positive self-regard and the actualising tendency is promoted. Dysfunctional behaviour on the part of the client decreases. Rogers states that for constructive personality change to occur, six conditions must exist and if they exist for a sufficient period of time they will be sufficient to produce constructive personality change (see Table 5.1).

In the first condition, psychological contact, Rogers is referring to a precondition which if not met would mean that the following five conditions were redundant. All he means by psychological contact is whether or not the two people are aware of each other, and that the behaviour of one impacts on the other. So, for example, with someone who is in a catatonic state it would be difficult to judge whether there was psychological contact. In the second condition, the client is in a state of anxiety and incongruence. Incongruence is explained as consisting of an incompatibility between underlying feelings and awareness of those feelings, or an incompatibility between awareness of feelings and the expression of feelings (Mearns and Thorne, 1999). For example, someone who appears anxious to an observer but has no awareness themselves of feeling anxious would be said to be incongruent in terms of their underlying feelings and their awareness of those feelings. Someone who is aware of their anxiety but says that they are feeling relaxed would be said to be incongruent between

Table 5.1   Rogers' necessary and sufficient conditions for
constructive personality change

1.   Two persons are in psychological contact.
2.   The first, whom we shall call the client, is in a state of incongruence, being vulnerable or anxious.
3.   The second person, who we shall call the therapist, is congruent or integrated in the relationship.
4.   The therapist experiences unconditional positive regard for the client.
5.   The therapist experiences an empathic understanding of the client's internal frame of reference and endeavours to communicate this experience to the client.
6.   The communication to the client of the therapist's empathic understanding and unconditional positive regard is to a minimal degree achieved.

(Rogers, 1957)

awareness and expression. In the third condition, the therapist is
congruent; that is to say, he or she is aware of their inner experience, e.g., feelings of anger, sadness, and is able to express this
openly if thought to be appropriate. In the fourth condition, the
therapist is able to provide unconditional positive regard; that is
to say, he or she is able to accept the client for who they are without
imposing conditions of worth on the client. In the fifth condition,
the therapist has empathic understanding; that is to say, he or she
is able to sense what the client's experience must feel like. Finally,
in the sixth condition, the client perceives the therapist's empathy
and unconditional acceptance (see Box 5.1).

Rogers (1957) believed that if these six conditions were in existence then constructive personality change would occur, but only
if all six were present. He also stated that the more that they were
present, the more marked the constructive personality change of
the client would be. His view was that this hypothesis applied to
all clients, regardless of the presenting problems (as long as condition one was met, i.e., that of psychological contact). He argued

> **Box 5.1**
>
> For Alex, who had grown up experiencing criticism from his father, it was important that he was able to feel unconditionally accepted by his therapist. It was only over time that he began to trust that his therapist would not respond to him in a critical way, and it was when this sense of safety had become established for him that he felt able to explore his inner conflicts and feelings openly and honestly.

that this was true regardless of which type of therapy was being delivered, and that these six conditions were able to produce constructive personality change in all relationships and not simply within the therapeutic relationship. The therapeutic relationship was simply one that tried to maintain these conditions at a heightened level of intensity. Contrary to other theoretical approaches, Rogers also claimed that these qualities did not require special intellectual knowledge and training in techniques of how to treat people, but were qualities of the person which could be acquired through experiential training.

The person-centred therapist does not attempt to change the client in some way, that is to say they do not set out to cure the client's depression or alleviate their anxiety for example. Rather their task is to maintain the attitudinal qualities described by Rogers, to hold unconditional positive regard, to be empathic, and to be congruent in the relationship. By doing just this, the therapist is thought to provide the client with the conditions necessary and sufficient for him or her to change in their own direction. It is believed that change will, because of the actualising tendency, be in a positive, social and constructive direction. One of the most important aspects of the person-centred approach was, however, Rogers' proposition that the best vantage-point for understanding behaviour is from the internal frame of reference of the individual themselves. Rogers (1951) argued that the only way we could understand another person's behaviour was to see the world through their eyes. Then, even the most seemingly bizarre behaviour would make sense.

Criticisms of the client-centred approach

The main criticism of the person-centred approach is focused on the concept of the actualising tendency itself, which is of course the foundation block of Rogers' theory. Some have called this assumption naïve (Ellis, 1959). Like Freud's concepts of id, ego, and superego, and other abstract psychological concepts which cannot be directly observed, it is not possible to ascertain whether an actualising tendency as described by Rogers actually exists in people. Others, although accepting the general principle of the actualising tendency, have viewed it as an insufficient basis on which to build a theoretical framework and approach to therapy, and consequently see a need for therapists to introduce other cognitive and behavioural techniques (Nelson-Jones, 1984).

Rogers has been criticised as presenting an overly optimistic view of human nature. Critics of the client-centred approach often point to the range of human suffering and ask how can there be so much suffering if people are basically trustworthy, social and constructive in nature. In response to such criticisms Rogers said:

> I am certainly not blind to all the evil and the terribly irresponsible violence that is going on ... There are times that I think I don't give enough emphasis on the shadowy side of our nature, the evil side. Then I start to deal with a client and discover how, when I get to the core, there is a wish for more socialization, more harmony, more positive values. Yes, there are all kinds of evil abounding in the world but I do not believe this is inherent in the human species any more than I believe that animals are evil. (Cited in Zeig, 1987, p. 202)

Other criticisms of Rogers' approach have been regarding the looseness of his language and the vagueness of his concepts which critics have argued do not lend themselves to empirical testing (Coffer and Appley, 1964). These criticisms are however somewhat ironic because it is also Rogers who is most often credited with introducing the field of psychotherapy research. For example, his early theoretical statements about the necessary and sufficient conditions for personality change were certainly presented as empirically testable hypotheses that could be subject to falsification as discussed by Popper (1959). Also, others have seen Rogers' understanding of how psychopathology develops through the internalisation of conditions of worth as simplistic (Nelson-Jones, 1984).

Going on to discuss the therapeutic implications of this, Nelson-Jones (1984) writes:

> Rogers' simplistic explanation of the genesis of people's problems has led to a unitary diagnosis: namely that of being out of touch with the valuing process inherent in the actualizing tendency. Consequently, he has restricted himself to what is essentially a single treatment approach. This is an inadequate way to approach the range of difficulties that people have in being personally responsible. (Nelson-Jones, 1984, pp. 15–16)

However, there are those who question this assumption that there are specific treatments for specific problems, and who argue that the research evidence is insufficient to draw such a conclusion (e.g., Bozarth, 1998).

Rogers was a psychologist and because of this background his earlier writings stressed the importance of subjecting the client-centred approach to empirical testing. However, although the early development of the client-centred tradition was fuelled by the results of scientific enquiry, later in his career Rogers moved away from working in academic psychological settings and the person-centred approach became less of a focus for research attention. Meanwhile, within academic psychological settings the cognitive-behavioural approach was gaining in popularity and attracting the interest of clinical research scientists. Consequently, the person-centred approach has been subject to less research in recent years than some other treatments, notably those from the cognitive-behavioural approach (Bozarth and Brodley, 1984). Today the person-centred approach is likely to less be a treatment of choice for many clients (see also Bohart, O'Hara, and Leitner, 1998). Also, many of those who became interested in the person-centred approach were not only less interested in conducting empirical research into the effectiveness of the therapy, but took the view that an empirical approach was inappropriate. It might therefore be argued that it is because of the anti-science approach of many of the humanistic practitioners that the person-centred approach has become less influential in recent years within academic psychology and psychiatry and even held in disdain (see DeCarvalho, 1991). Nevertheless, the approach remains popular within the fields of counselling and psychotherapy (see Thorne and Lambers, 1998).

Does client-centred therapy work?

Although evidence from research studies generally supports the view that these attitudinal qualities of the therapist, i.e., empathy, congruence, and unconditional positive regard, are important (e.g., Mitchell, Bozarth, and Krauft, 1977), Bozarth and Brodley (1984) argue that the paradigmatic difference between person-centred therapy and other therapies is that power and direction is centred on the client, but that this has become widely misunderstood with the consequence that there have been few studies which have actually tested the hypotheses of the person-centred approach (see also Bozarth, 1997; Levant and Shlien, 1984).

Also, humanistic therapists have not generally adopted the language of psychiatry, the *Diagnostic and Statistical Manual of Mental Disorders* published by the American Psychiatric Association. For this reason it might be argued that they have failed to gain credibility within the psychiatric and medical profession in the same way as cognitive and behavioural therapists. Despite the lack of empirical evidence person-centred therapy remains widely practised and remains a popular approach in the fields of counselling and psychotherapy (e.g., Mearns and Thorne, 1999; Thorne and Lambers, 1998). However, most outside commentators on the person-centred approach have concluded that the evidence is not persuasive that the necessary and sufficient conditions outlined by Rogers are indeed necessary and sufficient for personality change (e.g., Parloff, Waskow, and Wolfe, 1978). Nevertheless, few therapists of whatever persuasion would doubt that they represent important therapist qualities.

Some, like Bozarth (1998), would, however, still question this conclusion, asking whether the research which has been conducted has satisfactorily tested the hypothesis that the conditions are necessary and sufficient. One of the difficulties is finding appropriate methods with which to measure the proposed concepts of empathy, congruence, and unconditional positive regard, as well as the question of how to assess change in order to conduct traditional scientific research. Although empirical research data on the person-centred approach is sparse compared to the more medically oriented and cognitive-behavioural therapies, the evidence that does exist shows person-centred therapy to be as effective as any other therapy (e.g., Shapiro and Shapiro, 1982; Greenberg, Elliot, and Lietaer, 1994; Rice, 1988).

However, as researchers in the client-centred tradition do not generally adopt the medical model, research data on client-centred therapy for specific so-called psychiatric disorders is generally lacking. But some recent studies are beginning to address this gap in knowledge. For example, Greenberg and Watson (1998) have shown that humanistic person-centred therapies are effective for the treatment of depression. Despite the lack of research most commentators take the position that client-centred therapy is less effective for severe and chronic conditions. However, Rogers (1957) was of the opinion that the most essential ingredient for therapeutic change was the quality of the relationship between therapist and client, no matter what the client group was, and that client-centred therapy was useful even for psychotic clients. Until recently the use of client-centred therapy with psychotic clients has not received a great deal of attention. But this too is beginning to change.

Current directions

Pre-therapy

Recent writers in the person-centred tradition have begun to explore the use of client-centred therapy with psychosis and so-called personality disorders (Lambers, 1994a; 1994b; 1994c). *Pre-therapy* has been introduced as a way of working with clients who have difficulty maintaining contact, which is the first necessary condition according to Rogers for therapeutic change to take place (Prouty, 1976; 1990; Prouty and Kubiak, 1988). Pre-therapy involves the therapist reflecting to the client his or her awareness of the client's external world. For example, the therapist will reflect to the client about their facial expressions, body postures, and communication. By doing this the therapist is able to facilitate the client in engaging with the therapist so that more conventional client-centred therapy can take place.

Process-experiential approach

Several alternative therapeutic approaches based on Rogers' client-centred therapy have also been developed. One is the *process-experiential approach* pioneered by Greenberg and colleagues (Greenberg, Rice, and Elliot, 1993). The process-experiential approach emphasises an information-processing perspective, attempting to synthesise ideas from the client-centred tradition with those of the cognitive tradition.

Motivational interviewing

Another more recent approach is that of *motivational interviewing* (Rollnick and Miller, 1995). Motivational interviewing is based on the finding that the person-centred qualities of the therapist are important ingredients of therapy. However, motivational interviewing adds a more directive element by skilfully helping the client to explore the pros and cons of change in order to motivate the client towards making the necessary changes. Motivational interviewing has been described as a brief and directive form of person-centred counselling and has been shown to be effective with clients with substance-use problems (Miller, Zweben, DiClemente, and Rychtarik, 1992) (see Box 5.2).

Box 5.2

Although Alex found his experience in psychotherapy useful in understanding how his early and violent upbringing had led him to become the person he was now, he found it difficult to stop drinking and through the advice of his therapist he entered into therapy with someone specialising in motivational interviewing. The therapist using motivational interviewing techniques helped Alex to explore the pros and cons of his drinking and through this process Alex was able to make a decision to stop drinking.

Other variations include the experiential approach of Rennie (1998) which accepts the principle of non-directivity over the content of the client's material, but proposes a more directive approach to the process, using a range of experiential techniques to increase the client's self-awareness. Although not all therapists would agree that the conditions described by Rogers are necessary and sufficient for constructive personality change, most would probably agree that empathy, unconditional positive regard, and congruence are important therapist qualities, which are perhaps necessary if not sufficient for change. Indeed, studies show that these qualities are often evident in other therapists from psychodynamic and behavioural traditions, and some have argued that it is these factors which are important in promoting successful therapeutic change in all therapies. We shall go on to look at the common and non-specific factors in therapeutic healing in more detail in the final chapter.

As we have seen, the essence of person-centred therapy is not about what the therapist does but about the therapist's attitudinal qualities, the relationship which is formed between the therapist and the client, and thus the promotion of the actualising tendency. It is this trust in the ability of individuals to develop and grow in a positive direction that is the foundation of the humanistic approach and which is the unifying theme throughout all humanistic therapies. Person-centred therapy is perhaps the best known of the humanistic approaches, but it is not the only humanistic therapy. Two other notable humanistic-existential therapies are Gestalt therapy and transactional analysis, which we will now consider.

Other humanistic-existential approaches

Fritz Perls and Gestalt therapy

Fritz Perls (1893–1970), along with his wife Laura Perls and the philosopher Paul Goodman, founded what is known as *Gestalt therapy*. The word *Gestalt* is German and is taken to mean the total configuration of an object, the idea that an entity is more than the sum of the parts of which it is composed. The fundamental idea behind Gestalt therapy is that the client experiences and explores the total configuration of who they are. Gestalt therapy is a therapeutic approach which, like client-centred therapy, emphasises self-determination, choice and responsibility. However, in practise, Perls' approach contrasted sharply with that of Rogers as he advocated a more confrontational approach. In therapy the client is helped to maintain awareness and full contact with the present situation and the therapist interacts with the client in such a way as to facilitate the clients focus on the 'here and now'. For example, the therapist might ask the client to say what he or she is aware of right now, and to 'stay with' that awareness in order to train the client in present-centred attention. Other techniques used by Gestalt therapists are those which heighten the client's experience; the client may be asked to repeat what they are saying in an exaggerated way so as to enhance their experience. For example, someone who says that they are angry might be encouraged to shout it louder. Perhaps the most well known of all the Gestalt techniques is the 'empty chair', or 'two-chair' exercise which is often used to help clients resolve conflicts. Perhaps it is a conflict over an important decision that has to be made. The client sits facing the empty chair and imagines one part of the inner conflict to be sitting in the chair opposite. The client is encouraged to talk to that other part, to maintain a dialogue between the two parts of the inner conflict, until some integration between the two parts is achieved. The exercise can be used in a variety of ways; often people will use it to explore interpersonal conflicts (see Box 5.3).

But although Gestalt therapists employ a variety of techniques to heighten emotional awareness, what is more important to the Gestalt therapist is their ability to stay present with the client:

> To practise the Gestalt approach means that the counsellor uses himself or herself actively and authentically in the encounter with the other person. It is more a 'way of being and doing' than a set of techniques or a prescribed formula for counselling. Gestalt is characterised by a willingness on the part of the counsellor to be active, present as a person and interventionist in the counselling relationship. This is based on the assumption that treating the client as a human being with intelligence, responsibility and active choices at any moment in time is most likely to invite the client into autonomy, self-healing and integration. (Clarkson, 1989, pp. 19–20)

In contrast to client-centred therapy which has some scientific research base supporting its effectiveness as a form of therapy, Gestalt therapy has tended to attract little serious research interest.

Box 5.3

Alex's therapist helps him to explore his feelings towards his father using the two-chair exercise. Alex draws a picture of his father looking angry and sets it on the chair opposite and begins to talk to it. At first Alex is angry, shouting at his father for having treated him so poorly as a child. But as he switches seats and replies as his father, Alex begins to feel sadness too. Talking from his father's seat, Alex tells how he didn't want to hurt his son, how confused he was as a father, how he couldn't control his drinking and had no one to turn to himself, and how sorry he is for the pain he caused. Alex can still not forgive his father, although during this session he comes to understand for the first time how much psychological pain his father was experiencing after the separation with his wife and while struggling to bring Alex up on his own. At the end of the session, Alex goes over to the picture and redraws a sad face on the picture.

Eric Berne and transactional analysis

Eric Berne (1910–1970) introduced a system of therapy known as *transactional analysis* (TA) (Berne, 1971). Stewart (1989) says that the practice of TA is founded on three assumptions. The first of these is that at their core people are 'OK'. Although the therapist may not like the person's behaviour, the therapist values and esteems the client. Second, the TA therapist holds that each person has the capacity to think and make decisions about their life. Third, people can behave differently: the way we think, feel, and behave is our own choice. These are fundamental assumptions common to the humanistic approaches and for this reason transactional analysis has been included in the present chapter. However, Berne trained in classical psychoanalysis and some might instead include his work as a later development in psychodynamic theory.

Thinking Martian

One of things Berne encouraged people to do was to think *Martian*, to be able to observe human behaviour without preconceptions about what it means, to listen to how people say things as well as what they say. This involves the recognition that messages from one person to another can operate on two levels; what Berne referred to as the social level and the psychological level. The social level refers to what we say to one another, whereas the psychological level refers to what we really mean. For example, at a social level we might greet someone with the words, 'It's nice to see you', but the tone of our voice, or our eye contact, might say something else, such as 'Oh no, I was hoping you wouldn't be here, it really isn't nice to see you at all'. When the social and the psychological levels are incongruent in this way, the psychological message is said to be *ulterior*. Berne (1964; 1966; 1972) maintained that the psychological message was always the real message and it was this level that always determined what happened. In practice the role of the TA therapist is to be aware of, and to make the client aware of, the psychological level in his or her communication.

Ego states

Berne outlined a complex theoretical framework which therapists use to discuss with clients the nature of interpersonal communication. He outlined what he called the *ego state model* which consists of three ego states: the child; the parent; and the adult. In our child ego state we think and feel in a way as we did when we were children. In our parent ego state we think and feel in a way like those of the significant parental figures in our childhood. In our adult ego state we think and feel in ways that are direct responses to the here and now environment. Any behaviour is driven by the ego state which is in control of the personality at that moment. Feelings of inferiority as well as those of spontaneous joy are associated with the child. Criticism and orthodoxy are associated with the parent. Unemotional appraisal of the environment is associated with the adult. Normally we move in and out of these different ego states and psychopathology could be understood in terms of the functional breakdown of barriers between ego states. For example, delusional ideation occurs where there is a breakdown

between child and adult ego states such that child imagery conta-
minates the adult appraisal of the world. We can also analyse interpersonal interactions in terms of the communication between
individuals at an ego state level of analysis. Often at a social level
it might appear that we are talking adult to adult, but at the psychological level something else is happening, for example, we are
talking parent to child, or child to parent. Berne also described
the pathological games that people play in terms of stereotyped
ego state communication.

Life-script

Transactional analysis provides a very elaborate model of psychopathology, taking the view that psychological problems often
have their roots in childhood. Understanding our communication
with others also involves exploring the client's *life-script*. This is the
plan decided in early life by each person about the course of their
life, how it begins, what happens in the middle, and how it ends.
Berne said that the life script was laid down between the ages of
three and seven, and reflects one of four possible judgements
about the self and others:

1.   I'm OK and you're OK
2.   I'm not OK, but you're OK
3.   I'm OK, but you're not OK
4.   I'm not OK, and you're not OK.

Such feelings reflect parental introjections in infancy and form the
basis of the way the child experiences his or her life. As the intro-
jection of these parental messages takes place at such a young age
they are not the product of reasoned and logical thinking. The life-
script is likened to each person's own unfolding drama. In childhood, each of us develops our own personal life story, which is
referred to as the life-script. We carry these life-scripts into adulthood and play them out unconsciously, finding ways to confirm
our early decisions. The content of our scripts is unique to each
of us, although common script themes have been identified. For
example:

- I mustn't grow up
- I mustn't be important
- I mustn't exist
- I mustn't make it
- I mustn't feel
- I mustn't be me

The therapist endeavours to identify the client's script beliefs and to confront the life-script and encourage autonomy. The therapist aims to facilitate the client's recognition that they can now make different decisions in life (see Stewart, 1989). The life-script represents the infant's way of surviving and getting their needs met in what seems to be a hostile world. The child makes decisions, at an unconscious level, and as an adult the person plays out part of this script. For example, the child might perceive the parent as wanting them to be different. With parents who wanted a girl instead of a boy, for example, a child might come to decide that 'I mustn't be me'. This script belief might be expressed in a variety of ways, for example, a sense of the self as inferior, or through behaviour typical of the opposite sex. It might be that Alex's script was 'I mustn't feel'. Although transactional analysis has a wide appeal, it has not been subject to extensive scientific testing as a form of therapy.

Existential approaches

There is no doubt that Rogers' approach to therapy was influenced very much by his own personality and his experiences in life – particularly growing up in a strongly Christian family – as well as existential philosophy (see Thorne, 1992). Rogers often referred to the writings of two philosophers whose ideas he thought resonated with the person-centred approach, Buber and Kierkegaard. Indeed, to an extent, the person-centred approach, transactional analysis, and Gestalt therapy may be thought of as forms of *humanistic-existential* philosophy (Rogers, 1973). But perhaps the name most associated with the humanistic-existential approach is that of Victor Frankl.

Frankl (1905–1997) spent three years in the Nazi concentration camps during the Second World War during which time he experienced the deaths of his parents, wife, and brother. His experiences led him to emphasise the search for meaning in people's lives and to conclude that a fundamental purpose in life is to find meaning in a world which seems meaningless (Frankl, 1963; 1967). Meaning can come about through achievement, transcendent experience, and through suffering. Frankl developed a system of therapy known as *logotherapy* in which clients are helped to become fully aware of their own responsibilities, to develop choice over what attitudes are held, and to look at the existential vacuum of life. Using persuasion and reasoning as well as interpretations and confrontation, logotherapists attempt to raise the consciousness of their client. One particular technique is paradoxical intention, in which the client is encouraged to do what it is that they fear doing. Other notable existential therapists were Ludwig Binswanger (1881–1966) and Medard Boss (1903–1991) who endeavoured to understand the meaning of the client's experience, and used the discipline of philosophy rather than psychology to understand the human predicament. In more recent years, Yalom (1980) and Deurzen (1988; 1998) have helped to bring existential psychotherapy to our attention:

> Radical existential psychotherapy focuses on the inter-personal and supra-personal dimensions, as it tries to capture and question people's world views. Such existential work aims at clarifying and understanding personal values and beliefs, making explicit what was previously implicit and unsaid. Its practice is primarily philosophical and seeks to enable a person to live more deliberately, more authentically and more purposefully, whilst accepting the limitations and contradictions of human existence . . . Existential psychotherapy has to be reinvented and recreated by every therapist and with every new client. It is essentially about investigating human existence and the particular preoccupations of one individual and this has to be done without preconceptions or set ways of proceeding. There has to be complete openness to the individual situation and an attitude of wonder that will allow the specific circumstances and experiences to unfold in their own right. (Deurzen, 1998, pp. 13–14)

Issues raised in existential psychotherapy are bound up with questions about the meaning and purpose of life – what it is to be human. Existential therapy is also concerned with metaphysical issues to do with good and evil, life and death, and consequently existential therapy often overlaps with the field of transpersonal psychotherapy (Rowan, 1993).

Transpersonal psychotherapy

Towards the end of his life, Rogers became interested in altered states of consciousness and began to advocate a more spiritual understanding of human experience. Rogers stated that he found the view of Arthur Koestler that individual consciousness was a fragment of cosmic consciousness appealing (Rogers, 1980). Talking about what happened in therapy when he was most effective as a therapist, Rogers wrote:

> At those moments it seems that my inner spirit has reached out and touched the inner spirit of the other. Our relationship transcends itself and becomes part of something larger. Profound growth and healing and energy are present. (Rogers, 1980, p. 129)

Some recent writers have discussed spirituality within the person-centred approach (e.g., Purton, 1998; Thorne, 1991; 1994). Humanistic-existential approaches lend themselves more easily to an integration with spiritual ideas than, for example, the cognitive-behavioural approaches (see Payne, Bergin, and Loftus, 1992). But Rogers himself did not elaborate much further on a *transpersonal* approach, which is probably most closely associated with the work of Abraham Maslow, who is recognised as the founder of the transpersonal approach.

Abraham Maslow and the hierarchy of needs

Abraham Maslow, like Rogers, emphasised human beings as striving to fulfil their potential. But whereas Rogers saw behaviour as being driven by the self-concept, Maslow was concerned with the motives that drive people. He suggested that there were two kinds of motivations, which he called deficiency motivation, i.e., the need to reduce physiological tensions such as thirst and hunger, and growth motivation, i.e., the satisfaction of needs such as the need to be loved and esteemed, respectively. Maslow described a *hierarchy of human needs* (see Figure 5.1).

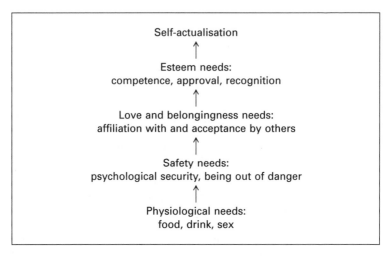

Figure 5.1   Maslow's hierarchy of needs

First, a person must meet physiological needs. When these needs have been met the person moves up to the next set of needs; safety and security needs. When these needs have then been met, the person moves up to the next set of needs; belongingness needs. Finally, when all the basic needs have been met, the person strives to meet their needs for self-actualisation. Achieving self-actualisation is not an all or nothing process – rather self-actualisation comes about over time by a matter of small changes. Maslow suggested that self-actualised individuals are self-directed, creative, independent, have an accurate view of themselves and other people, are willing to try and understand other people's points of view, and are open to new experiences:

> They listen to their own voices; they take responsibility; they are honest; and they work hard. They find out who they are and what they are, not only in terms of their mission in life, but also in terms of the way their feet hurt when they wear such and such a pair of shoes and whether they do or do not like eggplant . . . All this what the real self means. (Maslow, 1993, p. 49)

Self-actualised people (or fully functioning people in the language of Rogers), Maslow argued, are open to experiences, and one form of experience that particularly interested Maslow was what he called peak experiences. These are experiences that transcend ordinary human consciousness, often experienced as religious or spiritual in nature. Such experiences are seen as existing beyond the person, hence the term, transpersonal:

> I should say also that I consider Humanistic, Third Force Psychology to be transitional, a preparation for a still 'higher' Fourth Psychology, transpersonal, transhuman, centred in the cosmos rather than in human needs and interest, going beyond humanness, identity, self-actualization and the like. (Maslow, 1968, pp. iii–iv)

Stanislav Grof

Since Maslow's death, his colleagues have gone on to explore and map out the field of transpersonal psychology. One leading exponent is Stanislav Grof. Grof was a close friend of Maslow and together they helped found the International Transpersonal Association. Grof trained as a medical doctor going on to conduct psychiatric research into schizophrenic experiences and the potential value of LSD. From this work he developed interests in the transpersonal and in his career attempted to integrate Western science with the wisdom of the great spiritual systems. Grof has written about how experiences in the womb and during birth provide psychospiritual blueprints which guide the way we experience life and can become reflected in psychopathology. Grof also draws on the work of Jung, among others (e.g., Sheldrake, 1981), in linking our experience with those of a collective unconscious, one that exists beyond the boundaries of what we perceive as space and time:

> Over three decades of systematic studies of the human consciousness have led me to conclusions that many traditional psychiatrists and psychologists might find implausible if not downright incredible. I now firmly believe that consciousness is more than an accidental by-product of the neurophysiological and biochemical processes taking place in the human brain. I see consciousness and the human psyche as expressions and reflections of a cosmic intelligence that permeates the entire universe and all of existence. We are not just highly evolved animals with biological computers embedded inside our skulls; we are also fields of consciousness without limits, transcending time, space, matter, and linear causality. (Grof and Bennett, 1990, p. 18)

Grof reaches his conclusions from his observations of people experiencing trance states and spontaneous psychospiritual crisis, or those states achieved through meditation, hypnosis, psychedelic sessions, and experiential psychotherapy. Grof discusses Jung's concept of synchronicity:

> In a mechanical universe where everything is linked by cause and effect, there is no place for 'meaningful coincidences' in the Jungian sense. In the practice of traditional psychiatry, when a person perceives meaningful coincidences, he or she is, at best, diagnosed as projecting special meaning into purely accidental events; at worst he or she is diagnosed as suffering from hallucinations or delusions . . . As a result they may wrongly diagnose 'meaningful coincidences' as the result of serious pathology . . . Had those experiences been correctly understood and treated as manifestations of psycho-spiritual crisis those same people might have been quickly helped through approaches supporting spiritual emergence, rather than undergoing all the problems that unnecessary hospitalisation entails. (Grof and Bennett, 1990, p. 178)

Jung told of his experiences in states of non-ordinary consciousness and his communications with a spirit guide called Philemon. According to the criteria of the traditional scientific enquiry the evidence for these views is restricted to anecdotal accounts which cannot be verified. But, as with the humanistic approaches, Grof argues that the therapist must accept and trust the spontaneous unfolding of the process. This is a view in line with Jung's that there is an inner wisdom for healing which comes from the collective unconscious. What psychiatrists might view as mental illness can come to be seen in a different light. One writer, for example, who has provided some very interesting insights from his personal experience is Chadwick (1997), who writes:

> 'Schizophrenia', whatever it might mean, shows life in a blazing and terrifying light, it is difficult to believe that one is being enlightened at the same time as this cruel pain is searing through one's psyche. My argument here is that this is indeed the case . . . The psychotic experience takes one to the crags and ridges of human life and to the precipices of what consciousness can permit. It is very difficult after this to take on board the model of reality provided by science, which is like providing someone with a shoe box when they want an enclosure for an elephant. (Chadwick, 1997, pp. 39–40)

Running throughout this book has been the theme of scientific enquiry and how it relates to therapeutic practice. However, when we begin to discuss the ideas of the humanistic and transpersonal psychologists, we can see how some theorists within these traditions have come to doubt the value of traditional scientific enquiry for understanding what goes on in their domain of interest. Transpersonal psychologists often draw on quantum physics (e.g., Bohm, 1980) to provide a theoretical foundation for their work. For example, the ideas of Tart (1975) are important. Tart has argued that there are realms of awareness beyond those which we understand today. We can use science, he says, but

> the world we spend most of our time perceiving is not just any segment of the physical world, but a highly socialised part of the physical world that has been built into cities, automobiles, television sets. So our perception may indeed be realistic, but it is only with respect to a very tailored segment of reality, a *consensus* reality, a small selection of things we have agreed are 'real' and 'important.' Thus, within our particular cultural framework, we can easily set up what seem to be excellent scientific experiments that will show our perceptions are indeed realistic, in the sense that we agree with each other on these selected items from our consensus reality. (Tart, 1975, p. 39)

Levels of consciousness

According to Tart we are prisoners of our ordinary state of consciousness and Western science is challenged to recognise that our normal state of consciousness is a state of samsara. But perhaps the writer who has been most influential in recent years in helping to lay the foundations for transpersonal psychology is Ken Wilber, who has attempted to integrate the religious traditions of the East with the psychology of the West. Wilber, drawing upon many traditions, including Hinduism, has discussed how consciousness exists as a hierarchy of dimensional levels. Wilber describes six levels of consciousness:

1. Physical
2. Biological
3. Psychological
4. Subtle
5. Causal
6. Ultimate

First, there is the physical level, that of physics and chemistry; secondly, the biological level, which is concerned with living matter; and thirdly the psychological level, which is concerned with thinking and feeling, in much the same way as it was described in the previous chapters. Moving beyond these dimensions, however, we enter the transpersonal. Fourth, there is the subtle level, which Wilber says is the level of visionary insight, archetypal intuition, clarity of awareness, and higher experiences; fifth, the causal level, which is the realm of dissolution and transcendence of subject-object duality; and sixth, the ultimate, the highest level of consciousness. Therapy is about facilitating a person's development within the transpersonal realm of experience (Boorstein, 1980; Rowan, 1993).

Translation vs. transformation

There are similarities here with Buddhism, as a person comes to cease identifying with their construction of themselves, to realise at a profound level that there is no self. Wilber draws an interesting distinction between *translation* and *transformation*. Translation is when we come to think differently, and therefore to behave differently in the world as would be the case in cognitive therapy. Transformation, on the other hand, refers to completely and radically dismantling our way of seeing the world, shattering our perception of the world as we know it. Both translation and transformation are legitimate models of change Wilber argues, each being concerned with a different level of consciousness (see Wilber, 1998). Similarly, other writers have also focused on the relationship between Western psychotherapy and the ideas of Eastern religious traditions. Eastern thought also emphasises the interconnectedness of all things and how it is an illusion to see ourselves as separate from the world around us. Drawing on Eastern traditions, Brazier (1995) discusses how Zen is a form of therapy:

> The challenge which Zen poses us is to reach deeply into the experience of being alive to find something authentic . . . Zen is simply the awakening of one heart by another, of sincerity by sincerity. Although words can express it, and can point to it, they cannot substitute for it. It is the authentic experience which occurs when concern with all that is inessential drops away. (Brazier, 1995, pp. 12–13)

Eastern approaches to therapy, along with other transpersonal approaches, most often involve some form of meditation and altered states of consciousness. In discussing transpersonal therapy, Grof and Bennett (1990) write:

> In work with non-ordinary states of consciousness, the roles of therapist and client are quite different from those in traditional psychotherapy. The therapist is not the active agent who causes the changes in the client by specific interventions, but is somebody who intelligently co-operates with the inner healing forces of the client . . . It is also in agreement with C. G. Jung's approach to psychotherapy, wherein it is believed that the task of the therapist is to mediate for the client a contact and exchange with his or her inner self, which then guides the process of transformation and individuation. The wisdom for change and healing comes from the collective unconscious and surpasses by far the knowledge that is intellectually available to the therapist. (Grof and Bennett, 1990, p. 211)

Humanistic attitudes towards the medical model

In the previous chapter we saw that the cognitive-behavioural model, although not concerned with biological causes of abnormal psychological conditions, largely adopts the medical model in its attempt to understand the most effective forms of therapy for specific conditions as defined in DSM. In contrast, the humanistic approach is generally thought of as being antagonistic to the medical model of therapy described in Chapter 2. Maslow summed this up in describing the use of words such as patient:

> I hate the medical model that they imply because the medical model suggests that the person who comes to the counsellor is a sick person, beset by disease and illness, seeking a cure. Actually, of course, we hope that the counsellor will be the one who helps to foster the self-actualisation of people, rather than the one who helps to cure a disease. (Maslow, 1993, p. 49)

The humanistic approach has been less influenced by the use of diagnostic systems than the cognitive-behavioural approach, recognising that often any judgement of what is 'normal' or 'abnormal' is highly subjective and will rely on the clinician's own frame of reference. For example, a clinician must first of all judge what is a normal eating pattern before he or she can determine that someone is suffering from an eating disorder (Garfinkel, Kennedy, and Kaplan, 1995). Humanistic psychologists therefore tend not to use diagnostic systems such as DSM in their work. The role of the therapist is to let the client be themselves, to grow and to unfold in their own way, to break through their own defences and discover themselves. Some are wary of the implications of a medical model within counselling and psychotherapy. Mearns (1994), for example, is sceptical of the idea that working with particular client groups or issues requires prior training in that group or issue.

However, there are exceptions. Berne for example, despite being included here as a humanistic thinker, encouraged a medical perspective to psychotherapy. To illustrate what he meant he used the analogy of a man who gets splinter in his toe. The toe becomes infected and the man starts to limp. This leads his back and neck muscles to tighten up and in turn he develops headaches and a fever from the infection. How should we approach this person? What is needed, Berne argued, is a diagnosis of splinter in the toe followed by its removal with the result that all the symptoms quickly disappear:

> Running through this I think you will hear the dread medical model of psychotherapy, which scares the hell out of people – gives them night-mares. But I think it's a very good model. That's because it works for other conditions, and if you are going to cure people's heads I think you should use the medical model. (Berne, 1971, p. 12)

Conclusion

The influence of humanistic psychology remains a major force within the professions of counselling and psychotherapy and there seems to be a recent growth in interest towards the re-lated transpersonal and existential therapies. Indeed, the British Psychological Society now has a section of its membership devoted entirely to transpersonal psychology. However, the influence of humanistic and transpersonal psychology within the field of psy-chology remains minimal, and perhaps even less influential in the field of psychiatry. The reason for this lack of interest is often stated as the reluctance of many humanistic practitioners to put their model and their ways of working with clients to the test using the methods of empirical psychological science. For this reason many academic psychologists have viewed the humanistic per-spective with disdain. However, there is now a growing recognition that the discipline of psychology must also embrace more holistic approaches, and also of the importance of the positive psychology espoused by the humanistic writers.

Summary points

- Humanistic psychology has been referred to as the third force after psychoanalysis and behaviourism. Unlike these earlier approaches humanistic psychology emphasised personal responsibility and choice in people's lives.
- Rogers developed the client-centred approach to therapy which was based on the philosophical premise that there is a single motivational force towards constructive growth within each person, the actualising tendency. Psychopathology results when the actualising tendency is thwarted.
- The client-centred therapist endeavours to create a facilitative environment which nurtures the actualising tendency.
- In the early years of client-centred therapy the approach was subject to much research which supported its effectiveness, although in more recent years practitioners of the client-centred approach have tended not to emphasise the importance of traditional scientific research or to adopt the medical model.
- Other humanistic approaches include Gestalt therapy, developed by Perls, and transactional analysis, developed by Berne.
- After humanistic psychology, transpersonal psychology and psychotherapy has been called the fourth force. Transpersonal psychotherapy is about experiences which seem to transcend or go beyond the realms of ordinary human consciousness and experience.
- Leading figures in transpersonal psychotherapy include Maslow, Grof, and Wilber, who question our perceptions of reality.

6

Social and Cultural Approaches

Introduction

Each of the psychological therapies discussed in the previous chapters are, in one way or another, concerned with processes internal to human beings as the cause of psychopathology. In contrast, writers in the social and cultural approaches draw attention to how a person's psychological problems are manifestations of disturbances in the social structures. Psychopathology reflects the society in which the person has been raised and is living. First, there is the macro, or sociocultural, level of analysis which examines human behaviour from the standpoint of the social structure itself. Then there is the micro, or interpersonal, level which examines the interactions between individuals as they participate in that society. In this chapter we will first examine the notion of culture bound syndromes before considering the sociocultural origins of psychopathology and finally group and family approaches to therapy.

Cultural context

The sociocultural model challenges us to look across cultures for the similarities and differences in human experience. What might be seen as psychopathology in one culture might not be seen as such in another culture. Perceptions of psychopathology within a culture can change over time. A hundred years ago, for example, in Victorian England, masturbation was seen as a cause of madness. Children who persisted in masturbating despite warnings and punishment would sometimes be 'treated' surgically, by castration in boys and the removal of the clitoris in girls. Such practices rarely exist in our society today, although genital mutilation remains common in parts of the world (see Walker, 1993). This example illustrates well how important our cultural context is in shaping how we think about psychopathology. Another more recent example concerns psychiatrist's views of homosexuality over the past 30 years. The first edition of DSM classified homosexuality as a sexual deviation within the category of sociopathic personality disturbances. Homosexuality remained a sexual deviation in the second edition of DSM published in 1968, under the category of personality disorders. However, in 1973 the second edition of DSM was modified when the board of trustees of the American Psychiatric Association voted to eliminate the general category of homosexuality as a mental disorder, unless it was distressing to the person concerned. The exclusion of homosexuality from DSM came about as a result of political pressure from gay activist groups who maintained that its continued inclusion was inappropriate and oppressive. Within the American Psychiatric Association this was a controversial decision and the debate about the proper place of homosexuality within psychiatric classification continued. This illustrates that psychiatric classification is not necessarily value free, and some have argued that psychiatry and psychology embody the values of Western culture, affecting the way that forms of behaviour are perceived.

Culture-bound syndromes

If psychological problems are a function of the person's sociocultural context we would expect different problems in different cultures. This is indeed what is found. Many psychological problems have been described elsewhere that are unfamiliar in the Western context. *Koro* is a syndrome seen in Southeast Asia. In men, koro consists of anxiety and a fear that the penis is retracting into the abdomen and that death will result. In women koro consists of a sensation that the breasts and labia are shrinking. In order to prevent koro, men may try to prevent the shrinkage of their penis by stretching it by, for example, tying weights to it. Koro is extremely rare in Western society and in cases where it has been observed it has been associated with schizophrenia or drug use. However, in Asia there have been epidemics of koro such as happened in 1982 in India and in 1976 in Thailand. A woman in Bali might suffer from what is called *bebainin,* a syndrome that includes abdominal pain, headache, ringing in the ears, screaming, weeping and impaired vision. The onset of bebainin is sudden and the duration of an episode is short, after which the person has no memory of what has happened.

Another syndrome traditionally not seen in Western cultures is *amok.* The Malayan word amok means to engage furiously in battle. In the condition of amok men erupt, following a period of depression and brooding, into a sudden state of frenzied and unprovoked indiscriminate violence ending in exhaustion and amnesia. The affected person may run wildly about with a weapon such as a knife, killing those in his way, until he is overpowered, commits suicide, or is killed. The condition has traditionally been associated with the Malayan people and was relatively common a few hundred years ago, although it is rare today. Theorists have speculated that amok was related to the cultural values which placed heavy restrictions on adolescents and adults, and the belief in magical possession by demons and evil spirits. In Western culture we have seen in recent years several well-publicised episodes of behaviour which bear similarity to the condition of amok. These are only three culture-bound syndromes. There are many others (see Westermeyer, 1985).

Also, even when similar psychological problems are seen in different parts of the world, the way a particular syndrome is perceived might vary from culture to culture (Erinosho and Ayonrinde, 1981). What is also interesting is that we rarely think of the psychological problems we are more familiar with as culture bound. A complete list of culture-bound syndromes would include syndromes that we in Western society do not usually see as culture bound. Most notably, problems connected to eating are seen to be somewhat specific to Western cultures. It is worth looking at eating disorders and how they seem to be related to our cultural context.

Eating disorders
Perhaps the influence of sociocultural factors is most easily illustrated when we consider *eating disorders.* DSM-IV (American

Psychiatric Association, 1994) lists two major subtypes of eating disorder – anorexia nervosa and bulimia nervosa. People with anorexia nervosa starve themselves. They have a fear of gaining weight and of becoming fat. This is despite the fact they are often very underweight. People with bulimia nervosa will eat an excessive amount of food in a discrete period of time during which they lack control over their eating. This is then followed by purging behaviour, i.e., self-induced vomiting, misuse of laxatives, excessive exercise. Such behaviour is recurrent, happening on average twice a week. What is interesting is that both of these disorders are about ten times more common in females than in males, and most common in young women in their teens and early twenties. Also, it is more prevalent in women who have careers that place importance on appearance, such as modelling. Furthermore, research, which has looked at the risk of eating disorders in different generations of women, has concluded that it has become more prevalent in recent years (see Kendler *et al.*, 1991).

Racial and sexual prejudice

These findings have led many researchers to speculate that our cultural attitudes about appearance are central to understanding these disorders. Interestingly, recent research studies that have been carried out have found a high percentage of women are dissatisfied with some aspect of their physical appearance. For example, in one American survey, over 10 per cent were found to be dissatisfied with their face, over 20 per cent with their upper torso, over 40 per cent with their weight, and over 50 per cent with their mid torso (Cash and Henry, 1995). Also, differences in the prevalence of other so-called psychiatric disorders between men and women have been noted. For example, much evidence suggests that women are twice as likely as men to suffer from depression (see Comer, 1998). Several reasons have been suggested for this: for example, that women may lead more stressful lives. However, some would argue that such findings reflect underlying sex-related assumptions held by clinicians making the diagnoses. In an interesting study which supports such a view, Broverman and colleagues (1970) asked a mix of male and female psychiatrists, psychologists, and social workers to rate men and women along various dimensions, finding that women who were seen as submissive and dependent were also seen as healthier. Chessler (1972) argued that male-dominated psychiatry pathologised women's experiences in order to control their behaviour in line with stereotypes of femininity (see also Ussher, 1991).

There is concern about mental health professionals acting as agents of social control. In Britain, although only around 5 per cent of the population are black, 25 per cent of patients on psychiatric wards with a diagnosisis of schizophrenia are black (Banyard, 1996). Ethnic minorities such as Afro-Caribbean people are more likely to be detained under the mental health act (Pilgrim, 1997). Other studies suggest that Asian patients admitted to hospital are more likely to be diagnosed as psychotic and treated with electroconvulsive therapy than white patients (Shaikh, 1985). Why might this be? Several explanations are possible. On the one hand there are explanations to do with methodology rather than with any real group differences: for example, it has been suggested that psychiatrists, who are mostly white and middle class, misperceive what is normal behaviour within the Afro-Caribbean culture as abnormal (Banyard, 1996). On the other hand, there are explanations to do with real differences between the groups. Some might suggest genetic differences leading to an innate vulnerability to psychopathology among the Afro-Caribbean group. Others have suggested that higher rates of psychological disturbance in ethnic minorities are a response to racism and disadvantage (see Littlewood and Lipsedge, 1993).

Sociocultural origins of psychopathology

The modern emergence of the sociocultural model can be traced back to the publication of a landmark book, *Social Class and Mental Illness: A Community Study* by Hollingshead and Redlich (1958). These writers brought a sociological perspective to psychiatry. The sociocultural model recognises that sociocultural factors external to the person are important determinants of thoughts, feelings, and behaviour. Not surprisingly it is sociologists rather than psychologists who have drawn our attention to how our behaviour is shaped by the social structure. The French sociologist Emile Durkheim (1858–1917) was concerned with the way society has a set of values and norms which we usually behave in accordance with. When our own values no longer match those of the society in which we live, then our ties with that society are weakened resulting in what Durkhein called *anomie*. Durkheim related this loss of social cohesion to some forms of suicide. Sociologists have subsequently been interested in how feelings of anomie and alienation affect mental health, and during the past three decades there has been much research interest in trying to demonstrate the roles social factors play.

In perhaps the most famous study, a study of women living in London, it was found that those women who were diagnosed as depressed were more likely to have young children at home, less employment, and fewer people to talk to about their worries than those women who were not diagnosed as depressed (Brown and Harris, 1978). This landmark study was important in drawing attention to the social origins of depression. This and subsequent evidence leaves us with no doubt that psychopathology is related to social factors. Experiences of unemployment and economic hardship, for example, have been found to be associated with suicide attempts (e.g., Ahlburg and Shapiro, 1983). Poverty in particular has been shown to be related to psychopathology (e.g., Bruce, Takeuchi, and Leaf, 1991) and a review of the evidence shows that psychological problems are more prevalent in those people who are lower in social class (see Argyle, 1994). This is most evident in a psychiatric hospital, where a large proportion of patients will usually be from lower social class backgrounds. It is also known that people from a lower social class background are more likely to be diagnosed as schizophrenic (see Goldberg and Huxley, 1992). Why might this be?

In an attempt to explain these data it has been suggested that those who are less able to function in society end up in the lowest social strata (and those who are well able to function effectively move up the social strata). This is called the *downward drift hypothesis* and most commentators would agree that this process plays at least a small part in explaining the relationship between social class and health (see Williams, 1990). However, this explanation does not seem to fully account for the relationship between social class and psychopathology, and it is also thought that those with lower social status are subject to more life-stressors and are therefore more likely to experience psychological problems. Certainly, there is evidence supporting the idea that those people of lower social status experience greater life-stress (e.g., Gunnell, Peters, Kammerling, and Brooks, 1995; McLeod and Kessler, 1990) and engage in poorer health behaviours, such as smoking and taking less exercise (e.g., Blaxter, 1990), which in turn might contribute to poorer psychological health. Such health detrimental behaviours are, of course, linked to wider social factors such as education and financial security, and draw our attention to what Smail (1996a) has described as the impress of power.

Impress of power

Smail (1996a) has argued that the working of social power is central to understanding psychological problems. He sees individual distress as the outcome of a social process in which psychological problems have their origin in powerful factors, often distant in the person's life history, of politics, economics, and culture. It is the misuse of power which is ultimately at the core of people's difficulties (see also, Hagan and Smail, 1997a; 1997b). Smail argues that the aim of therapy should be to attempt to increase power and resources available to clients.

What sets the sociocultural perspective so far apart from all the other perspectives considered in this book is that it is not focused on the individual, but on society. Psychological therapy, whether it be psychodynamic, cognitive-behavioural, or humanistic, largely attempts to help the person to live in society as it is. However, sociocultural explanations emphasise the way in which we are products of our culture, and the fact that by changing our culture we are best positioned to create a healthy population (e.g., Newnes, 1996). For this reason, the sociocultural model is less concerned with the question of what constitutes psychiatric disorder and how it should be treated. Rather, it is concerned with changing society. Sociocultural theorists are concerned with questions about what aspects of our culture need to change to create a healthy population. For example, how does our education system create and maintain divisions in society? What might an alternative education system look like?

One aspect of the sociocultural viewpoint that is perhaps of most interest to psychological therapists is the question of the extent to which the mental health professions themselves are part of the oppressive social forces operating on people, and whether the business of therapy itself needs to change. Certainly, there are those who have strongly argued that this is the case. For example, an Italian psychiatrist Franco Basaglia came to view psychiatric hospitals as instruments of social control and violence, and went on to help introduce community care (see Tansella and Williams, 1987). However, the most well-known critic of the psychiatric profession, and its adherence to a biomedical model, is Thomas Szasz.

Thomas Szasz and the myth of mental illness

Szasz (1961) argued that the biomedical model, when applied to psychological problems, was simply metaphorical. Psychological problems are not, he argued, illnesses, in the same way as the flu is an illness. Szasz (1961) argued that to claim psychological problems were an illness in the same way as the flu is an illness was to make a metaphorical statement:

> I hold that mental illness is a metaphorical disease; that, in other words, bodily illness stands in the same relation to mental illness as a defective television receiver stands to an objectionable television programme. To be sure, the word 'sick' is often used metaphorically. We call jokes 'sick', economies 'sick', sometimes even the whole world 'sick' – but only when we call minds 'sick' do we systematically mistake metaphor for fact; and send to the doctor to 'cure' the illness. It's as if a television viewer were to send for a TV repairman because he disapproves of the programme he is watching. (Szasz, 1974, p. 11)

Mental illness, Szasz argued, was a concept invented to control and change people whose behaviour threatens the social order. As we saw in Chapter 2, one of the tasks of the medical model is to classify and provide a description of the various psychiatric disorders. Szasz has this to say about psychiatric classification:

> Psychiatric diagnoses are stigmatising labels phrased to resemble medical diagnoses and applied to persons whose behaviour annoys or offends others. Those who suffer from and complain of their own behaviour are usually classified as 'neurotic'; those whose behaviour makes others suffer, and about whom others complain, are usually classified as 'psychotic'. (Szasz, 1974, p. 26)

Although such views are perhaps less common today than when Szasz was writing in the 1970s, there are those who still remain strongly critical of the idea that psychological problems are best understood as illnesses or diseases, and best treated within the medical model. Smail (1996), for example, writes:

> Psychiatry's obsession with cataloguing the phenomena of distress into diagnostic syndromes of illness is rendered ultimately futile precisely because the supposed victims of such illness are not carriers of clear-cut cultures of disease, but in essence ordinary human beings struggling to cope with a disordered world. The continued efforts of psychiatry to define ever more tightly and exclusively the varieties of illness it thinks are to be discerned in emotional suffering borders, at the end of the twentieth century, on farce. Psychiatrists seem to hope that if, like Victorian gentleman scholars sorting out butterflies, they refine their descriptions carefully enough, they will identify species of disease which can be treated medically in the same way that, for instance, tuberculosis can. Widespread criticism of this approach, not to mention its evident fruitlessness, has done nothing over the past hundred years to diminish the enthusiasm of those who engage in it. (Smail, 1996a, pp. 49–50)

Furthermore, Albee (1996) has written of how our concepts of mental disorder are developed in such a way as to support the rulers of an exploitative society. Taking up this theme in relation to the psychiatric diagnosis of schizophrenia, Marshall (1996) writes:

> I am interested in the way that what is termed 'schizophrenia' first becomes seemingly scientifically validated as an 'illness' or 'disease', and then becomes reified into a preponderantly genetic disorder which then justifies a hunt for specifically causative genes. It is my thesis that much of what passes for science here is a myth-making process which develops a momentum of its own, powered by a variety of interests, and supported by a lack of real analysis and an inclination to provide results which support a biologically determinist stance. (Marshall, 1996, p. 5)

Marshall goes on to discuss evidence supporting his thesis. For example, he questions the use of certain statistical techniques in some studies purporting to show the heritability of schizophrenia. He quotes Rose (1990) as saying that 'the fact is that any conceivable set of data can be manipulated to fit some sort of genetic model if one tries hard enough – and there have been many decades of trying'. Acknowledging Breggin's (1993) book *Toxic Psychiatry*, he also raises the question of the relationship between the psychiatric profession and the psycho-pharmaceutical industry and reminds us of Mark Twain's comment that when money talks then truth is silenced. Marshall concludes by saying:

> Genetic and biological explanations provide a ready apersonal, ahistorical, and asocial focus. In reality, the consensus genetic beliefs are based upon illegitimate statistical and methodological manoeuvres, misreports of misreports, distortions of data, misrepresentations and selectivity, all of which signify a neglect of scientific thinking of such magnitude ... Socio-economic and historical perspectives on disordered behaviour and distress have already been ousted as unscientific and politically motivated. Now psychological and psychotherapeutic perspectives are in the process of being marginalized as peripheral to genetic and biological explanations. It is difficult to avoid the impression that science, ideology and belief have become intermeshed. (Marshall, 1996, p. 12)

I have used these few quotes to capture what I see as the essence of the sociocultural criticisms. It seems to me that three criticisms are raised. First, that the application of traditional scientific methods to understanding psychopathology is corrupt and influenced by self-serving concerns. Second, that psychological problems are not organic in nature, but are instead products of social forces. Third, that the classification of psychopathology is futile and unnecessary. Taking these criticisms in turn, although science may aspire to principles of objectivity, there is no doubt that in practice scientific research may be influenced by wider political agendas of funding and sometimes driven by self-interest and other more human frailties, rather than a search for truth. Therapy research is no different in this respect (Goldfried, 2000). Nevertheless, psychological scientists have accumulated a great deal of research findings (see e.g., Bergin and Garfield, 1994) and we would, I think, be foolish to throw the baby out with the bathwater. We have also seen in Chapter 2 that there is some convincing evidence that at least some forms of psychopathology may be organic in nature. Work in the last ten to twenty years has suggested that genetic factors might be involved in the development of psychopathology, that psychological distress is associated with levels of neurotransmitters, and new neuroimaging techniques are pointing us towards an understanding of which areas of the brain are responsible for which psychological functions. We can not simply dismiss all this evidence. Some forms of psychopathology are likely, at least in part, to be biological in origin, and best treated biomedically.

However, even if we were to accept that these critics are right about this and that so-called psychiatric disorders are nothing more than metaphors, this does not mean that the classification of psychological problems is not a potentially useful goal. It is, I would argue, a potentially valuable scientific exercise to be able to describe the different ways in which psychological suffering manifests itself. Often those supporting an anti-medical model stance to understanding psychopathology confuse the medical model with scientific method. The two are not synonymous. Certainly those working within the medical model adopt the scientific method, but the scientific method is potentially applicable to testing aspects of all therapeutic approaches. So, classification and description are useful scientifically. What is potentially dangerous is how such a classification system is used.

Labelling theory

Critics have pointed to how diagnosis can lead to *labelling*. The most famous study to illustrate the difficulties of diagnosis, as well as difficulties in distinguishing normal from abnormal behaviour, was conducted by David Rosenhan (1973). Rosenhan's research team of eight 'normal' people visited twelve different mental hospitals saying that they were experiencing auditory hallucinations and hearing voices saying words like 'dull', 'thud', and 'empty'. This was part of the experiment. They were not really hearing voices, and they proceeded to answer all the other questions they were asked by the medical staff honestly. However, most of Rosenhan's team were admitted to hospital and diagnosed as schizophrenic. Once inside, the task of the research team (now pseudo-patients) was to convince the hospital staff that they were 'sane'. While inside the hospital the pseudo-patients behaved 'normally' and insisted on their 'sanity'. The pseudo-patients were hospitalised for between 7 to 52 days with an average length of stay of 19 days. When discharged the members of the research team were diagnosed as schizophrenic in remission. But what was most interesting was that while they were inside, their 'normal' behaviours were perceived by staff as indicating evidence of schizophrenia. Interestingly, however, some of the other patients were able to identify the pseudo-patients as impostors.

The next step in Rosenhan's research was perhaps even more interesting. Rosenhan informed psychiatric hospitals that pseudo-patients would again present themselves at the hospitals over the next few months. This time, however, there were no pseudo-patients. But, around one-fifth of patients admitted during this time were actually identified by staff as being pseudo-patients (Rosenhan, 1975). The studies by Rosenhan are often taken as evidence for how diagnosis is uncertain and can lead to labelling, and how once a label is attached to a person it becomes a self-fulfilling prophecy.

Therapy as oppression

Therapists will differ in the extent to which they are aware of cultural diversity and how sociocultural factors are important in shaping both their own and their clients' life experiences (Ponterotto, 1988). An awareness of cultural diversity is central to working as a therapist. The sociocultural model questions our perceptions of what is normal and abnormal, and our use of power over others. According to some critics, psychological therapy, of whatever theoretical orientation, is an oppressive and abusive force which maintains the political status quo (see, e.g., Masson, 1988). Although this is perhaps an extreme view, it is worth considering the political differences between therapies based on the biomedical model, psychological therapies, and sociocultural therapies. George Albee, a prominent American psychologist, recently wrote this about the current practice of clinical psychology:

> There are major political differences between a medical/organic/brain-deficit model to explain mental disorders and a social-learning, stress-related model. The former is supported by the ruling class because it does not require social change and major readjustments to the status quo. The social model, on the other hand, seeks to end or to reduce poverty with all its associated stresses, as well as discrimination, exploitation, and prejudices as other major sources of stress leading to emotional problems. By aligning itself with the conservative view of causation, clinical psychology has joined the forces that perpetuate social injustice. (Albee, 2000, p. 248)

Psychological therapies, naturally, vary in the extent to which they adopt medical vs. social models of causation, with perhaps the cognitive-behavioural approaches being most adoptive of the medical model and humanistic-existential approaches being least adoptive of the medical model. However, both cognitive-behavioural and humanistic-existential approaches, as well as psychodynamic approaches are chiefly concerned with internal processes rather than sociocultural processes. All forms of psychotherapy are largely concerned with changing the person rather than changing society. The question raised by some is the extent to which therapy simply serves to help people function effectively in a 'sick' society. Certainly, other writers such as the social philosopher and psychoanalyst Eric Fromm (1900–1980) have also highlighted how Western society fosters an orientation towards 'having' as opposed to 'being' (Fromm, 1993) and how change must come about not only through the individual, but also through social and economic structures.

So, sociocultural approaches to therapy reject standard medical interventions and question the medicalisation of psychological suffering, pointing instead to the social values and abuses of power which shape psychopathology. Therefore the concern is not so much with therapy for changing the individual to fit better within the existing society, but with changing society itself. Smail (1996a) discusses the alternative of a more ethically based society in which people are cared for. In our society psychopathology is largely a function of the social and environmental forces operating on us and psychotherapy, Smail argues, offers only a limited freedom within the constraints in which we live.

What therapists can do to change society might be limited, although in the 1960s therapeutic communities based on existential approaches were developed to provide a safe and secure environment for clients to continue on what was seen as their voyage of self-discovery (see e.g., Cooper, 1967). The idea was to create small communities within society which provided the members of that community with acceptance, affirmation, and authentic relating between persons. But whether or not such attempts at empowerment were successful is another question, and relatively few therapeutic communities of this sort exist today. Community psychology is a more recent initiative in which techniques, such as mass media campaigns or educational programmes in schools, are applied to help prevent problems from arising in groups of people. However, it is difficult to evaluate the effectiveness of community psychology given that programmes are carried out in the real world.

Finally, it is worth noting that many of the values we hold in Western society about what therapy should aim to achieve are themselves potentially culture specific. For example, other non-Western cultures take a different approach to therapy. Whereas our culture largely focuses on the individual and therapy is about restoring their sense of autonomy and independence, these are culture specific goals. A Hindu in India, for example, might instead be helped to reintegrate within their social group and to restore the sense of interdependence rather than independence.

Group therapy

Understanding that we are social beings and that our psychological problems may be a mirror of the wider social structures and the interpersonal interactions which take place within those social structures has led to an interest in *group therapy*. In group therapies individuals who may not have met before come together and by observing the relationships and ways of behaving that each member develops in the group, the therapist is able to understand more about how each person is in the world. There is no one single approach to group therapy. A variety of therapeutic orientations can inform the way the group is run. The choice of theoretical orientation might be guided by the goal of the group, whether it be to help people adapt better to their environment, for the reconstruction of personality dynamics, alteration of behaviours through mechanisms of conscious control, or the relief of specific symptoms. For example, the transactional analysis approach developed by Berne discussed in the previous chapter is particularly suitable for the purpose of altering behaviour through reality testing and interpreting behaviours in the here-and-now. Transactional analysis provides a complex theoretical system with which to understand the nature of interactions between people. Client-centred or Gestalt group therapy might be useful for clients who find it difficult to get in touch with their feelings and who need to learn to be able to express themselves more openly and honestly. For those suffering from more severe psychological problems, behavioural and psychoeducational approaches might be useful (see Box 6.1).

Box 6.1

During Matt's stay in hospital he attended several group therapy sessions with other patients. The main focus of the group was social skills training, using principles such as modelling drawn from the behavioural approach. The group was largely a psychoeducational one in which Matt and the other patients were instructed in aspects of day to day living that could cause them difficulties following discharge from the hospital. Role play excercises were also used in which Matt would, for instance, play going into shops to ask for things. Through such exercises Matt greatly improved his interpersonal skills, learning, for example, how to make better eye contact, and to express himself more clearly.

Generally, weekly groups lasting around 90 minutes and consisting of around eight to ten people are considered most appropriate. It is also thought that the more heterogeneous the group is with respect to age, sex, educational background, social class, the better, although of course there will be exceptions to this.

Encounter groups

In contrast to the sort of groups discussed above, which are concerned with the amelioration of some specific psychological problem, encounter groups, sometimes called T-groups (T for training), refer to groups of individuals who come together to heighten their self-awareness and promote their personal development. Members of an encounter group focus on the present and their interpersonal relations.

Family therapy

It is difficult to reject the general idea that the person can only be fully understood in context and that our families are important in shaping our personalities and particular psychopathologies. Evidence shows that those seeking counselling are more likely to come from families which could be considered as dysfunctional (King and Mallinckrodt, 2000). According to the family systems model, each family is a unique social system in which all the elements are interconnected, and changes in one element of the system affect all other elements of the system. Families develop patterns of interacting and expressing themselves and the psychological problems of any one member can be understood by stepping back and observing the family system and the dynamics of interaction. The family systems model has lent itself to various forms of therapy in which families can be helped to find new and more adaptive ways of interacting.

Early concepts
Although family therapists work in a variety of different ways, some employing psychodynamic, cognitive-behavioural, and humanistic approaches, they all share the same assumption that disturbances in the social and familial context are important to the well being of the individual. The idea that family members can contribute to psychopathology dates back to Fromm-Reichman (1948) who first put forward the idea of the schizophrenic mother who is domineering, cold, rejecting, and guilt inducing. She suggested that such parents drove their children to schizophrenia. A similar theme was advanced by Bateson and colleagues (e.g., Bateson, Jackson, Haley, and Weakland, 1956) who put forward the *double bind* theory of schizophrenia. According to Bateson, schizophrenia was the result of parents who send contradictory verbal and non-verbal signals to their children, e.g., a parent who tells his or her child that they love them but simultaneously looks at them with disgust. Children who experience such double binds, Bateson argued, are put in a no win situation and begin to lose touch with reality, unable to trust their own perceptions, and retreat inwards as a way of dealing with the situation, resulting in signs and symptoms characteristic of schizophrenia. Similar views have been put forward over the years by others (e.g., Wynne, Singer, Bartko, and Toohey, 1977) and the misunderstandings in interpersonal communication that take place between people were explored by the psychiatrist R. D. Laing (1966; 1970). Laing was concerned with

the social and familial contexts in which psychopathology takes place, and used the following example to illustrate the idea behind family therapy:

> If one has a 'referral', say, from a hockey team, because the left back is not playing properly, one wouldn't think only of getting the left back round to one's office, taking a history, and giving a Rorschach. At least I hope not. One would also go to see how the team plays hockey. (Laing, 1976, p. 28)

Although the idea that families, and mothers in particular, cause severe psychiatric conditions is largely disputed today, recent work has shown the importance of communication patterns in the family, with critical and hostile remarks, along with expressions of over-involvement being related to symptom relapse (e.g., Falloon, Boyd, and McGill, 1984). Thus, more recent approaches to family therapy must be contrasted to the earlier approaches of Fromm-Reichman and Bateson and colleagues which implicated family structure and communication in the aetiology of schizophrenia.

Family therapy recognises that the elements of the family are interrelated and can be best understood not in isolation but in relation to the system. More recent approaches emphasise how illness within the family can be stressful to all involved and how increased stress in turn can impair the family's ability to cope, which in turn can be involved in the relapse of the recovering person (Falloon, Proporta, Fadden, and Craham-Hole, 1993). Therapists will provide a range of interventions and educational packages to help the family system cope (see Box 6.2).

The family therapist is therefore concerned with working with the family as well as the client. He or she will endeavour to understand the relationships between members of the family, and will treat the family as an organism, and attempt to change the family system. The therapist is interested in identifying problematic patterns of communication within the family, how misunderstandings arise, and who plays what roles in the family and why. Satir (1964), one of the founders of family therapy, developed an experiential approach known as *conjoint family therapy*, in which the entire family meet together and the therapist draws attention to the communication difficulties she or he observes. Satir viewed normal family functioning as consisting of open and clear communication with

Box 6.2

Matt and his parents were provided by the clinical psychologist with an educational package about the nature, course, and treatment of schizophrenia. The information was that schizophrenia was an illness with both physical and psychological components. Matt's parents were reassured that families do not cause schizophrenia but their role in helping him reach recovery was also emphasised along with the importance of adherence to medication. The family attended for several sessions and following this first educational session the psychologist helped the family explore their feelings, and learn new ways of coping with stress and dealing with family tensions. The psychologist drew heavily on behavioural skill-based techniques.

flexible and appropriate rules. The dysfunctional family, on the other hand, consists of dysfunctional communication and incongruent non-verbal messages. The goal of therapy was to create a system with direct and clear communication and provide an environment for growth through shared experience. One of the techniques used by family therapists is *family sculpting*. Here each member of the family makes use of modelling materials to create a representation of the family, showing their view of personal relationships. The therapist can help the family understand the meaning of the sculpture, and may modify it to show new forms that the relationship might take. Another technique associated with the Bowen model of family systems (Bowen, 1978) is the use of the *genogram*. Genograms are used to sketch out the map of the family over several generations using specific symbols to represent individuals and the nature of their relationships.

Conclusion

According to the sociocultural model psychopathology reflects the society in which the person has been raised and is living. We are challenged to look across cultures for the similarities and differences in human experience. Some culture-bound syndromes were considered. The sociocultural model is concerned with the question of how can we improve society. The sociocultural model therefore poses questions for a strictly medical view of psychopathology, which holds that psychological problems are the result of physical or even psychological disturbances. Some sociocultural theorists warn of the dangers of psychiatric classification, and therapy itself has been seen as an oppressive force. An approach to therapy which focuses not only on the individual but on his or her social relationships and cultural context is encouraged.

Summary points

- Notions of what constitute psychopathology vary depending on the historical and cultural context. Several culture-bound syndromes have been identified.
- Racial and sexual prejudice have been implicated in the development of psychopathology as well as in the way psychopathology is perceived in psychological minority groups.
- Sociologists have brought to our attention the relationship between social factors, such as poverty and unemployment, and the development of psychopathology.
- Sociocultural theorists such as Szasz have been critical of the biomedical model, claiming that mental illness is a concept invented to control and oppress people whose behaviour threatens the social order.
- Other sociocultural theorists like Rosenhan have warned of the dangers of labelling and stigmatising people with psychological problems.
- Sociocultural theorists are concerned with changing the nature of society as opposed to the idea of changing people to fit better within a society.

7

Evidence-based Practice, Eclectic and Integrated Approaches

Introduction

Each of the seven models of psychopathology examined in the previous chapters provide a set of assumptions about human nature. Historically, proponents of each of the perspectives have tried to explain all of human psychopathology within their perspective. For most of the latter half of the twentieth century, psychologists were concerned with which of these models, or paradigms, were correct and some bitter conflicts between proponents of particular approaches resulted. However, most would now accept that all of the models tell us something useful about human experience. In this final chapter, I want to say a little more about the thinking behind eclecticism and integrationism and some current trends in therapeutic approaches. The most obvious of these trends is that of evidence-based practice.

Fundamental to the idea of evidence-based practice is the attempt to discover specific treatments for specific disorders leading to an eclectic therapeutic approach based on the medical model. There can be no doubt that experimental research can provide important data about which therapies are effective for which problems, and such research evidence is now taken very seriously indeed within the NHS in the UK. Throughout this book I have tried to demonstrate what scientific research is about, why it is carried out, and why counsellors and psychotherapists should be interested in it. I hope through reading the previous chapters the reader has come to understand the scientific function of assessment, classification, and diagnosis in psychotherapy and counselling; why psychodynamic and psychoanalytic ideas have been criticised for their unscientific nature; how this has led to the rise of behavioural and cognitive approaches with their emphasis on observability and scientific testability, and how some theorists within the humanistic and transpersonal models question the relevance of the traditional scientific approach to their domains of interest.

Which therapy?

There is no doubt that theoretical allegiances exist and a room filled with counsellors, psychologists, psychotherapists, psychoanalysts, and psychiatrists, would contain a lot of conflicting views about the nature of psychopathology and how best to treat it. But, adopting the view that free speech is each individual's right within a democracy, then everyone should have the right to teach and practise what they believe as long as it is not harmful (Pokorny, 1991). Few would argue with this, in which case our concern should be directed towards the consumer of therapy and the service with which they are being provided. There is also an obligation to the tax payer when that service is publicly provided to ensure that they are having their money spent wisely.

This book has looked at the major models in abnormal psychology, which form the theoretical basis for a variety of different therapeutic practices. Indeed it has been noted that there are at least 400 different 'schools' of psychotherapy (Karasu, 1992; Kazdin, 1994). Given that many people who choose to go into therapy are not informed of the different models, not to mention the vast number of specific types of psychotherapy, should we be concerned? Does it make any difference which theoretical perspective informs therapeutic practice? Can we reconcile the different models? Although there are no straightforward answers to these questions, in this chapter we will look at some of the work that has tried to address these issues. As already mentioned in Chapter 1, various attempts at integrating the differing therapy approaches have been proposed. I will go on to discuss this shortly, but first it might be useful to look at one of the most influential current models of psychopathology which promises to provide a framework for future therapeutic integration, the biopsychosocial model.

Biopsychosocial model

Rather than viewing the different models of psychopathology as competitive, it is now generally agreed that some aspects of human experience are better looked at from one perspective, other aspects from another, and that our understanding of human experience must be based on different levels of understanding (see Schneider, 1998). Within psychology, there has been a move towards adopting a systems-based approach to understanding health. Recognising that psychopathology often has multiple causes – a combination of biological, psychological, and social factors – the challenge is to integrate what we know into a coherent approach to understanding psychopathology. Biological, psychological, and social factors are conceptualised as different levels of analysis within the *biopsychosocial model*.

Reductionism versus holism

Thus, rather than viewing biological, psychological, and social approaches as providing competitive explanations for human behaviour, we might view each of these approaches as providing a partial understanding of psychopathology at a particular level of analysis. Therefore, a central principle of the biopsychosocial approach is holism, the idea that the whole is greater than the sum of its parts. Contrast this with reductionism, the idea that the whole is the sum of the parts and that explanations are found when problems are reduced to their smallest parts. Much of modern psychiatry is reductionistic with its search for biochemical causes of psychopathology (Cacioppo and Bernston, 1992).

Holism, however, views smaller units of explanation as subsystems within a larger system, such that no one explanation provides the correct answer. All levels of explanation are correct, but are concerned with different levels of analysis. The biological, the psychological, and the social are all different ways of analysing the same problem and the challenge is to understand their interaction, and how changes at one level are reflected by changes at another level. For example, it has been shown that self-disclosure and talking about upsetting events is associated with healthier immune functioning (Pennebaker, Kiecolt-Glaser, and Glaser, 1988) and improved liver enzyme function (Francis and Pennebaker, 1992). Changes at one level in the system are mirrored by changes at another level in the system.

Although the biopsychosocial model helps us to think about psychopathology, the exact relationship between biological, psychological, and social factors remains to be specified. If we are to formulate therapeutic approaches based on the biopsychosocial model, we need to hypothesise how the various factors interact with each other to produce psychopathology.

One example of this approach is the model of depression advocated by Dinan (1994; 1998). In Chapter 2, evidence was mentioned for an association between depression and low levels of the neurotransmitters serotonin and noradrenaline, and it has been hypothesised that low levels of these neurotransmitters might be a cause of depression. In Chapter 6, however, evidence was presented that stressful life-events cause depression. On the one hand it would seem that depression has a biological cause, and on the other that it has a social cause. However, perhaps these explanations are not mutually exclusive. Dinan has suggested that low levels of these neurotransmitters may be a proximal (i.e., closer in time) cause of depression, but that the low levels of these neurotransmitters are themselves caused by more distal (i.e., more distant in time) stressful life-events (see Figure 7.1). Evidence for Dinan's suggestion remains to be gathered and approaches to counselling and psychotherapy based on such integrative approaches remain in their infancy. Specifying the relationships between the various factors that cause psychopathology is problematic and calls for massive research interest. Much interest has focused on specifying diathesis-stress models of psychopathology.

Diathesis-stress model

Diatheses refer to predisposing factors and stress refers to current environmental factors. This model has probably received the great-

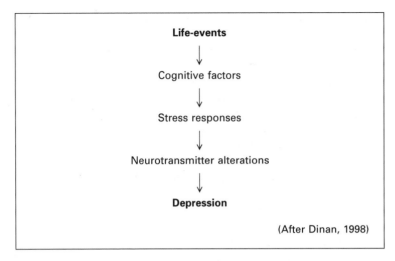

Figure 7.1   Biopsychosocial model of depression

est attention with respect to the psychiatric diagnosis of schizo-phrenia. Meehl (1962), for example, suggested that although only people with a genetic predisposition will develop schizophrenia, not all those with a genetic predisposition will develop schizo-phrenia, only those who are also exposed to some form of detri-mental learning environment and stressful life experience. Here, the diathesis is a genetic predisposition and the stress is a stressful life experience. For other psychological problems the diathesis could be a particular personality disposition and the stress an infection, for example. But what is important is that neither the diathesis, nor the stress, is sufficient on their own to produce psychological problems. When the stress is added to the diathesis, then problems occur. Certainly, research evidence would suggest that multiple factors are involved in the onset and maintenance of psychopathology.

However, although we might speculate on how a combination of genetic factors, childhood experience factors, patterns of thinking, personality, stressful life-events, and so on all interact to produce psychopathology, the difficulty is in conducting the research to test out such ideas. To illustrate, one study conducted by Card (1987) collected data from over 400 Vietnam veterans to see who had developed post-traumatic stress. These veterans were also people who had taken part in a large survey over 20 years previously when they were children, and at that time had completed various psychological measures of their personality. What this enabled Card to do was investigate whether personality in childhood, in conjunction with later war experiences, was a determinant of post-traumatic stress. What he found was that those with lower self-esteem as children were more likely to develop posttraumatic stress as adults following the experience of combat compared with those who had higher self-esteem in childhood. Such research is, of course, not easy to carry out, is time consuming, and expensive to fund.

For this reason, questions that might appear on the surface fairly simple to answer remain largely unanswered. For example, although we know that irrational thinking as discussed by Ellis and Beck is associated with depression, we are less certain of whether irrational thinking causes depression as opposed to irrational thinking being a result of depression. Often it has been assumed that causation operates in one direction only. However, the bio-psychosocial model, with its emphasis on systems theory, leads us to understand causality as bi-directional. Changes in one level are accompanied by changes in another level. To address such questions usually calls for a massive research effort involving large samples of participants taking part in studies over lengthy periods of time.

Evaluating evidence-based practice

One of the confusions that often arises concerns the difference between the medical model and the scientific method. The two are not the same. The medical model adopts the scientific method and most research tends to be carried out by those working in the medical model – whether they focus on biological, learning, or cognitive explanations for psychopathology. However, the scientific method can be applied to any therapeutic approach so long as clear and testable hypotheses are formulated. Historically, those conducting the research have tended to belong to the professions of psychiatry and psychology, and for this reason psychodynamic and humanistic approaches have tended to receive less interest.

Nevertheless, because biomedical and behavioural approaches to treatment lend themselves well to research, they have gained in popularity as clinicians aspired to provide therapy with proven effectiveness. Subsequently, these models of psychopathology and related therapeutic approaches have become widely researched and shown to be effective in various circumstances. However, as counsellors and psychotherapists begin to conduct more research we might expect the balance of research interest to shift with the possibility that psychodynamic and humanistic approaches begin to find greater support again.

Historically many of those involved in counselling and psychotherapy have not agreed with the value of traditional scientific research. However, *evidence-based practice* is important. After all, if we go to someone for help we want to be reassured that what we get from the helper is likely to work. When we go to see the GP we want to know that they are aware of the latest developments in their field and are able to offer us the treatment which is most likely to help us. We might be very unsettled if we thought that they were doing otherwise. Why should counselling and psychotherapy be any different? This is the argument put forward by advocates of evidence-based practice. Within the NHS, there is an emphasis on the identification of those therapies which research has shown to be effective. This follows trends in America, where an emphasis on evidence-based practice has been in place for some time. The American Psychological Association is in the process of developing a list of those therapies which are empirically validated in a move towards 'certification of specific psychotherapies by governmental, profession, and insurance bodies' (Elliot, 1998, p. 115). The American Psychiatric Association has produced lists of empirically supported therapies and practice guidelines for a number of psychological problems (American Psychiatric Association, 1993; 1994; 1995; 1996; 1997).

There are obvious merits to evidence-based practice. However, the role of the traditional scientific method in the context of counselling and psychotherapy also has its critics. Information from randomised controlled experimental designs to test for differences between treatment groups is limited in what it can tell us about the broader context of people's lives and their day to day experiences (see Schneider, 1998). It has been argued that some therapies lend themselves better to traditional scientific research, or are simply more popular among those who are research orientated, such as psychologists, with the implication that other therapies which are less well validated, but might be at least equally effective, or useful for certain groups of people, will likely fall by the wayside (Bohart, O'Hara, and Leitner, 1998). However, given the demands for evidence-based practice within the NHS, the onus is now on those who argue for psychodynamic and humanistically oriented therapies to make their case using traditional scientific evidence.

As already mentioned, one of the goals of an evidence-based practice approach is to identify what therapies work best for what problems. The question of whether there are specific treatments most suitable for specific problems is an important one. However, it is a question most often shaped by a medical research context in which effectiveness comes to be defined in terms of changes in clients on indices defined by the DSM classes of psychiatric disorder. With psychiatry and psychology this has become an established way of conducting therapy research. As we have seen, there are critics of DSM, like Szasz, Smail, and Marshall, who argue that it is inappropriate to treat psychological problems as if they are physical illnesses and who point towards the stigmatising effects of psychiatric diagnosis. Others, like Goldfried (2000) are also wary of this approach, and for many therapists working outside the medical model the imposition of DSM criteria poses a difficulty for them in conducting research. But we have also seen that the purpose of classification is to aid scientific enquiry. People have problems in living of one sort or another and it is potentially scientifically valuable to understand the different ways in which psychopathology is expressed:

> It is of course possible to arrive at broad descriptions of the kinds of distress that human beings are prone to. As embodied creatures, we have only a limited number of ways to react to the blows life inflicts upon us: the way we express our thoughts and feelings will depend on the physical structure of our bodies. For example, I weep with sadness because that is how human beings are constructed to express the feeling we call sadness. (Smail, 1996a, p. 50)

Similarly, Stevens and Price (1996) are critical of DSM, but go on to say:

> This does not mean, however, that examining patients and classifying their mental symptoms are futile activities. Observation, differentiation, and classification are natural modes of intellectual progression: they are the means by which our cognitive facilities seek to impose order on

chaos. Phenomena have to be recognised and distinguished before they can be explained. (Stevens and Price, 1996, p. 3)

Evolutionary psychology

How might we go about classifying psychological problems in a different way which might be more acceptable to those who agree with the critics of DSM? Eysenck's (1986) suggestion that we base our classification of psychopathology on what we know about the basic structure of human personality is an interesting one which would lead to a very different system to that of DSM.

However, perhaps the most fruitful avenue to understanding the different ways in which we react to the blows of life comes from recent thinking in the area of *evolutionary psychology*. An evolutionary approach to psychopathology proposes that psychological problems are manifestations of ancient adaptive strategies which are not necessarily adaptive any longer. Stevens and Price (1996) argue that an evolutionary approach to psychopathology provides a powerful fundamental model that can guide the development of therapeutic work. Stevens and Price (1996) discuss human archetypal needs for two social resources: attachment and rank. Attachment refers to the ties of affection and affiliation between people, and rank refers to status and power within the group. Stevens and Price believe that these two archetypal systems provide the basis for understanding the nature of psychopathology. Different expressions of psychopathology are related to the extent to which people achieve these two social resources. They go on to discuss how frustrations of these archetypal needs result in psychopathology. Although Stevens and Price (1996) view the evolutionary approach to psychopathology as a challenge to the current psychiatric classification system, they also state that an evolutionary analysis upholds some of the major distinctions within DSM.

Pseudoscience?

We have already seen that those conducting the research often tend to be psychiatrists and psychologists interested in the biomedical and cognitive-behavioural models, meaning that therapies derived from other models are likely to fall by the wayside.

However, there are other concerns too. There remain those who question what we think we know. It has been suggested that much of the traditional scientific research we rely on is not of sufficient high quality to make decisions (Orford, 2000) and that many current recommendations for which therapies are most effective are premature (Garfield, 1996).

Also, there are the questions about the extent to which the scientific method can supply the answers to the questions about human experience and psychological suffering (Henry, 1998). One of the criticisms is that counselling, psychology, and psychotherapy, far from being scientific disciplines, are in fact examples of pseudoscience. Mahrer (1998) writes:

> Most scientists believe that if something is real, it can be measured. Psychotherapists are quixotically unique in their certainty that if they can devise a measure of it, then it must of course be real. We have the idea backwards, but we are energetic at our pseudoscience . . . We are convinced that there really are things like schizophrenia, altruism, introversion, conceptual schemata, egos, and hundreds of other things mainly because we have thousands of measures, scales, and tests, all of which are subjected to the highest rigorous standards of science. Set our scientific measure-makers on the task and they can prove the existence of schizophrenia, devil possession, elves and goblins, witches, and warlocks. (Mahrer, 1998, p. 22)

Even if counselling, psychology, and psychotherapy are pseudoscientific, Mahrer (1998) goes on to argue that the results of psychotherapy research have essentially made no significant differences to the field of psychotherapy anyway:

> Most [therapeutic] approaches that seek to become respectable have their own researchers producing friendly studies on behalf of the approach. If anyone doubts that psychotherapy is truly a scientific field, put the doubter in the room filled with thousands of published studies . . . Psychotherapists can be proud of their researchers because the researchers don't really bother practitioners much. Every so often researchers grumble that practitioners pay little attention to their findings, and they are right. In general, the practice of psychotherapy is essentially undisturbed by whatever researchers do. The practice of psychotherapy would probably be insignificantly different if researchers had instead spent their time playing volleyball. (Mahrer, 1998, p. 26)

Mahrer (1998) is not alone in thinking that practitioners pay little attention to the work of researchers (see e.g., Goldfried, 2000; Morrow-Bradley and Elliot, 1986). Nevertheless, evidence-based practice is the foundation stone of clinical practice within the NHS and is the central theme in training as a psychiatrist and psychologist, although what constitutes evidence remains a controversial subject. The letters page of *The Psychologist*, the house journal of the British Psychological society, has recently been devoted to this debate. Some have argued, along the lines of those arguments in Chapter 2, that therapists must be provided with quantitative research data using randomised controlled trials, for example, on the effectiveness of therapy (e.g., Bailey and Shevlin, 1999). In response, others have argued that the therapeutic process is not easily understood using the techniques of traditional scientific research. Dorahy and Millar (2000), for example, argue that traditional scientific research tells us only about the average response of groups of participants rather than how a particular person with a particular problem will respond to a particular therapist using a particular approach. They conclude that although the traditional scientific method has its uses, it also has its limitations and must be coupled with other (often qualitative) research methods which can capture the individual's point of view. No one suggests that we abandon the traditional scientific method. Rowe (1996) puts it this way:

> What I do encounter are those therapists who have abandoned scientific method for the realms of magic. They have learned nothing from the history of philosophy and psychology. What they show is sloppy thinking, self-serving hypotheses and a failure of nerve in the face of real life . . . they think that if a number of people hold a certain idea then that idea must inevitably relate to something real . . . Although we can never know external reality directly, if we are wise we try to create meanings which reflect reality as accurately as possible . . . To create such accurate meanings we need to use logic and scientific method . . . It can be pleasant to enter the realm of magic and pretend we have access to knowledge and power unknown to ordinary mortals, but to tell ourselves that this is real, is stupid and base. (Rowe, 1996, p. 38)

However, Rowe also goes on to warn us that

> It is equally stupid to believe that whatever meanings we create must have their counterpart in reality. We form patterns to help us understand, but the patterns are tools, not reality in itself, whatever that might be. Freud's patterns of id, ego, and superego have proved to be very useful tools in helping us understand ourselves, but anyone who thinks we are walking around with an id, an ego and a superego inside us is just being silly. (Rowe, 1996, p. 38)

Finally, Marshall (1996) has argued that much of science has become intermeshed with ideology and has itself become the victim of its own self-serving hypothesis, and for many there is now a deep distrust of the traditional scientific method. Nevertheless, it is true to say that the traditional scientific method remains important in determining how people are treated within the NHS. It looks like it will become increasingly important as therapists are trained to deliver specific treatments for specific problems, in response to moves similar to those in America towards certification of specific psychotherapies. It is within this context that counsellors and psychotherapists must strive to find their voice.

Eclectic and integrative approaches to therapy

Eclectic approaches

Providing specific treatments for specific problems is an *eclectic approach*. Many therapists now describe their way of working as eclectic (e.g., Lazarus, 1989; O'Sullivan and Dryden, 1990; Zook and Walton, 1989). Eclecticism can be defined as

> Choosing what is best from diverse sources, styles, and systems; using techniques and rationales based on more than one orientation to meet the needs of the individual case; the systematic use of a variety of therapeutic interventions in the treatment of a single patient and the pragmatics of selecting a variety of procedures and wider interventions for specific problems. The common thread is that technical eclecticism is relatively atheoretical, pragamatic and empirical. (Norcross and Greencavage, 1990, p. 10)

The idea behind eclecticism is that no one therapeutic approach is adequate for all of the different psychological problems that a client may bring. Psychologists and psychiatrists, drawing on the research literature, are trained to provide those treatments which have been shown to be effective with particular problems, and a range of cognitive-behavioural treatment programmes have been manualised for use with several of the so-called psychiatric disorders listed in DSM. However, there is concern that many psychological therapists who describe themselves as working eclectically do so in an unstructured way, using a mix of approaches in a theoretically incoherent way. Technical eclecticism is relatively atheoretical and although this might be appropriate in some contexts, working in this way with one client over a period of time could be extremely confusing for the client:

> Unless the counsellor is experienced and creative enough to meld different approaches and assumptions into a new and consistent synthesis, the result may be extremely confusing. Clients may pick up the message that life is confusing and that the counsellor does not really have a clue about which direction to follow. (Deurzen-Smith, 1988, p. 3)

It has been argued that the profusion of alternative and incompatible models suggests a state of crisis for counselling and psychotherapy (e.g., Janov, 1982). However, in answer to such criticisms, it has been argued that those working in an eclectic way should use each approach discretely and in a planned sequence to avoid confusion (Messer, 1986). To do this requires a model with theoretical coherence. Several such models have now been proposed. For example, the stages of change model proposed by Prochaska and DiClemente (1984) provides such theoretical coherence.

Stages of change

It is important to recognise the insights of existing therapies as well as their shortcomings, so some attempts have been made to develop a theoretically based eclectic approach. It has been suggested that psychological change consists of a progression through various stages, from a stage in which the person has no intention to change, through stages in which the person contemplates change, prepares for change, takes action towards making change, to maintaining that change (Prochaska and DiClemente, 1983; 1984). At each stage, the client or patient requires help with different processes. As Prochaska and Norcross (1999) write:

> The therapist's stance at different stages can be characterised as follows: with precontemplators, often the role is like a nurturing parent joining with a resistant and defensive youngster who is both drawn to and repelled by the prospects of becoming more independent. With contemplators, the role is akin to a Socratic teacher who encourages clients to achieve their own insights into their condition. With clients who are in the preparation stage, the stance is more like that of an experienced

coach who has been through many crucial matches and can provide a fine game plan or can review the person's own plan. With clients who are progressing into action and maintenance, the psychotherapist becomes more of a consultant who is available to provide expert advice and support when action is not progressing as smoothly as expected. (Prochaska and Norcross, 1999, p. 510)

Prochaska and Norcross (1999) propose five stages involved in making changes in behaviour. These are:

- Precontemplation
- Contemplation
- Preparation
- Action
- Maintenance

Such a model shows how different therapeutic orientations might be useful at different stages. For example, a psychodynamic approach during the precontemplation stage might be useful in helping the client become more aware of the need to change. When the client has moved into the contemplation stage, a person-centred approach might be used to help the client think through the changes they want to make. During the preparation stage a more cognitive approach might be employed to help the client think through how they might make changes. When the client has moved into the action stage a more behavioural approach might be used to implement those changes. It would seem that by understanding the clients needs at each stage of process, the therapist is able to provide an appropriate therapeutic intervention. Several other theorists have also proposed models which show how therapies can be incorporated into an eclectic treatment model. The most well known of these other models are those proposed by Egan (1982) and by Stiles and colleagues (1990).

Egan's stages

Egan (1982) suggests that therapy can be broken down into three stages: exploration; interpretation; and action. In the exploration stage a client-centred approach might be most useful, as the therapist builds up rapport with the client and gets to understand their experience and what has brought them to therapy. In the interpretation stage the therapist wishes to make a formulation of the problem and psychodynamic and cognitive approaches might be useful. In the action stage behavioural strategies, such as homework assignments, are suggested as useful. Alex's therapist worked very much in an eclectic way, using the client-centred approach to establish rapport and trust with Alex and then using psychodynamic insights to explore the role of his early experiences in shaping his adult personality and to make new choices in life. Following this, Alex found motivational interviewing useful for helping him deal with his alcohol problems.

Assimilation of problematic experiences

Stiles and colleagues (1990) propose stages of emotional assimilation, ranging from stage 0, where problematic experiences are warded off and the client is unaware of emotional discomfort, through unwanted thoughts and feelings beginning to break into awareness (stage 1), acknowledgement of problematic experiences coupled with an inability to formulate the problem clearly (stage 2), making a clear statement of the problem (stage 3), understanding and insight (stage 4), working on the problem (stage 5), successful resolution of the problem (stage 6), and finally to generalisation of the solution to other problem areas (stage 7). As with the stages of change model, and Egan's model, it has been suggested that more psychodynamic and humanistic approaches might be more useful during the earlier stages and more cognitive and behavioural techniques in the later stages (Stiles, Barkham, Shapiro, and Firth-Cozens, 1992).

Models such as these provide some answers to those therapists who are concerned that eclecticism is confusing to the client. However, as already mentioned, some would argue that therapeutic interventions should simply be based on scientific evidence about what treatments work for what problems. Remember the hypothetical experiment described in Chapter 2. A group of people with depression were treated with a new drug and another group of people with depression were given a placebo. Later on the two groups were compared and it was found that the group given the new drug had decreased in depression compared to the group given the placebo. The results of this would tell us that, on average, the new drug alleviates depression. Although this is an example of a rather simple experimental research design, it is only through such methods that we are able to get answers to the question of whether therapy is effective. Based on knowledge from such experiments, therapists can be trained to provide whatever help is known to be most suitable for the client's problem. Essentially, this is the medical model and provides the background philosophy of psychology training as well as much counselling and psychotherapy training.

However, as we have seen there are those, like Orford (2000), who are critical of what the research evidence is actually able to tell us. Others, like Bozarth (1998), claim that the evidence base for specific treatments for specific problems is a myth, one that works to bolster the status of those who believe in it. Also, what such research doesn't necessarily tell us is that the particular therapeutic intervention works for all people all of the time. The methods of research are such that if a small number of those given the active drug were actually to get worse because of the drug we would not necessarily find that out. This is an extremely important consideration. Potentially, all therapies are dangerous in that they can exacerbate problems (see Palmer, 1999). However, under what circumstances therapies may be dangerous is a question rarely addressed by research. This is because research is generally concerned with whether or not people do better on average. When confronted with an individual we might not know the best thing to advise them to do. Although research evidence might say that on average people with a particular psychological problem seem to benefit from a particular therapy, this does not necessarily imply that this particular person will benefit from that therapy.

Common factors

In contrast to the medical model of psychological therapy, the humanistic person-centred therapist works on the assumption that it is the client who will know best what it is they need to do and not the therapist, although the extent of this non-directivity varies from therapist to therapist. As Bozarth, a well-known exponent of the person-centred approach writes:

I resonate with Rogers' comment that if I thought that I knew what would help, I'd tell the person. Since I seldom think that I know another person's best directions, I am seldom tempted to offer such advice. (Bozarth, 1997, p. 23)

The person-centred approach is certainly radical in holding this view, and because of this underlying philosophical stance, the person-centred therapist works with all clients in the same way. He or she attempts to hold unconditional positive regard for their client, be congruent in the relationship, and communicate empathy towards their client, regardless of their presenting problem. Although sometimes viewed as a superficial approach to therapy, few would deny the importance of these attitudinal qualities in a therapist and their importance in developing a solid working relationship between therapist and client. Indeed, Rogers (1957) proposed that these attitudinal qualities were the common ingredients in all successful therapy, regardless of what approach the therapist was adopting. Certainly, empirical studies show that therapist qualities like empathy are important in predicting client outcome (e.g., Burns and Nolen-Hoeksema, 1992).

Common factors in EMDR

Proponents of person-centred therapy might therefore argue that other therapies are effective, not because of what the therapist says he or she does, but because of the relationship and alliance that forms between therapist and client. In an interesting example of such an argument, Hyer and Brandsma (1997) argue that *eye movement desensitisation and reprocessing therapy* (EMDR) is efficacious, not because it induces eye movements, but because it applies common and generally accepted principles of psychotherapy.

EMDR is a relatively new therapy on the scene. It was introduced by Shapiro (1989a; 1989b; 1995) who noticed that her own distressing and intrusive thoughts began to diminish while she was out jogging. She linked this to rapid movements of her eyes, and following further investigations she went on to develop the EMDR procedure. Briefly, the EMDR procedure involves the client creating in his or her mind a visual image of the upsetting event and then isolating a word or phrase which represents a belief about the visual image. For example, 'I am helpless' or 'I have no control'. The client then repeats these phrases while bilateral saccadic eye movements are induced by following the therapist's fingers which are moved rapidly back and forth across the visual field. The negative belief statements are then replaced with positive belief statements such as 'I am in control', or 'I am worthy'. After 20 or so passes, the therapist will ask the client to rest. Case studies testify that clients often report that their distress reduces, and the strength of upsetting images fades. It has been suggested that eye movements are connected to the way in which information is consolidated in the brain (e.g., Levin, Lazrove, and Van der Kolk, 1999). For example, it has been suggested that EMDR activates a similar process to that occuring during rapid eye movement (REM) sleep, when it is thought that information is being processed and consolidated within the brain. This may well be the case and reports of EMDR are generally encouraging. Current evidence suggests that the EMDR protocol is an effective therapy and is now a treatment of choice for people suffering from posttraumatic stress disorder (e.g., Chambless *et al.*, 1998; Chemtob, Tolin, and van der Kolk, 2000; Van Etten and Taylor, 1998; Vaughan, Wiese, Gold, and Tarrier, 1994). However, the exact role of the eye movements remains a focus for enquiry (e.g., Renfrey and Spates, 1994) and it is not certain why EMDR works (Dyck, 1993).

Reviewing this and other literature on EMDR, Hyer and Brandsma argue that EMDR might simply work because it involves the application of some basic psychotherapeutic principles. For example, Hyer and Brandsma argue that EMDR rests on the principle that clients move toward positive growth and that EMDR, although directive over process, is non-directive with regard to content and allows the client to follow his or her own direction rather than that of the therapist. What this illustrates is that although different therapies might on the surface appear very different, perhaps the differences between the psychotherapies are only skin deep. It is likely that similar processes occur in all psychological therapies. It remains to be seen therefore whether Shapiro has in fact stumbled across something new or whether EMDR is a repackaging of existing therapeutic techniques. However, if indeed there is an accelerated information processing linked to eye movements, then EMDR is probably one of the most important therapeutic discoveries of all time.

Similar common factor arguments have been put forward by proponents of other approaches as well as person-centred theorists. Proponents of the psychodynamic approach might say that person-centred therapy only works because it unintentionally provides insight and clarification. Alternatively, proponents of cognitive-behavioural approaches might say that person-centred therapy only works because it unintentionally provides a corrective learning experience or desensitises the client to fearful experiences. What all of this illustrates is that although there is research evidence for the effectiveness of different psychological therapies for various psychological problems, it is often unclear why that therapy works. We should not necessarily conclude that just because a treatment works this tells us about the cause of the problem. This is the treatment-aetiology fallacy mentioned in Chapter 2.

In addition, although evidence suggests that some therapeutic approaches may be more suitable than others for specific forms of psychopathology, no therapy stands out as greatly superior to any other in effectiveness overall. This was the conclusion originally reached by Smith and Glass (1977) who examined the results of 375 studies of therapy outcome, using a *meta-analysis* approach, concluding that all forms of psychotherapy – humanistic, cognitive, behavioural, cognitive-behavioural, and psychodynamic – were equally effective. Meta-analysis is a statistical technique that allows one to reach a conclusion from reviewing the results of many separate research studies. A later study by Shapiro and Shapiro (1982) tried to improve on Smith and Glass's research design by only looking at studies with well-defined treatment and control groups, and found similar results. Although some questioned this conclusion (e.g., Prioleau, Murdock, and Brody, 1983), further research has confirmed the general equivalence of therapies from different schools (Stiles, Shapiro, and Elliott, 1986). It is now generally accepted that in terms of overall effectiveness no therapy is any better than any other (Lambert and Bergin, 1994), although people seem to do better with long-term treatment rather than short-term treatment (Seligman, 1995). These data support the idea that all therapies are, therefore, doing essentially the same thing, and that therapeutic effectiveness is the result of nonspecific factors, i.e., those factors common to all therapies.

Many would argue that similar processes occur in all psychological therapies regardless of what their proponents claim are the specific ingredients. The identification of factors common to all therapies, and those which promote psychological change, has become the focus for much research interest (see Roth and Fonagy, 1996). Indeed, it has even been suggested that therapies might be developed on the basis of this knowledge (Garfield, 1992). We have already seen that Rogers' (1957) core conditions provide one common factors model. Subsequently, there have been other attempts to delineate the factors that are common to all psychological therapies. For example, Jerome Frank (1961; 1971) also argued that it is through the non-specific factors common to all therapies that change comes about. The first non-specific factor identified by Frank was that of the an intense, emotionally charged, confiding relationship with a helping person.

Therapeutic relationship

Most would now agree that one commonality which is important is the *therapeutic relationship* (Grencavage and Norcross, 1990), and it has been argued that positive change is attributable to the healing effects of a benign human relationship (Russell, 1995). Research results certainly support the idea that the relationship between client and therapist, the therapeutic alliance, is important (Horvath and Luborsky, 1993; Horvath and Symonds, 1991; Krupnick *et al.*, 1996; Lambert, 1992). Interestingly, the recognition of the importance of the therapeutic relationship as an agent of healing is clearly resonant with Rogers' person-centred approach to psychotherapy which sees the therapeutic relationship as the process which produces psychological change. Rogers (1951) wrote:

> It is clear, however, that the stress is upon a direct experiencing in the relationship. The process is not seen as primarily having to do with the client's memory of his past, nor with his exploration of the problems he is facing, nor with the perceptions he has of himself, nor the experiences he has been fearful of admitting into awareness. The process of therapy is, by these hypotheses, seen as being synonymous with the experiential relationship between client and therapist. Therapy consists in experiencing the self in a wide range of ways in an emotionally meaningful relationship with the therapist. The words – of either client or counsellor – are seen as having minimal importance compared with the

present emotional relationship which exists between the two. (Rogers, 1951, pp. 171–2)

What exactly the common ingredients of therapeutic change are remains a controversial question, although the therapeutic relationship would seem to be one important condition. As well as an emotional bond between client and therapist, the therapeutic alliance is thought to comprise a collaboration on the goals and tasks of treatment (e.g., Agnew-Davies *et al.*, 1998; Hovarth and Luborsky, 1993). However, despite the importance of the therapeutic alliance it may not be sufficient for therapeutic change. Thus, as well as emphasising the therapeutic relationship, Frank also identified five other non-specific factors:

- Providing a rationale which explains the client's distress and strengthens the client's confidence in the therapist.
- Providing new information concerning the nature and sources of the client's problems and possible alternative ways of dealing with them.
- Strengthening the client's expectations of help through the personal qualities of the therapist.
- Providing experience of success that further heightens the client's hope and enhances their sense of mastery and interpersonal competence.
- The facilitation of emotional arousal.

Other researchers have also sought to identify the common factors, and over 80 commonalities have now been suggested (Grencavage and Norcross, 1990). One of the most mentioned of these commonalities is that of positive expectations. This refers to the idea that those clients who expect to improve are more likely to do so. However, although it would seem that positive expectations are important, research would not lead us to believe that psychological change is the result of nothing more than the client possessing a positive expectation (e.g., Roberts, Kewman, Mercier and Hovell, 1993). It is beyond the scope of this book to go into great detail on all of the various common factors which have been mentioned in the literature, but one general area of interest in recent years concerns how clients come, through therapy, to construct new meanings.

Construction of meaning

All forms of counselling and psychotherapy involve at least some level of self-disclosure. Is it simply that talking about distressing experiences is therapeutic? In recent years social psychologists have carried out very interesting research into the health benefits of self-disclosure and there is now much evidence that talking about upsetting events is associated with better adjustment. For example, Pennebaker and O'Heeron (1984) found that spouses who had been bereaved through suicide or accidents and who talked with friends about the death had a lower rate of illness than those who did not talk to friends. Perhaps more surprising is that the evidence also seems to suggest that even writing about traumatic events when no one is going to read the accounts is associated with better functioning. Pennebaker and Beall (1986) asked students to write about either a trivial topic or a personally upsetting event for several consecutive days and then compared groups on the number of visits to the health centre in the following months. What they found was that those who wrote about the upsetting events made fewer visits to the health centre.

Pennebaker and his colleagues' work on the expression of emotional material has a long history dating back to the Greeks, who believed that catharsis was an important means of alleviating psychological suffering. The idea was that emotional tensions built up inside and had somehow to be released or else the pressure would build up and result in somatic complaints. Catharsis is one explanation. More recently, however, theorists have tended to look at self-disclosure in terms of information processing models, and how the person comes to create new meanings through their self-disclosure. In a review of the research he and his colleagues conducted, Pennebaker (1993) concluded that what is important is that the person is not only able to express their negative emotions, but that they are also able to construct a coherent story. So, it is not just emotional expression per se which is important, but expression which involves some sort of cognitive working through. Theorists from a wide variety of other traditions also agree on this (see also Bohart, 1980; Nichols and Efran, 1985). Brewin and Power (1997) write all psychological therapies share a commitment to transforming the meanings that clients have attached to their symptoms, relationships and life problems. This common purpose has, we believe, been obscured by the use of different terminologies, by different conceptualisations of meaning, and by a tendency to focus on what divides therapies rather than on what unifies them. (Brewin and Power, 1997, p. 1)

Integrative approaches

By focusing on this common purpose, Brewin and Power are able to provide what seems to be an important step towards understanding how *integration* might take place. The recognition that counselling and psychotherapy involves a translation or transformation of meaning, whether it be changes in how we think about our relationships with others, and other more everyday concerns, or changes at a more profound and existential level, the modification of meaning is seen as the most important therapeutic activity by therapists from different approaches. Brewin and Power (1997) suggest that it is possible to integrate different psychotherapies at a theoretical level in terms of processes of meaning translation and transformation. One can see how different therapies help an individual remodel their view of themselves and other people within the world. But although a better understanding of the psychological change processes involved in therapy would be desirable, their aim is an ambitious one. Although most commentators would agree that the translation and transformation of meaning is central to psychological change, it is difficult to see how some of the bedrock assumptions of all psychological therapies could come to be reconciled, and how an understanding of change processes could lead us to an integrated and more effective means of conducting therapy. As Arnold Lazarus (1989) writes:

In their attempt to avoid ideological rigidity, integrationists try to meld disparate ideas and conflicting schools into a co-operative and harmonious whole . . . The main problem here is that, upon close scrutiny, what seems to be interchangeable among different theories, often turns out to be totally irreconcilable. (Lazarus, 1989, pp. 248–58)

Feltham (1997) further invites us '. . . to consider the idea that integrationism or integrative psychotherapy may be a myth or, in spite of good intentions, simply another orientation or group of orientations in the making' (Feltham, 1997, p. 5). However, although it might be difficult to find ways of integrating all the psychological therapies, more circumscribed integration is certainly possible. We have already seen that the cognitive and the behavioural perspectives can be integrated. A more recent development is *cognitive analytic therapy* (CAT) (Ryle, 1990) which attempts to integrate ideas of cognitive therapy with psychodynamic ideas, in particular those of the object relations school. Another development is *dialectical behaviour therapy* (DBT) (Linehan, 1987; 1993). DBT is a cognitive-behavioural technique developed for the treatment of people diagnosed with borderline personality disorder which attempts to integrate ideas from Zen Buddism and client-centred therapy.

Integrating ideas from different therapies in a theoretically consistent way is therefore possible with those therapies which share similar basic assumptions about human nature, or at least between those theories which do not contain conflicting assumptions. Cognitive analytic therapy, for example, seems to possess much of the richness in thinking associated with the psychodynamic approach coupled with the clear scientifically testable methods of the cognitive-behavioural approach to produce a brief therapeutic approach. But it is also true that some attempts at integrationism end up with what seems to be a lack of clear theoretical basis and a miscellaneous collection of counselling techniques.

Culley (1991), in her description of integrated counselling, makes the point that integrative counsellors must be able to be explicit about the basic theoretical assumptions. Some of the assumptions she makes are:

- Individuals are deserving of acceptance and understanding because they are human.
- Individuals are capable of change.
- Individuals create their own meaning.
- Individuals are experts on themselves.
- Individuals want to realise their potential.
- The behaviour of individuals is purposeful.
- Individuals will work harder to achieve goals which they have set for themselves.

Self-healing

Similarly, O'Brien and Houston (2000) hold as a fundamental assumption the capacity for *self-healing* and it is probably around this assumption that integration is most difficult. If we believe that people have an innate drive towards health, as the more humanistic approaches hold, then our task as therapists is to help promote this drive and to remove whatever blocks there exist to self-healing. It is not only the humanistically oriented therapies though that share this assumption. EMDR, for example, rests on the assumption that there is a self-healing mechanism and the therapist is like a guide who is helping the person move in an adaptive direction. Consequently, many humanistically oriented therapists will feel comfortable integrating EMDR within their ways of working. However, other therapists do not share the belief that there are self-healing processes. Many behavioural and cognitive therapists, for example, will be directive over content as well as process in the belief that the client does not have an inner capacity for healing, and unless they are directed towards exploring material that the therapist views as important, no change will result. The assumption of whether or not there is a self-healing process is the foundation stone on which our choice of therapeutic style rests and it is perhaps around this question that therapeutic style most diverges.

But although many therapists describe themselves as working in an eclectic or integrative way there are some therapists who, in my experience, when questioned as to what they mean exactly by this do not seem to have thought fully about these issues, and do not understand the difference between working in an eclectic way and working in an integrated way. Others sometimes describe themselves as employing a creative synthesis. It might be recommended that potential clients of therapists who describe themselves in this way check with the therapist what exactly they mean, and what sort of training they have had. For example, some therapists will describe themselves as working in both psychodynamic and person-centred ways and although there have been interesting attempts to integrate these approaches at a theoretical level, both of these approaches contain some very different fundamental assumptions about human nature. The person-centred approach emphasises the actualising tendency of the individual as the central motivating drive with the consequent belief that the therapist should follow the direction of the client. This belief is in contrast to the psychodynamic approach, or at least the more Freudian approaches within this tradition, which emphasise unconscious drives and a striving to fulfil id impulses which need to be kept in check by the ego. Consequently, the therapist's task is to bring to awareness these unconscious forces to enable interpretion of the client's behaviour, not from the client's frame of reference, but from the frame of reference of psychoanalytical theory. Asking the therapist how they either integrate or use these approaches eclectically might be useful for the new client.

Moral and ethical questions

The more humanistic, existential, and transpersonal therapies, in contrast to the more biomedical, behavioural, and cognitive therapies, are explicitly concerned with moral issues, and questions about the meaning of life (Bergin, 1980). As counsellors and psychotherapists we must be aware of our own value systems. In the context of this discussion on the future development of counselling and psychotherapy, we might also be aware that what we do is a moral and ethical endeavour. As Deurzen (1998) writes:

> Those who take on this profession end up debating the big issues of life and the universe, often without any systematic training in the field of philosophy. Approaches to psychotherapy represent distinct value systems and belief systems although they remain non-explicit about their own philosophical and spiritual guidance role. The calibre of a lot of the thinking is therefore low. There is a risk that psychotherapists end up making interpretations from a background of unassimilated home-spun, popular philosophy . . . Woven in with the personal and psychological problems that our clients bring are other deeper layers of difficulty which are to do with the perennial questions about the meaning of life and the moral issues about how a good human life should be lived. (Deurzen, 1998, pp. 5–7)

How we decide what constitutes a good life is beyond the boundaries of scientific enquiry. Christopher (1996) has argued that we should give up pretensions to objectivity and value neutrality and acknowledge that psychological intervention is a morally imbued activity. Therapists, he argues should:

(a) Acknowledge our cultural embeddedness,
(b) seek to continually clarify and question the moral visions that motivate us,
(c) relentlessly attempt to discern how moral visions affect our work as counsellors, and
(d) regularly engage in public discourse on the nature and appropriateness of our moral visions. (Christopher, 1996, p. 23)

However, Christopher goes on to say that

> this does not necessarily thrust us into a debilitating relativism in the face of which we must conclude that every moral vision or way of life is equally 'good' and that there are no grounds for criticising values and practices that we deem oppressive, racist, sexist, or otherwise unworthy . . . We need to define a middle ground or third way beyond objectivism and relativism based on a search for truth and moral insight with full awareness that no final or certain formulations of them are possible (or even desirable) . . . Our maturity as counsellors deepens when we recognise that our responsibility comes with uncertainty; we can never be certain that our theories, diagnoses, conceptualisations, and interventions are right . . . When, as counsellors, we interact with clients or engage in research or theorising, we will be adopting a stance, presupposing a moral vision. Whether we admit it or not in our work with clients, we are engaging in a conversation about the good. Ultimately, counseling is part of a cultural discussion about ethos and world view, about the good life and the good person, and about moral visions. The only real choice becomes how honest we are with ourselves about our inescapable moral visions. (Christopher, 1996, p. 24)

Conclusion

Although, on average, it would seem that all therapies are more or less equally effective, it has also been argued that some therapies are more suited for some problems than others. Since the Smith and Glass (1977) study, as we have seen, there has been an increased emphasis on which type of therapy is most effective for which psychological problem (Lambert and Bergin, 1992; Roth and Fonagy, 1996) and within the health service there is an emphasis on evidence-based practice and the delivery of therapies which have been shown to be effective. However, the role of traditional scientific research in evaluating therapies remains contentious, with some claiming that it can only provide us with limited knowledge of what works for whom. More recently, however, researchers and clinicians have been interested in developing ways of understanding psychopathology which incorporate the different models. The biopsychosocial model emphasises the interplay between biological, psychological, and social forces acting upon the person. Researchers have attempted to specify models of the interactions between various factors. Based on such ideas, therapists have begun to adopt eclectic and integrative ways of working with clients, rather than confining themselves to particular models. Researchers have attempted to understand the common factors that lead to therapeutic change. For example, recent theorists have emphasised that psychological therapies all involve, in some way, the transformation of meaning. At a practical level it has been suggested that different therapeutic approaches might be more or less appropriate depending on the person's stage of readiness to change. Finally, we must not forget that therapy is also a moral endeavour.

Summary points

- The biopsychosocial model adopts a holistic view, conceptualising biological, psychological, and social factors not as competitive, but as providing explanations at different but related levels of analysis.
- Modern psychological research often adopts a diathesis-stress model to investigate the interaction between different factors and how they cause psychopathology.
- Evidence-based practice is becoming increasingly important in deciding which approaches to therapy can be delivered within the National Health Service.
- Criticisms of evidence-based practice can be made and there remains debate over what constitutes evidence.
- Evidence-based practice is based on the idea that there are specific treatments for specific problems. Therapists working in such a way describe themselves as eclectic. Integrative therapists attempt to meld the ideas from two or more models or approaches to therapy.
- Factors common to all therapies have been identified. The therapeutic alliance is one such factor and is believed

to play an important part in the healing process in all therapies.

- Psychological therapy is also a morally imbued activity which raises questions for us about how a good human life should be lived.

References

Adler, A (1931) Compulsion neurosis, *International Journal of Individual Psychology* **9**: 1–16.

Adler, A (1964) *Social Interest: A challenge to mankind*, New York: Capricorn.

Agnew-Davies, R, Stiles, W B, Hardy, G E, Barkham, M, and Shapiro, D A (1998) Alliance structure assessed by the Agnew Relationship Measure (ARM), *British Journal of Clinical Psychology* **37**: 155–72.

Ahlburg, D A, and Shapiro, M O (1983) The darker side of unemployment, *Hospital and Community Psychiatry* **34**: 389.

Albee, G W (1996) The psychological origins of the white, male patriarchy in psychology, *The Journal of Primary Prevention* **17**: 1.

Albee, G W (2000) The boulder model's fatal flaw, *American Psychologist* **55**: 247–8.

Allyon, T, and Azrin, N (1968) *The Token Economy: A motivational system for therapy and rehabilitation*, New York: Appleton Century Crofts.

American Psychiatric Association (1952) *Diagnostic and Statistical Manual of Mental Disorders* (1st edn), Washington, DC: American Psychiatric Association.

American Psychiatric Association (1968) *Diagnostic and Statistical Manual of Mental Disorders* (2nd edn), Washington, DC: American Psychiatric Association.

American Psychiatric Association (1980) *Diagnostic and Statistical Manual of Mental Disorders* (3rd edn), Washington, DC: American Psychiatric Association.

American Psychiatric Association (1987) *Diagnostic and Statistical Manual of Mental Disorders* (rev. 3rd edn), Washington, DC: American Psychiatric Association.

American Psychiatric Association (1993) Practice guidelines for the treatment of major depressive disorder in adults, *American Journal of Psychiatry* **150** (4): 1–26.

American Psychiatric Association (1994) *Diagnostic and Statistical Manual of Mental Disorders* (4th edn), Washington, DC: American Psychiatric Association.

American Psychiatric Association (1994) Practice guidelines for the treatment of patients with bipolar disorder, *American Journal of Psychiatry* **151** (12): 1–36.

American Psychiatric Association (1995) Practice guidelines for the treatment of patients with substance use disorders: Alcohol, cocaine, opioids, *American Journal of Psychiatry* **152** (11): 1–59.

American Psychiatric Association (1996) Practice guidelines for the treatment of patients with nicotine dependence, *American Journal of Psychiatry* **153** (10): 1–31.

American Psychiatric Association (1997) Practice guidelines for the treatment of patients with schizophrenia, *American Journal of Psychiatry* **154** (4): 1–63.

Anderson, E M, and Lambert, M J (1995) Short-term dynamically orientated psychotherapy: A review and meta-analysis, *Clinical Psychology Review* **15**: 503–14.

Argyle, M (1994) *The Psychology of Social Class*, London: Routledge.

Arnkoff, D B, and Glass, C R (1982) Clinical cognitive constructs: Examination, evaluation, and elaboration. In Kendall, P C (ed.), *Advances in Cognitive-behavioral Research and Therapy*, Vol 1, New York: Academic Press.

Bailey, and Shevlin, M (1999) Letter, *The Psychologist*, December 1999.

Bandura, A (1969) *Principles of Behavior Modification*, New York: Holt, Rinehart, & Winston.

Bandura, A, and Walters, R H (1963) *Social Learning and Personality Development*, New York: Ronald Press.

Banyard, P E (1996) *Applying Psychology to Health*, London: Hodder & Stoughton.

Barker, C, Pistrang, N, and Elliott, R (1994) *Research Methods in Clinical and Counselling Psychology*, Chichester: Wiley.

Barker, C, Pistrang, N, Shapiro D A, and Shaw, I (1990) Coping and help seeking in the UK adult population, *British Journal of Clinical Psychology* **29**: 271–85.

Barlow, D H (1988) *Anxiety and its Disorders*, New York: Guilford.

Barlow, D H, Craske, M G, Cerny, J A, and Klosko, J S (1989) Behavior treatment of panic disorder, *Behavior Therapy* **20**: 261–82.

Bassett, A S, McGillivray, B C, Jones, B D, and Pantzar, J T (1988) Partial trisomy chromosome 5 cosegregating with schizophrenia, *Lancet* **108**: 799–801.

Bateson, G, Jackson, D, Haley, J, and Weakland, J (1956) Toward a theory of schizophrenia, *Behavioural Science* **1**: 251–64.

Beck, A T (1963) *Depression: Clinical, experimental and theoretical aspects*, New York: Harper and Row.

Beck, A T (1967) *Depression, Causes and Treatment*, Philadelphia: University of Philadelphia Press.

Beck, A T (1974) The development of depression: A cognitive model. In Friedman R J, and Katz, M (eds) *The Psychology of Depression: Contemporary theory and research*, New York: Wiley.

Beck, A T, and Emery, G (1985) *Anxiety Disorders and Phobias: A cognitive perspective*, New York: Basic.

Beck, A T, and Freeman, A (1990) *Cognitive Therapy of Personality Disorders*, New York: Guilford.

Beck, A T, and Weishaar, M (1989) Cognitive therapy. In Freeman, A, Simon, K M, Beutler, L E, and Arkowitz, H (eds) *Comprehensive Handbook of Cognitive Therapy*, New York: Plenum Press.

Bergin, A E (1971) The evaluation of therapeutic outcomes. In Bergin, A E, and Garfield, S L (eds) *Handbook of Psychotherapy and Behavior Change*, New York: Wiley.

Bergin, A E, and Garfield, S L eds (1994) *Handbook of Psychotherapy and Behavior Change* (4th edn), New York: Wiley.

Bergin, A E (1980) Psychotherapy and religious values, *Journal of Consulting and Clinical Psychology* **48**: 95–105.

Berne, E (1964) *Games People Play*, New York: Grove Press.

Berne, E (1966) *Principles of Group Treatment*, New York: Oxford University Press.

Berne, E (1971) Away from a theory of the impact of interpersonal interaction on non-verbal participation, *Transactional Analysis Journal* **1**: 6–13.

Berne, E (1972) *What Do You Say After You Say Hullo?*, New York: Grove Press.

Blaxter, M (1990) *Health and Lifestyle*, London: Routledge.

Bohart, A (1980) Toward a cognitive theory of catharsis, *Psychotherapy: Theory, Research, and Practice* **17**: 192–201.

Bohart, A C, O'Hara, M, and Leitner, L M (1998) Empirically violated treatments: disenfranchisement of humanistic and other psychotherapies, *Psychotherapy Research* **8**: 141–57.

Bohm, D (1980) *Wholeness and the Implicate Order*, London: Routledge and Kegan Paul.

Boorstein, S (ed.) (1980) *Transpersonal Psychotherapy*, Palo Alto, CA: Science and Behavior.

Bowen, M (1978) *Family Therapy in Clinical Practice*, New York: Jason Aronson.

Bowlby, J (1969) *Attachment and Loss: Volume 1: Attachment*, London: Hogarth Press.

Bowlby, J (1973) *Attachment and Loss: Volume 2: Separation: Anxiety and Anger*, London: Hogarth Press.

Bowlby, J (1980) *Attachment and Loss: Volume 3: Loss, Sadness and Depression*, London: Hogarth Press.

Boyle, M (1993) *Schizophrenia – A Scientific Delusion*, London: Routledge.

Bozarth, J D (1997) The person-centered approach. In Feltham, C (ed.) *Which Psychotherapy?*, London: Sage.

Bozarth, J (1998) *Person-centred Therapy: A revolutionary paradigm*, Ross-on-Wye: PCCS Books.

Bozarth, J D, and Brodley, B T (1984) Client-centered/person-centered psychotherapy: a statement of understanding, *Person-centered Review* **1**: 262–5.

Brazier, D (1995) *Zen Therapy*, London: Constable.

Breggin, P (1993) *Toxic Psychiatry*, London: Fontana.

Brewin, C R, and Power, M J (1997) Meaning and psychological therapy: Overview and introduction. In Power, M, and Brewin, C R (eds) *The Transformation of Meaning in Psychological Therapies: Integrating theory and practice*, Chichester: Wiley.

British Association for Counselling (1996) *Code of Ethics and Practice*, Rugby: British Association for Counselling.

Broverman, I K, Broverman, D M, Clarkson, F E, Rosenkrantz, P S, and Vogel, S R (1970) Sex-role stereotypes and clinical judgements of mental health, *Journal of Consulting and Clinical Psychology* **34**: 1–7.

Brown, G W, and Harris, T (1978) *The Social Origins of Depression*, London: Tavistock Press.

Bruce, M L, Takeuchi, D T, and Leaf, P J (1991) Poverty and psychiatric status: longitudinal evidence from the New Haven Epidemiological Catchment Area Study, *Archives of General Psychiatry* **48**: 470–74.

Bucher, B, and Lovaas, O I (1967) Use of aversive stimulation in behavior modification. In Jones, M R (ed.) *Miami Symposium on the Prediction of Behavior 1967: Aversive stimulation* (pp. 77–145), Coral Gables, FL: University of Miami Press.

Burns, D D, and Nolen-Hoeksema, S (1992) Therapeutic empathy and recovery from depression in cognitive behavioural therapy: a structural equation model, *Journal of Consulting and Clinical Psychology* **60**: 441–9.

Cacioppo, J T, and Bernston, G G (1992) Social psychological contributions to the decade of the brain: Doctrine of multilevel analysis, *American Psychologist* **47**: 1019–28.

Card, J J (1987) Epidemiology of PTSD in a national cohort of Vietnam veterans, *Journal of Clinical Psychology* **43**: 6–17.

Cash, T F, and Henry, P E (1995) Women's body images: The results of a national survey in the USA, *Sex Roles* **33**: 19–28.

Chadwick, P K (1997) Recovery from schizophrenia: The problem of poetic patients and scientific clinicians, *Clinical Psychology Forum* **103**: 39–43.

Chambless, D L, and Gillis, M (1993) Cognitive therapy with anxiety disorders, *Journal of Consulting and Clinical Psychology* **61**: 248–60.

Chambless, D L, Baker, M J, Baucom, D H, Beutler, L E, Calhoun, K S, Crits-Christoph, P, Daiuto, A, DeRubeis, R, Detweiler, J, Haaga, D A F, Bennett Johnson, S, McCurry, S, Mueser, K T, Pope, K S, Sanderson, W C, Shoham, V, Stickle, T, Williams, D A, and Woody, S R (1998) Update on empirically validated therapies, II, *The Clinical Psychologist* **51**: 3–16.

Chemtob, C M, Tolin, D F, Van der Kolk, B A, and Pitman, R K (2000) Eye movement desensitization and reprocessing. In Foa, E A, Keane,

T M, and Friedman, M J (eds) *Effective treatments for PTSD: Practice Guidelines from the International Society for Traumatic Stress Studies* (pp. 139–55), New York: Guilford.

Chessler, P (1972) *Women and Madness*, New York: Harcourt Brace Jovanovich.

Christopher, J C (1996) Counseling's inescapable moral visions, *Journal of Counseling and Development* **75**: 17–25.

Clarkson, P (1989) *Gestalt Counselling in Action*, London: Sage.

Coffer, C N, and Appley, M (1964) *Motivation: Theory and Research*, New York: Wiley.

Cohen, S, and Wills, T A (1985) Stress, social support, and the buffering hypothesis, *Psychological Bulletin* **98**: 310–57.

Comer, R J (1998) *Abnormal Psychology* (3rd edn), New York: Freeman.

Cook, J D, and Bickman, L (1990) Social support and psychological symptomatology following natural disaster, *Journal of Traumatic Stress* **3**: 541–56.

Cooper, D (1967) *Psychiatry and Antipsychiatry*, London: Paladin.

Coppen, A J, and Doogan, D P (1988) Serotonin and its place in the pathogenesis of depression, *Journal of Clinical Psychiatry* **49**: 4–11.

Crits-Christoph, P (1992) The efficacy of brief psychodynamic psychotherapy: A meta-analysis, *American Journal of Psychiatry* **149**: 151–8.

Culley, S (1991) *Integrative Counselling Skills in Action*, London: Sage.

Dakof, G A, and Taylor, S E (1990) Victims' perceptions of social support: What is helpful from whom?, *Journal of Personality and Social Psychology* **58**: 80–89.

Dale, A J D (1980) Organic mental disorders associated with infections. In Kaplan, H I, Freedman, A M, and Sadock, B J (eds) *Comprehensive Textbook of Psychiatry*, Vol 2 (3rd edn), Baltimore: Williams & Wilkins.

Dalgleish, T, Joseph, S, Thrasher, S, Tranah, T, and Yule, W (1996) Crisis support following the Herald of Free Enterprise disaster: a longitudinal perspective, *Journal of Traumatic Stress* **9**: 833–45.

Davey, G C L (1992) Classical conditioning and the acquisition of human fears and phobias: a review and synthesis of the literature, *Advances in Behaviour Research and Therapy* **14**: 29–66.

DeCarvalho, R (1991) *The Founders of Humanistic Psychology*, New York: Praeger.

Deurzen-Smith, E van (1988) *Existential Counselling in Practice*, London: Sage.

Deurzen-Smith, E van (1998) Beyond psychotherapy, *Psychotherapy Section Newsletter of the British Psychological Society* **23**: 4–18.

Dinan, T G (1994) The role of steroids in the genesis of depression: a psychobiological perspective, *British Journal of Psychiatry* **164**: 365–72.

Dinan, T G (1995) Treatment approaches to therapy-resistant depression, *Journal of Psychopharmacology* **9**: 199–204.

Dinan, T G (1998) Physical treatments for depression. In O'Mahony, G, and Lucey, J V (eds) *Understanding Psychiatric Treatment: Therapy for serious mental health disorder in adults* (pp. 59–75), Chichester: Wiley.

Dobson, K S (1989) A meta-analysis of the efficacy of cognitive therapy for depression, *Journal of Consulting and Clinical Psychology* **57**: 414–19.

Dorahy, M J, and Millar, R (2000) Letter, *The Psychologist* **13**: 121.

Duggan, C E, Marks, I, and Richards, D (1993) Clinical audit of behavior therapy training in nurses, *Health Trends* **25**: 25–30.

Durkheim, E (1897) *Le Suicide*, Paris: Alcan.

Dyck, M J (1993) A proposal for a conditioning model of eye movement desensitization treatment for posttraumatic stress disorder, *Journal of Behaviour Therapy and Experimental Psychiatry* **24**: 201–10.

Egan, G (1982) *The Skilled Helper* (2nd edn), Monterey, CA: Brooks/Cole.

Ellenberger, H (1970) *The Discovery of the Unconscious: The history and evolution of dynamic psychiatry*, New York: Basic.

Elliot, R (1998) Editors introduction: a guide to the empirically supported treatments controversy, *Psychotherapy Research* **8**: 115–25.

Ellis, A (1959) Requisite conditions for basic personality change, *Journal of Consulting Psychology* **23**: 538–40.

Ellis, A (1962) *Reason and Emotion in Psychotherapy*, New York: Stuart.

Ellis, A (1973) Rational-emotive therapy. In Corsini, R (ed.) *Current Psychotherapies*, Itasca, IL: Peacock.

Ellis, A (1979) Toward a new theory of personality. In Ellis, A, and Whiteley, J M (eds) *Theoretical and Empirical Foundations of Rational-emotive Therapy*, Monterey, CA: Brookes/Cole.

Erikson, E H (1959) *Identity and the Life Cycle*, New York: Norton.

Erikson, E H (1963) *Childhood and Society* (2nd edn), New York: Norton.

Erikson, E H (1968) *Identity, Youth and Crisis*, New York: Norton.

Erinosho, O, and Ayonrinde, A (1981) Educational background and attitude to mental illness among the Yoruba in Nigeria, *Human Relations* **34**: 1–12.

Evans, R (1969) *Dialogue with Erik Erikson*, New York: Dutton.

Evans, M D, Hollon, S D, DeRubeis, R J, Piasecki, J M, Grove, W M, Garvey, M J, and Tuason, V B (1992) Differential relapse following cognitive therapy and pharmacotherapy for depression, *Archives of General Psychiatry* **49**: 802–08.

Eysenck, H J (1952) The effects of psychotherapy: an evaluation, *Journal of Consulting Psychology* **16**: 319–24.

Eysenck, H J (1960) *Handbook of Abnormal Psychology*, London: Pitman.

Eysenck, H J (1965) The effects of psychotherapy, *International Journal of Psychiatry*, 1: 97–142.

Eysenck, H J (1986) A critique of contemporary classification and diagnosis. In Millon, T, and Klerman, G L (eds) *Contemporary Directions in Psychopathology: Towards the DSM-IV*, New York: Guilford.

Eysenck, H J, and Wilson, G D (1973) *The Experimental Study of Freudian Theories*, London: Methuen.

Fairbairn, W (1952) *An Object-relations Theory of the Personality*, New York: Basic.

Falloon, I R H, Boyd, J L, and McGill, C W (1984) *Behavioral Family Management of Mental Illness: Enhancing family coping in community care*, New York: Guilford.

Falloon, I R H, Laporta, M, Fadden, G, and Graham-Hole, V (1993) *Managing Stress in Families*, London: Routledge.

Feltham, C (1997) Introduction: Irreconcilable psychotherapies (pp. 1–11) In Feltham, C (ed.), *Which Psychotherapy?*, London: Sage.

Fisher, S, and Greenberg, R P (1996) *Freud Scientifically Reappraised: Testing the theories and therapy*, New York: Wiley.

Flannery, R B (1990) Social support and psychological trauma: A methodological review, *Journal of Traumatic Stress* 3: 593–611.

Foa, E B, Rothbaum, B O, Riggs, D S, and Murdock, T B (1991) Treatment of posttraumatic stress disorder in rape victims: A comparison between cognitive-behavioral procedures and counselling, *Journal of Consulting and Clinical Psychology* 59: 715–23.

Fowler, D, Garety, P, and Kuipers, E (1995) *Cognitive Behaviour Therapy for Psychosis: Theory and practice*, Chichester: Wiley.

Francis, M E, and Pennebaker, J W (1992) Putting stress into words: The impact of writing on physiological, absentee, and self-reported emotional well-being measures, *American Journal of Health Promotion* 6: 280–7.

Frank, J (1961) *Persuasion and Healing: A comparative study of psychotherapy*, New York: Schocken.

Frank, J (1971) Therapeutic factors in psychotherapy, *American Journal of Psychotherapy* 25: 350.

Frankl, V (1963) *Man's Search for Meaning*, New York: Washington Square.

Frankl, V (1967) *Psychotherapy and Existentialism: Selected papers on logotherapy*, New York: Washington Square.

Freud, S (1900) *The Interpretation of Dreams*, Standard Edition of the Complete Psychological Works of Sigmund Freud, Vols 4 and 5, edited and translated by J Strachey (1953), London: Hogarth Press and the Institute of Psychoanalysis.

Freud, S (1901) *The Psychopathology of Everyday Life*, Standard Edition of the Complete Psychological Works of Sigmund Freud, Vol 6, edited and translated by J Strachey (1960), London: Hogarth Press and the Institute of Psychoanalysis.

Freud, S (1917) *Mourning and Melancholia*, London: Hogarth Press.

Freud, S (1933) *New Introductory Lectures on Psychoanalysis*, Standard Edition of the Complete Psychological Works of Sigmund Freud, Vol 22, edited and translated by J Strachey (1964), London: Hogarth Press and the Institute of Psychoanalysis.

Freud, S (1940/1969) *An Outline of Psycho-analysis*, New York: Norton.

Fromm, E (1993) *The Art of Being*, London: Constable.

Fromm-Reichman, F (1948) Notes on the development of treatment of schizophrenics by psychoanalytic psychotherapy, *Psychiatry* 11: 263–73.

Fuller, R, Walsh, P N, and McGinley, P (1997) A *Century of Psychology: Progress, paradigms and prospects for the new millennium*, London: Routledge.

Garfield, S L (1992) Eclectic psychotherapy: A common factors approach. In Norcross, J C, and Goldfried, M R (eds) *Handbook of Psychotherapy Integration*, New York: Basic.

Garfield, S L (1996) Some problems associated with 'validated' forms of psychotherapy, *Clinical Psychology: Science and Practice* 3: 218–29.

Garfinkel, P E, Kennedy, S H, and Kaplan, A S (1995) Views on classification and diagnosis of eating disorders, *Canadian Journal of Psychiatry* 40: 445–56.

Gewirtz, J L, and Pelaez-Nogueras, M (1992) B F Skinner's legacy to human infant behavior and development, *American Psychologist* 47: 1411–22.

Goldberg, D, and Huxley, P (1992) *Common Mental Disorders: A biosocial model*, London: Tavistock Routledge.

Goldfried, M R (2000) Consensus in psychotherapy research and practice: Where have all the findings gone?, *Psychotherapy Research* 10: 1–16.

Gottesman, I I, and Shields, J (1972) *Schizophrenia and Genetics: A Twin Study Vantage Point*, New York: Academic Press.

Gottesman, I I (1991) *Schizophrenia Genesis: The origins of madness*, New York: Freeman.

Grawe, K, Donati, R, and Bernauer, F (1998) *Psychotherapy in Transition*, Seattle: Hogrefe & Huber.

Greenberg, L S, Elliott, R, and Lietaer, G (1994) Research on experiential psychotherapy. In Bergin, A E, and Garfield, S L (eds) *Handbook of Psychotherapy and Behavior Change* (4th edn), New York: Wiley: 509–39.

Greenberg, D, and Marks, I (1982) Behavioural therapy of uncommon referrals, *British Journal of Psychiatry* 141: 148–53.

Greenberg, L S, Rice, L N, and Elliot, R (1993) *Facilitating Emotional Change: The moment-by-moment process*, New York: Guilford.

Greenberg, L S, and Watson, J (1998) Experiential therapy of depression: differential effects of client-centred relationship conditions with and without process experiential interventions, *Psychotherapy Research* **8**: 210–24.

Grencavage, L M, and Norcross, J C (1990) Where are the commonalities among the therapeutic common factors?, *Professional Psychology: Research and Practice* **21**: 372–8.

Grof, S, and Bennett, H Z (1990) *The Holotropic Mind: The three levels of human consciousness and how they shape our lives*, San Francisco: HarperCollins.

Gunnell, D J, Peters, T J, Kammerling, R M, and Brooks, J (1995) Relation between parasuicide, suicide, psychiatric admissions, and socioeconomic deprivation, *British Medical Journal* **311**: 226–30.

Gusella, J F, Wexler, N S, Conneally, P M, Naylor, S L, Anderson, M A, Tanzi, R E, Watkins, P C, Ottina, K, Wallace, M R, Sakaguchi, A Y, Young, A B, Shoulson, I, Bonilla, E, and Martin, J B (1983) A polymorphic DNA marker genetically linked to Huntington's disease, *Nature* **306**: 234–8.

Hagan, T, and Smail, D (1997a) Power mapping – I. Background and basic methodology, *Journal of Community and Applied Social Psychology* **7**: 257–67.

Hagan, T, and Smail, D (1997b) Power mapping – II. Practical application: The example of sexual abuse, *Journal of Community and Applied Social Psychology* **7**: 269–84.

Harlow, J M (1868) Recovery from the passage of an iron bar through the head, *Publication of the Massachussetts Medical Society* **2**: 327 ff.

Hartmann, H (1958) *Ego Psychology and the Problem of Adaptation*, New York: International Universities Press.

Henry, W P (1998) Science, politics and the politics of science: the use and misuse of empirically validiated treatment research, *Psychotherapy Research* **8**: 126–40.

Heston, L L (1970) The genetics of schizophrenia and schizoid disease, *Science* **167**: 249–56.

Heston, L L (1992) *Mending Minds: A guide to the new psychiatry of depression, anxiety, and other serious mental disorders*, New York: Freeman.

Hollingshead, A B, and Redlich, F C (1958) *Social Class and Mental Illness: A community study*, New York: John Wiley & Sons.

Hollon, S D, and Beck, A T (1994) Cognitive and cognitive-behavioural therapies. In Bergin, A E, and Garfield, S L (eds) *Handbook of Psychotherapy and Behavior Change* (4th edn), New York: Wiley.

Horvath, A O, and Luborsky, L (1993) The role of the therapeutic alliance in psychotherapy, *Journal of Consulting and Clinical Psychology* **61**: 561–73.

Horvath, A O, and Symonds, B D (1991) Relationship between working alliance and outcome in psychotherapy: a meta-analysis, *Journal of Counseling Psychology* **38**: 139–49.

Hyer, L, and Brandsma, J M (1997) EMDR minus eye movements equals good psychotherapy, *Journal of Traumatic Stress*, **10**: 515–22.

Janov, A (1982) *Prisoners of Pain*, London: Abacus.

Jensen, J A (1994) An investigation of eye movement desensitization and reprocessing (EMDR) as a treatment for posttraumatic stress disorder (PTSD) symptoms of Vietnam combat veterans, *Behavior Therapy* **25**: 311–25.

Jones, M C (1925) A laboratory study of fear: the case of Peter, *Pedagogical Seminary* **31**: 308–15.

Joseph, S, Andrews, B, Williams, R, and Yule, W (1992) Crisis support and psychiatric symptomatology in adult survivors of the Jupiter cruise ship disaster, *British Journal of Clinical Psychology* **31**: 63–73.

Joseph, S, Yule, W, Williams, R, and Andrews, B (1993) Crisis support in the aftermath of disaster: a longitudinal perspective, *British Journal of Clinical Psychology* **32**: 177–85.

Kantorovich, F (1930) An attempt at associative reflex therapy in alcoholism, *Psychological Abstracts* 4282.

Karasu, T B (1992) The worst of times, the best of times, *Journal of Psychotherapy Practice and Research* **1**: 2–15.

Kazdin, A E (1994) Methodology, design, and evaluation in psychotherapy research. In Bergin, A E, and Garfield, S L (eds) *Handbook of Psychotherapy and Behavior Change* (4th edn) (pp. 19–71), New York: Wiley.

Kazdin, A E, and Wilcoxin, L A (1976) Systematic desentization and nonspecific treatment effects: A methodological evaluation, *Psychological Bulletin* **83**: 729–58.

Keefe, F J, Dunsmore, J, and Burnett, R (1992) Behavioral and cognitive-behavioral approaches to chronic pain: Recent advances and future directions, *Journal of Consulting and Clinical Psychology* **60**: 528–36.

Kendler, K S, MacLean, C, Neale, M, Kessler, R, Heath, A, and Eaves, L (1991) The genetic epidemiology of bulimia nervosa, *American Journal of Psychiatry* **148**: 1631.

Kernberg, O F (1976) *Object-relations Theory and Clinical Psychoanalysis*, New York: Jason Aronson.

Kessler, R C, McGonagle, K A, Zhao, S, Nelson, C R, Highes, M, Eshleman, S, Wittchen, H, and Kendler, K S (1994) Lifetime and 12-month prevalence of DSM-II-R psychiatric disorders in the United States. Results from the National Comorbidity survey, *Archives of General Psychiatry* **51**: 8–19.

King, J L, and Mallinckrodt, B (2000) Family environment and alexithymia in clients and non-clients, *Psychotherapy Research* **10**: 78–86.

Klein, M (1932) *The Psychoanalysis of Children*, London: Hogarth.

Kleinman, J E, Karson, C N, Weinberger, D R, Freed, W J, Berman, K F, and Wyatt, R J (1984) Eye-blinking and cerebral ventricular size in chronic schizophrenic patients, *American Journal of Psychiatry* **141**: 1430–32.

Kohut, H (1971) *The Analysis of the Self*, New York: International Universities Press.

Korpi, E R, Kleinman, J E, Goodman, S I, Phillis, I, DeLis, L E, Linnoil, M, and Wyatt, R J (1986) Serotonin and 5-hydroxyindoleacetic acid in brains of suicide victims, *Archives of General Psychiatry* **43**: 594–600.

Krupnick, I J, Sotsky, S M, Simmens, S, Moyer, J, Elkin, I, Watkins, J, and Pilkonis, P A (1996) The role of the therapeutic alliance in psychotherapy and pharmacology outcome: findings in the National Institute of Mental Health Treatment of Depression collaborative Research Programme, *Journal of Consulting and Clinical Psychology* **64**: 532–9.

Laing, R D (1966) *Self and Others*, Harmondsworth: Penguin.

Laing, R D (1970) *Knots*, Harmondsworth: Penguin.

Laing, R D (1976) *The Politics of the Family and Other Essays*, Harmondsworth: Penguin.

Lambers, E (1994a) Borderline personality disorder. In Mearns, D (ed.) *Developing Person-centred Counselling*, London: Sage

Lambers, E (1994b) Psychosis. In Mearns, D (ed.), *Developing Person-centred Counselling*, London: Sage.

Lambers, E (1994c) Personality disorder. In Mearns, D (ed.) *Developing Person-centred Counselling*, London: Sage.

Lambert, M J (1992) Psychotherapy outcome research: Implications for integrative and eclectic therapists. In Norcross, J C, and Goldfried, M R (eds) *Handbook of Psychotherapy Integration*, New York: Basic.

Lambert, M J, and Bergin, A E (1992) Achievements and limitations of psychotherapy research. In Freedheim, D K (ed.) *History of Psychotherapy: A century of change*, Washington, DC: American Psychological Association.

Lambert, M J, and Bergin, A E (1994) The effectiveness of psychotherapy. In Bergin, A E, and Garfield, S L (eds) *Handbook of Psychotherapy and Behavior Change*, New York: Wiley.

Lang, P, and Melamed, B (1969) Case report: avoidance conditioning therapy of an infant with chronic ruminative vomiting, *Journal of Abnormal Psychology* **74**: 1–8.

Lazarus, A A (1989) Why I am an eclectic (not an integrationist), *British Journal of Guidance and Counselling* **17**: 248–58.

Levant, R F, and Shlien, J M (eds) (1984) *Client-centered Therapy and the Person-centred Approach*, New York: Praeger.

Levin, P, Lazrove, S, and Van der Kolk, B (1999) What psychological testing and neuroimaging tell us about the treatment of post-traumatic stress disorder by eye movement desensitization and reprocessing, *Journal of Anxiety Disorders* **13**: 159–72.

Lewinsohn, P M (1974) A behavioral approach to depression. In Friedman, R, and Katz, M (eds) *The Psychology of Depression: Contemporary Theory and Research*, Washington, DC: Winston/Wiley.

Lieberman, J A, Kinon, B J, and Loebel, A D (1990) Dopaminergic mechanisms in idiopathic and drug-induced psychosis, *Schizophrenia Bulletin* **16**: 97–110.

Linehan, M H (1987) Dialectical behavior therapy for borderline personality disorder, *Bulletin of the Menninger Clinic* **51**: 261–76.

Linehan, M H (1993) *Cognitive-behavioral Treatment for Borderline Personality Disorder*, New York: Guilford.

Littlewood, R, and Lipsedge, M (1993) *Aliens and Alienists: Ethnic minorities and psychiatry* (3rd edn), London: Routledge.

Lovaas, O (1977) *The Autistic Child: Language development through behavior modification*, New York: Irvington.

Mahrer, A P (1998) Embarrassing problems for the field of psychotherapy, *Psychotherapy Section Newsletter of the British Psychological Society* **23**: 19–29.

Margraf, J, Barlow, D H, Clark, D M, and Telch, M J (1993) Psychological treatment of panic: Work in progress on outcome, active ingredients, and follow up, *Behaviour Research and Therapy* **31**: 1–8.

Marks, I M (1987) *Fears, Phobias and Rituals*, New York: Oxford University Press.

Marks, I M (1990) Behavioral therapy of anxiety states. In Sartorius, N, Andreoli, V, Cassano, G, Eisenberg, L, Kielholz, P, Pancheri, P, and Racagni, G (eds) *Anxiety: Psychological and clinical perspectives*, New York: Hemisphere.

Marks, I M, Gelder, M G, and Bancroft, J (1970) Sexual deviants two years after electrical aversion, *British Journal of Psychiatry* **117**: 73–85.

Marks, I M, and O'Sullivan, G (1988) Drugs and psychological treatments for agoraphobia /panic and obsessive-compulsive disorders: A review, *British Journal of Psychiatry* **153**: 650–58.

Marshall, J R (1996) Science, 'schizophrenia' and genetics: the creation of myths, *Clinical Psychology Forum* **95**: 5–13.

Maslow, A (1968) *Toward a Psychology of Being* (2nd edn), New York: Harper & Row.

Maslow, A H (1970) *Motivation and Personality* (2nd edn), New York: Harper & Row.

Maslow, A H (1993) *The Farther Reaches of Human Nature*, London: Penguin Arkana.

Masson, J (1988) *Against Therapy*, London: Collins.

Mattick, R P, Andrews, G, Hadzi-Pavlovic, D, and Christensen, H (1990) Treatment of panic and agoraphobia: an integrative review, *Journal of Nervous and Mental Disease* **178**: 567–76.

McGuffin, P, and Katz, R (1989) The genetics of depression and manic-depressive disorder, *British Journal of Psychiatry* **155**: 294–304.

McLeod, J D, and Kessler, R C (1990) Socioeconomic status differences in vulnerability to undesirable life events, *Journal of Health and Social Behavior* **31**: 162–72.

McNeal, E T, and Cimbolic, P (1986) Antidepressants and biochemical theories of depression, *Psychological Bulletin* **99**: 361–74.

Mearns, D (ed.) (1994) *Developing Person-centred Counselling*, London: Sage.

Mearns, D, and Thorne, B (1999) *Person Centred Counselling in Action*, London: Sage.

Meehl, P E (1962) Schizotaxia, schizotypy, schizophrenia, *American Psychologist* **17**: 827–38.

Meichenbaum, D H (1977) *Cognitive-behavior Modefication*, New York: Plenum.

Menzies, R, and Clarke, J (1993) A comparision of in vivo and vicarious exposure in the treatment of childhood water phobia, *Behaviour Research and Therapy* **31**: 9–15.

Messer, S B (1986) Eclectism in psychotherapy: Underlying assumptions, problems and trade-offs. In Norcross, J C (ed.) *Handbook of Eclectic Psychotherapy*, New York: Brunner/Mazel.

Miller, W R, Zweben, A, DiClemente, C C, and Rychtarik, R G (1992) *Motivational Enhancement Therapy Manual: A clinical research guide for therapists treating individuals with alcohol abuse and dependence*, Rockville, MD: National Institute on Alcohol Abuse and Alcoholism.

Mitchell, K, Bozarth, J, and Krauft, C (1977) A reappraisal of the therapeutic effectiveness of accurate empathy, nonpossessive warmth and genuineness. In Gurman, A, and Razin, A (eds) *Effective Psychotherapy*, Oxford: Pergamon Press.

Morrow-Bradley, C, and Elliot, R (1986) Utilization of psychotherapy research by practicing psychotherapists, *American Psychologist* **41**: 188–97.

Mowrer, O (1947) On the dual nature of learning, *Harvard Educational Review* **17**: 102–48.

Mowrer, O, and Mowrer, W (1938) Enuresis: A method for its study and treatment, *American Journal of Orthopsychiatry* **8**: 436–9.

Nelson-Jones, R (1984) *Personal Responsibility Counselling and Therapy: An integrative approach*, London: Harper & Row.

Newnes, C (1996) The development of clinical psychology and its values, *Clinical Psychology Forum* **95**: 29–34.

Nichols, M P, and Efran, J S (1985) Catharsis in psychotherapy: A new perspective, *Psychotherapy: Theory, Research, and Practice* **22**: 46–58.

Nolen-Hoeksema, S (1990) *Sex Differences in Depression*, Stanford, CA: Stanford University Press.

Norcross, J C (1990) An eclectic definition of psychotherapy. In Zeig, J K, and Munion, W M (eds) *What is Psychotherapy?*, San Francisco: Jossey-Bass.

Norcross, J C, and Greencavage, L M (1990) Eclecticism and integration in counselling and psychotherapy: major themes and obstacles. In Dryden, W, and Norcross, J C (eds) *Eclecticism and Integration in Counselling and Psychotherapy* (pp. 1–33), Loughton: Gale Centre.

Norcross, J C, Prochaska, J O, and Farber, J A (1993) Psychologists conducting psychotherapy: New findings and historical comparisons on the Psychotherapy Division Membership, *Psychotherapy* **30**: 692–7.

O'Brien, M, and Houston, G (2000) *Integrative Therapy: A practitioner's guide*, London: Sage.

O'Callaghan, E, Sham, P C, Takei, N, Murray, G K, Hare, E H, and Murray, R M (1991) Schizophrenia following prenatal exposure to influenza epidemics between 1939 and 1960, *British Journal of Psychiatry* **160**: 461–6.

O'Callaghan, E, Sham, P C, and Takei, N (1993) Schizophrenia after prenatal exposure to 1957 A2 influenza epidemic, *The Lancet* **337**: 1248–50.

O'Connell, R A, Mayo, J A, Flatow, L, Cuthbertson, B, and O'Brien, B E (1991) Outcome of bipolar disorder on long-term treatment with litium, *British Journal of Psychiatry* **159**: 123–9.

O'Mahony, G O, and Lucey, J V (eds) (1998) *Understanding Psychiatric Treatment: Therapy for serious mental health disorder in adults*, Chichester: Wiley.

Orford, F (2000) Letter, *The Psychologist* **13**: 64.

O'Sullivan, G, and Marks, I (1991) Follow-up studies of behavioral treatment of phobic and obsessive compulsive neuroses, *Psychiatric Annals* **21**: 368–73.

O'Sullivan, K R, and Dryden, W (1990) A survey of clinical psychologists in the South East Thames Region: activities, role and theoretical orientation, *Counselling Psychology Forum* **29**: 21–6.

Owen, M, Craufurd, D, and St Clair, D (1990) Localization of a susceptibility locus for schizophrenia on chromosome 5, *British Journal of Psychiatry* **157**: 123–7.

Pakenham, K I, Dadds, M R, and Terry, D J (1994) Relationships between adjustment to HIV and both social support and coping, *Journal of Consulting and Clinical Psychology* **62**: 1194–203.

Palmer, S (1999) Can counselling and psychotherapy be dangerous?, *Counselling* **10**: 179–80.

Palmer, S, and Ellis, A (1993) In the counsellor's chair: Stephen Palmer interviews Dr Albert Ellis, *Counselling* **4**: 171–4.

Parloff, M B, Waskow, I E, and Wolfe, B E (1978) Research on therapist variables in relation to process and outcome. In Bergin, A E, and Garfield, S L (eds) *Handbook of Psychotherapy and Behavior Change* (2nd edn), New York: Wiley.

Pavlov, I P (1928) *Lectures on Conditioned Reflexes*, New York: Liveright.

Payne, L R, Bergin, A E, and Loftus, P E (1992) A review of attempts to integrate spiritual and standard psychotherapy techniques, *Journal of Psychotherapy Integration* **2**: 171–92.

Pennebaker, J W (1993) Putting stress into words: Health, linguistic, and therapeutic implications, *Behaviour Research and Therapy* **31**: 539–48.

Pennebaker, J W, and Beall, S (1986) Confronting a traumatic event: Toward an understanding of inhibition and disease, *Journal of Abnormal Psychology* **95**: 274–81.

Pennebaker, J W, Kiecolt-Glaser, J K, and Glaser, R (1988) Disclosures of traumas and immune functioing: Health implications for psychotherapy, *Journal of Consulting and Clinical Psychology* **56**: 239–45.

Pennebaker, J W, and O'Heeron, R C (1984) Confinding in others and illness rates among spouses of suicide and accidental death victims, *Journal of Abnormal Psychology* **93**: 473–6.

Persaud, R (1998) *Staying Sane: How to make your mind work for you*, London: Metro.

Pilgrim, D (1997) *Psychotherapy and Society*, London: Sage.

Piper, W E, Azim, H F, McCallum, M, and Joyce, A S (1990) Patient suitability and outcome in short-term individual psychotherapy, *Journal of Consulting and Clinical Psychology* **58**: 475–81.

Pokorny, M (1991) United Kingdom Standing Conference for Psychotherapy. Conference January 1991: Chairman's address, *British Journal of Psychotherapy* **7**: 303–06.

Ponterotto, J (1988) Racial consciousness development among white counselor trainees, *Journal of Multicultural Counseling and Development* **16**: 146–56.

Popper, K R (1959) *The Logic of Scientific Discovery*, New York: Basic.

Prioleau, L, Murdock, M, and Brody, N (1983) An analysis of psychotherapy versus placebo studies, *The Behavioural and Brain Sciences* **2**: 275–85.

Prochaska, J O, and DiClemente, C C (1983) Stages and processes of self-change of smoking: towards an integrative model of change, *Journal of Consulting and Clinical Psychology* **51**: 390–95.

Prochaska, J O, and DiClemente, C C (1984) *The Transtheoretical Approach: Crossing the traditional boundaries of therapy*, Homewood, IL: Dow Jones-Irwin.

Prochaska, J O, and Norcross, J C (1999) *Systems of Psychotherapy: A transtheoretical analysis* (4th edn), Monterey, CA: Brooks/Cole.

Prouty, G F (1976) Pre-therapy, a method of treating pre-expressive psychotic and retarded patients, *Psychotherapy: Theory, Research and Practice* **13**: 290–95.

Prouty, G F (1990) A theoretical evolution in the person-centered/ experiential psychotherapy of schizophrenia and retardation. In Lietaer, G, Rombauts, J, and Van Balen, R (eds) *Client-centered and*

Experiential Psychotherapy in the Nineties (pp. 645–85), Leuven: Leuven University Press.

Prouty, G F, and Kubiak, M A (1988) The development of communicative contact with a catatonic schizophrenic, *Journal of Communication Therapy* 4: 13–20.

Purton, C (1998) Unconditional positive regard and its spiritual implications. In Thorne, B, and Lambers, E (eds) *Person-centred Therapy: A European perspective*, London: Sage.

Rapaport, D (1958) The theory of ego autonomy: A generalization, *Bulletin of the Menninger Clinic* 22: 13–35.

Renfry, G, and Spates, C R (1994) Eye movement desensitization and reprocessing: A partial dismantling procedure, *Journal of Behaviour Therapy and Experimental Psychiatry* 25: 231–9.

Rennie, D L (1998) *Person-centred Counselling: An experiential approach*, London: Sage.

Rice, L N (1988) Integration and the client-centred relationship, *Journal of Integrative and Eclective Psychotherapy* 7: 291–302.

Roberts, A H, Kewman, D G, Mercier, L, and Hovell, M (1993) The power of non-specific effects in healing. Implications for psychosocial and biological treatments, *Clinical Psychology Review* 13: 375–91.

Robson, C (1993) *Real World Research: A resource for social scientists and practitioner-researchers*, Oxford: Blackwell.

Rogers, C R (1942) *Counseling and Psychotherapy*, Boston: Houghton Mifflin.

Rogers, C R (1951) *Client-centred Therapy*, London: Constable.

Rogers, C R (1957) The necessary and sufficient conditions of therapeutic personality change, *Journal of Consulting Psychology* 21: 95–103.

Rogers, C R (1959) A theory of therapy, personality, and interpersonal relationships as developed in the client-centered framework. In Koch, S (ed.) *Psychology, the Study of a Science, Vol. 3: Formulations of the Person and the Social Context* (pp. 184–256), New York: McGraw Hill.

Rogers, C R (1961) *On Becoming a Person: A therapist's view of psychotherapy*, Boston: Houghton Mifflin.

Rogers, C R (1973) My philosophy of interpersonal relationships and how it grew, *Journal of Humanistic Psychology* 13: 3–15.

Rogers, C R (1980) *A Way of Being*, Boston: Houghton Mifflin.

Rollnick, S, and Miller, W R (1995) What is motivational interviewing?, *Behavioral and Cognitive Psychotherapy* 23: 325–34.

Rose, S (1990) The euphoria fades, *The Guardian*, 20 July.

Rosenhan, D L (1973) On being sane in insane places, *Science* 179: 250–58.

Rosenhan, D L (1975) The contextual nature of psychiatric diagnosis, *Journal of Abnormal Psychology* 84: 442–52.

Roth, A, and Fonagy, P (1996) *What Works for Whom? A critical review of psychotherapy research*, New York: Guilford.

Rowan, J (1993) *The Transpersonal: Psychotherapy and counselling*, London: Routledge.

Rowe, D (1996) Science and imagination, *Clinical Psychology Forum* **95**: 38–9.

Russell, R (1995) What works in psychotherapy when it does work?, *Changes* **13**: 213–18.

Russo, D C, Carr, E G, and Lovaas, O I (1980) Self-injury in pediatric populations. In Ferguson, J, and Taylor, C R (eds) *Comprehensive Handbook of Behavioral Medicine, Vol. 3: Extended Applications and Issues*, Holliswood, NY: Spectrum.

Ryle, A (1990) *Cognitive Analytic Therapy: Active participation in change*, Chichester: Wiley.

Salkovskis, P M, and Kirk, J (1997) Obsessive-compulsive disorder. In Clark, D M, and Fairburn, C G (eds) *Science and Practice of Cognitive Behaviour Therapy* (pp. 179–209), Oxford: Oxford Medical Publications.

Samelson, F (1980) J B Watson's Little Albert, Cyril Burt's twins, and the need for a critical science, *American Psychologist* **35**: 619–25.

Sarason, B R, Sarason, I G, and Pierce, G R (eds) (1990) *Social Support: An interactional view*, New York: Wiley.

Satir, V (1964) *Conjoint Family Therapy*, Palo Alto, CA: Science and Behavior.

Schaap, C, Bennun, I, Schinder, L, and Hoogduin, K (1993) *The Therapeutic Relationship in Behavioural Psychotherapy*, Chichester: Wiley.

Schneider, K J (1998) Toward a science of the heart: Romanticism and the revival of psychology, *American Psychologist* **53**: 277–89.

Seligman, M E P (1995) The effectivness of psychotherapy, *American Psychologist* **50**: 965–74.

Shaikh, A (1985) Cross-cultural comparison: psychiatric admission of Asian and indigenous patients in Leicestershire, *International Journal of Social Psychiatry* **31**: 3–11.

Shapiro, D A, and Shapiro, D (1982) Meta-analysis of comparative therapy outcome studies. A replication and refinement, *Psychological Bulletin* **92**: 581–604.

Shapiro, F (1989a) Efficacy of the eye movement desensitization procedure in the treatment of traumatic memories, *Journal of Traumatic Stress* **2**: 199–223.

Shapiro, F (1989b) Eye movement desensitization: A new treatment for Post-Traumatic Stress Disorder, *Journal of Behaviour Therapy and Experimental Psychiatry* **20**: 211–17.

Shapiro, F (1995) *Eye Movement Desensitization and Reprocessing: Basic Principles, protocols and procedures*, New York: Guilford.

Sheldrake, R (1981) *A New Science of Life*, Los Angeles: J P Tarcher.

Skinner, B F (1953) *Science and Human Behavior*, New York: Macmillan.

Skinner, B F (1971) *Beyond Freedom and Dignity*, New York: Vintage.

Skinner, B F (1990) Can psychology be a science of the mind?, *American Psychologist* **45**: 1206–10.

Smail, D (1987) *Taking Care: An alternative to therapy*, London: Dent.

Smail, D (1996a) *How to Survive without Psychotherapy*, London: Constable.

Smail, D (1996b) J Richard Marshall, *Clinical Psychology Forum* **95**: 14–17.

Smith, M L, and Glass, G V (1977) The meta-analysis of psychotherapy outcome studies, *American Psychologist* **32**: 752–60.

Snaith, R P (1994) Psychosurgery: Controversy and Enquiry, *British Journal of Psychotherapy* **161**: 582–4.

Starr, P (1982) *The Social Transformation of American Medicine*, New York: Basic.

Stevens, A, and Price, J (1996) *Evolutionary Psychiatry: A new beginning*, London: Routledge.

Stewart, I (1989) *Transactional Analysis Counselling in Action*, London: Sage.

Stiles, W B, Barkham, M, Shapiro, D A, and Firth-Cozens, J (1992) Treatment order and thematic continuity between contrasting psychotherapies: Exploring an implication of the assimilation model, *Psychotherapy Research* **2**: 112–24.

Stiles, W B, Elliot, R, Llewelyn, S P, Firth-Cozens, J A, Margison, F R, Shapiro, D A, and Hardy, G (1990) Assimilation of problematic experiences by clients in psychotherapy, *Psychotherapy* **27**: 411–20.

Stiles, W B, Shapiro, D A, and Elliott, R K (1986) Are all psychotherapies equivalent?, *American Psychologist* **41**: 165–80.

Stravynski, A, Marks, I, and Yule, W (1982) Social skills problems in neurotic outpatients: social skills training with and without cognitive modification, *Archives of General Psychiatry* **39**: 1378–85.

Sutherland, S (1992) *Irrationality: The enemy within*, London: Penguin.

Sutherland, S (1998) *Breakdown: A personal crisis and a medical dilemma* (2nd edn), Oxford: Oxford University Press.

Svartberg, M, and Stiles, T C (1991) Comparative effects of short-term psychodynamic psychotherapy: a meta-analysis, *Journal of Consulting and Clinical Psychology* **5**: 704–14.

Szasz, T S (1961) *The Myth of Mental Illness*, New York: Hoeber.

Szasz, T S (1974) *The Second Sin*, London: Routledge & Kegan Paul.

Tansella, M, and Williams, P (1987) The Italian experience and its implications, *Psychological Medicine* **17**: 283–9.

Tart, C T (1975) *States of Consciousness*, New York: E P Dutton & Co., Inc.

Thompson, L W, Gallagher, D, and Breckenridge, J S (1987) Comparative effectiveness of psychotherapies for depressed elders, *Journal of Consulting and Clinical Psychology* **55**: 385–90.

Thorndike, E L (1898) Animal intelligence: An experimental study of the associative processes in animals, *Psychological Monographs* **2** (No. 8).

Thorne, B (1991) *Person-centred Counselling: Therapeutic and spiritual aspects*, London: Whurr.

Thorne, B (1992) *Carl Rogers*, London: Sage.

Thorne, B (1994) Developing a spiritual discipline. In Mearns, D (ed.) *Developing Person-centred Counselling*, London: Sage.

Thorne, B, and Lambers, E (1998) (eds) *Person-centred Therapy: A European perspective*, London: Sage.

Ussher, J (1991) *Women's Madness*, London: Harvester Wheatsheaf.

VandenBos, G R, and Stapp, J (1983) Service providers in psychology: Results of the 1982 APA human resources survey, *American Psychologist* **38**: 1330–52.

Van Etten, M L, and Taylor, S (1998) Comparative efficacy of treatments for posttraumatic stress disorder: a meta-analysis, *Clinical Psychology and Psychotherapy* **5**: 126–44.

Vaughan, K, Wiese, M, Gold, R, and Tarrier, N (1994) Eye-movement desensitization: Symptom change in post-traumatic stress disorder, *British Journal of Psychiatry* **164**: 533–41.

Walker, A (1993) *Warrior Marks: Female genital mutilation and the sexual blinding of women*, New York: Harcourt Brace.

Warren, R, and Zgourides, G D (1991) *Anxiety Disorders: A rational-emotive perspective*, New York: Pergamon Press.

Watson, J B (1913) Psychology as the behaviourist views it, *Psychological Review* **20**: 158–77.

Watson, J B, and Rayner, R (1920) Conditioned emotional reactions, *Journal of Experimental Psychology* **3**: 1–14.

Weiner, R D, and Crystal, A D (1994) The present use of electroconvulsive therapy, *Annual Review of Medicine* **45**: 273–81.

Westermeyer, J (1985) Psychiatric diagnosis across cultural boundaries, *American Journal of Psychiatry* **142**: 798–805.

White, J (2000) Cognitive therapy – what is left when you remove the hype?, *Proceedings of the British Psychological Society* **8**: 16.

Wilber, K (1998) *The Essential Ken Wilber: An introductory reader*, Boston: Shambha.

Williams, D R (1990) Socioeconomic differentials in health: A review and redirection, *Social Psychology Quarterly* **53**: 81–99.

Williams, J B W, Gibbon, M, First, M B, Spitzer, R L, Davies, M, *et al.* (1992) The Structured Clinical Interview for DSM-III-R (SCID): 2. Multisite test-retest reliability, *Archives of General Psychiatry* **49**: 630–36.

Winston, A, Pollack, J, McCullough, L, Flegenheimer, W, Kestenbaum, R, and Trujillo, M (1991) Brief dynamic psychotherapy of personality disorders, *Journal of Nervous and Mental Disease* **179**: 188–93.

Wolpe, J (1958) *Psychotherapy and Reciprocal Inhibition*, Stanford, CA: Stanford University Press.

Wolpe, J (1990) *The Practice of Behavior Therapy* (4th edn), New York: Pergamon.

Wolpe, J, and Rachman, S (1960) Psychoanalyitic evidence: A critique based on Freud's case of Little Hans, *Journal of Nervous and Mental Disease* **131**: 135–45.

Woody, G E, Luborsky, L, McLellan, A T, and O'Brien, C P (1990) Corrections and revised analyses for psychotherapy in methadone maintenance patients, *Archives of General Psychiatry* **47**: 788–9.

Woolfe, R, and Dryden, W (eds) (1996) *Handbook of Counselling Psychology*, London: Sage.

World Health Organisation (1992) *Tenth Revision of the International Classification of Diseases*, Geneva: WHO.

Wynne, L C, Singer, M T, Bartko, J J, and Toohey, M L (1977) Schizophrenics and their families: Recent research on parental communication. In Tanner, J M (ed.) *Developments in Psychiatric Research*, London: Hodder & Stoughton.

Yalom, I D (1980) *Existential Psychotherapy*, New York: Basic.

Zeig, J K (1987) *The Evolution of Psychotherapy*, New York: Brunner/Mazel.

Zigler, E, and Phillips, L (1961) Psychiatric diagnosis and symptomatology, *Journal of Abnormal Psychology* **63**: 69–75.

Zilboorg, G, and Henry, G W (1941) *A History of Medical Psychology*, New York: Norton.

Zook, A, and Walton, J M (1989) Theoretical orientations and work settings of clinical and counseling psychologists: A current perspective, *Professional Psychology* **20**: 23–31.

Index